UNIVERSITY OF LONDON

INSTITUTE OF COMMONWEALTH STUDIES

*

COMMONWEALTH PAPERS

General Editor

PROFESSOR W. H. MORRIS-JONES

24

INTERNATIONAL
LABOUR MIGRATION

INTERNATIONAL
LABOUR MIGRATION

INTERNATIONAL LABOUR MIGRATION

HISTORICAL PERSPECTIVES

*

EDITED BY

SHULA MARKS

Institute of Commonwealth Studies
and School of Oriental and African Studies
University of London

AND

PETER RICHARDSON

University of Melbourne

PUBLISHED FOR THE
INSTITUTE OF COMMONWEALTH STUDIES
BY MAURICE TEMPLE SMITH

First published in Great Britain 1984
by Maurice Temple Smith Limited
Jubilee House, Chapel Road
Hounslow Middlesex TW3 1XT

The maps appearing on pages 172 and 174 are reproduced by permission of the
publisher from *Chinese Mine Labour in the Transvaal* (Macmillan, 1982)
by Peter Richardson.

International labour migration.—(Commonwealth studies; 24)
1. Migrant labor—Congresses   I. Marks, Shula   II. Richardson, Peter,
    1948—   III. Series 305.5'62   HD5855

ISBN 0-85117-238-5

Typeset by George Street Studios, Hounslow, Middlesex
Printed and bound in Great Britain by the Camelot Press, Southampton.

CONTENTS

FOREWORD

There is, notoriously, no guarantee that an interesting seminar series will lead to a good book. In this case, however, the organisers have done more than bring together a valuable set of papers originally presented at meetings held during 1977-1982. Consistently over the period they were seeking to work out a set of fresh approaches and consequently the whole group came to share a common intellectual excitement. Moreover, as editors, they have not been content to place the papers as they stood before readers; revisions apart, they have devoted considerable effort to the preparation of an introduction which integrates each motif in a coherent and arresting pattern. The field of labour migration is no doubt an important segment of social and economic history as well as a central part of the imperial experience. The editors have succeeded in producing a fresh and challenging contribution to this field.

W. H. Morris-Jones

EDITOR'S PREFACE

This volume originated in a seminar on labour migration in the British Empire and Commonwealth held at the Institute of Commonwealth Studies between 1977 and 1982. Although it has been impossible to include in this collection all the contributions presented in the series, all the papers and the very stimulating discussions have undoubtedly shaped the present volume, and we would like to thank the participants for their generosity with time and ideas.

Composite volumes present special headaches for authors, publishers, and editors. We would like to thank Margaret Beard and Keith Williams who read through the manuscript meticulously and helped tidy up a number of loose ends, and Sonja Jansen for her help not only in the organisation of the seminar but also with the typing of this volume. Finally, we would like to thank our contributors for their patience in the face of the unavoidable delays in the volume's publication, and their promptitude in answering our queries.

Shula Marks
Peter Richardson

CONTRIBUTORS

Gill Burke is Senior Lecturer in Social Administration, Polytechnic of Central London

Francine de Clercq worked on the South Africa Project of the Sociology Department of the University of Warwick

Donald Denoon is Senior Research Fellow, Department of Pacific and Southeast Asian History, Australian National University

Pieter Emmer is Senior Lecturer, Centre for the History of European Expansion, University of Leiden

Charlotte Erickson is Paul Mellon Professor of American History, Cambridge University

Adrian Graves is Lecturer in Economic History, University of Edinburgh

Martin Legassick now works for the South African Labour Education Project, London

Shula Marks is Director of the Institute of Commonwealth Studies and Reader in the History of Southern Africa, University of London

Colin Newbury is University Lecturer in Commonwealth History and Fellow of Linacre College, Oxford University

Peter Richardson is Research Fellow in Economic History, University of Melbourne

David Souden is Fellow of Emmanuel College, Cambridge University

Hugh Tinker is Professor Emeritus of the University of Lancaster

INTRODUCTION

SHULA MARKS AND PETER RICHARDSON

I

SINCE the beginnings of a recognisable world economy in the seventeenth
century the international deployment of capital has been paralleled by an
international movement of labour. The era of industrial capitalism in
particular witnessed what Eric Hobsbawm has termed 'the greatest
migration of peoples in history'.[1] Nor has the advent of advanced capitalism seen an end to the phenomenon; contrary to the declaration of Brinley
Thomas in the *International Encyclopaedia of the Social Sciences* in 1968 that
'international migration no longer plays the role in economic growth that
it did in the nineteenth century',[2] the enormous expansion of the world
economy since World War II has been accompanied by a movement of
people which rivals that of the nineteenth and early twentieth centuries in
magnitude, even if the major movements tend now to be intra- rather than
inter-continental. The current recession in the core capitalist countries and
the enforced return of the large numbers of *gastarbeiter,* with all that implies
for the supplier countries, is a further pointer to the continued significance
of the process in the contemporary world.

It was in part to come to terms with the nature of this process in its
historical specificity and to try to advance our theoretical understanding of
labour migration in the past and the present by juxtaposing the different
historical experiences of the imperial metropole and the Third World that
we launched a series of seminars at the Institute of Commonwealth
Studies, University of London, between February 1977 and December
1981. This book is its outcome.

The focus of our fortnightly meetings was the migration of labour
within the British Empire/Commonwealth from 1780 to the present. For
both practical and intellectual reasons, however, the seminar was never
strictly confined to regions which have experienced or acknowledged
British sovereignty since the end of the eighteenth century. The difficulty
of finding contributors who were able to slot neatly into this mould
combined with the obvious advantages of comparative studies to ensure
that the seminar benefited from a wide range of contributions during its
four-year existence.

Both chronologically and geographically the seminar broke its bounds.
The seminar covered a large number of regions of international economic

1

activity, many of which lay outside areas of formal British sovereignty, if not of British economic interest, while some contributions went back as far as the seventeenth century. Thus, early in its existence, the seminar took a close look at the migration of indentured servants from Britain to colonial north America. Later it also looked in detail at Maryland and Virginia in the second half of the seventeenth century. The range of areas covered included north and south America, central, west and southern Africa, Australasia, south and east Asia, and western Europe. Among the more contemporary papers were contributions on the inter-relationship between migration and urban development in Latin America in the 1970s, and migrant labour in agricultural sectors of the United States economy.

The bulk of the papers, however, fell within the more limited time period and geographical scope of the Empire/Commonwealth which mirrored more faithfully the original boundaries of the seminar. Generally speaking nineteenth and twentieth century migration in a wide variety of imperial contexts made up most of the contributions and the essays selected for inclusion in this volume reflect this. Despite the breadth of its scope, not all regions were treated in the same way, nor with equal depth. Notable omissions were a consistent reminder of the challenge and difficulty of this type of thematically based international study.

Despite our deliberate emphasis both in the seminar and in this volume on labour migration, from an early stage it became apparent that the conventional distinction between 'colonisation' in the areas of 'white settlement' and 'labour migration' to the tropics ran a real risk of artificially stunting the whole reach of our discussions and contributions. Here we were influenced by Colin Newbury's remarks in a seminal article on 'Labour Migration in the Imperial Phase', published in 1975:

In a sense, most of Europe's fifty million emigrants were labour recruits, destined for positions as wage-earners in the small towns and cities of the New World, rather than as prairie homesteaders or out-back sheep farmers. For most of them land settlement remained, perhaps, a desirable goal, but not one frequently achieved in the first generation. On the other hand, many of the indentured labourers became small farmers and leaseholders in the sugar colonies . . . . African migrant labour has remained for a variety of reasons close to its origins and sources of rural income. The imperial Open Spaces produced rapid urbanisation and the imperial tropics remained largely agricultural . . . .[3]

Our comparative insights were enhanced by dropping this distinction and considering in a single forum both the European, especially the British,

2

experience and that of the Third World, and it was this juxtaposition which participants found one of the most fruitful aspects of the seminar. In so doing, we moved across a whole range of experiences associated not only with the movement of 'free' and constrained labour, but also with questions of subsidised and unsubsidised family, male and female settlement, and temporary migration, of ideology and literature, both in Britain and in the Empire/Commonwealth. It is for this reason, too, that the essays on the British experience form such an important core of the present volume — a third of all our contributions.

II

The original justification for the seminar's existence was our appreciation of the formidable problems presented by the current literature and debate on the whole question of labour migration, both historically and in the present. In the light of the experience of the seminar, the justification still stands and remains the rationale behind the publication of this volume. There are essentially two aspects to this problem. The first concerns the state of historical literature on migration, a subject with which we are particularly concerned. To quote Newbury's 1975 article once again:

The historical literature [on migration] is richer in parochial studies than comparative works, in filiopietism and the literature of group settlement, than composite pictures of the universal migrant labourer.[4]

We would contest his view, however, that 'on the whole, the economists and demographers have made bolder and more intelligent expeditions in these regions of social mobility and change than historians . . .': their timeless 'universal migrant labourer' is as far away from the complex realities of the phenomenon as is the general run of historical studies. It is only through a theoretically-informed, historically specific approach that a more comprehensive and satisfactory account of labour migration can be produced, although experience of the seminar over the past four years has shown that this is a more difficult task than we anticipated. We shall return to this point, which is in essence both analytical and ideological.[5]

The failures of historians, demographers, economists, and geographers in tackling the issue are not unrelated to the state of the predominant theoretical literature on migration. The conventional approach to migrant labour is derived largely from the marginalist school of economics, which undertakes discussion 'within a theoretical framework based on the hypothesis that factors of production (labour, capital, natural resources and land) are given *a priori*'. This ahistorical approach ignores the fact that distribution of so-called factors of production is the result of economic strategy, as Samir Amin has pointed out.[6] It explains labour migration in terms of an oversupply acting as a 'natural mechanism' working in everyone's best interest to restore some kind of notional 'balance'.

Yet demography cannot be divorced in this way from the productive capacity of society and its social relations. The illogicality of so doing is illuminated by a recent study of the Puerto Rican experience of labour migration to the United States. Since World War II experts on Puerto Rico have believed that 'the Island could not sustain a population of a million and it was obviously necessary to export Puerto Ricans'. Critics of the government policy of exporting labour comment:

From this moment on the talk of population growth as an inexorable and catastrophic process was unceasing. Comparative population density statistics were citied to evoke cataclysmic images. Puerto Rico had in this period a density of 618 persons per square mile, as compared with 47 persons per square mile in the United States. It was noted that if the United States had a similar density it would hold more than three-quarters of the world's population, but it was rarely mentioned that the majority of Puerto Ricans in their flight from this human avalanche, were destined to land in New York City, where the population was around 90,000 per square mile. No work on migration in the United States raised any serious question as to the validity of the basic premise that Puerto Ricans are in the United States because they do not fit on the Island.[7]

Marx illustrated this point theoretically most clearly in his introduction to the *Grundrisse* when, in discussing the method of political economy, he argued that, although it would seem to be correct to begin with something as concrete as the numerical aspect of population in the initial stages of economic investigation, this is in fact a distortion:

Population is an abstract if I leave out, for example, the classes of which it is composed. These classes in turn are an empty phrase if I am not familiar with the elements on which they rest, e.g. wage labour, capital etc. These latter in turn presuppose exchange, division of labour, prices etc . . . Thus if I were to begin with population, this would then, by means of further determination, move analytically towards even more simple concepts, from the imagined concrete towards even thinner abstractions until I arrived at the simplest determinations. From there the journey would have to be retraced until I finally arrived at the population again, but this time not as a chaotic conception of a whole, but as a rich totality of many relations and determinations.[8]

The surplus population theory has its counterpart in the individualistic school of migration analysis which seeks to explain movement in terms of the attraction of better pay for work elsewhere, without reference to the society from which the emigrant leaves. This society is assumed to be a conglomeration of individuals who exercise free choice in leaving or staying; the assumption eliminates all discussion of the organisation of the society from which they come. A similar set of difficulties arises with dualist models of labour migration, especially whose which talk of the 'backward sloping curve of labour'. This theory, widely propogated in relation to migrant labour in Africa, holds that migrants are essentially single target workers, and therefore raising wages has a negative effect on the supply of labour because workers can earn their 'targets' — usually identified with taxes and simple, 'one-off', commodities like bicycles or sewing machines — in a shorter period of time. Although this approach has the undoubted merit of attempting to confront some of the problems of the society of origin and the conditions prevailing in the host country, its essential defect is not so much its abstract and ahistorical character as its failure to deal with interactive and disruptive effects of expansive and intrusive capitalism.[9]

These persistent tendencies within the economic literature to reify as social forms isolated or individual instances of migration, or to argue from *a priori* bases have often led to unhelpful or even irrelevant conclusions for historians of migration. An example of this which is dealt with in many of the contributions to this volume is the question of motivation. Why did people emigrate in the multifarious circumstances that have been analysed here? Are the explanations which the migrants gave for their movement acceptable as bases for a satisfactory historical explanation of the general phenomenon of their mobility? These are, of course, among the most intractable issues for historians, and indeed all social scientists. Edward Thompson has described this as 'the crucial ambivalence of our human presence in our own history, part subjects, part objects, the voluntary agents of our own involuntary determinations'.[10]

Yet most studies of labour migration have treated as wholly unproblematic the extent to which human actors are aware of the structural preconditions for what appear to be their freely-willed actions. The historical respectability that these individualistic explanations of mobility has received in the past derives, we would suggest, from the theoretical domination that the marginalist school of economic theory has enjoyed among historians until quite recently. As Brinley Thomas has observed, however:

History shows the influence of the threat of starvation, political oppression, religious persecution, eviction, avoidance of military service, a sense of adventure, an urge to make a fortune, a desire to join relatives or to get away from those at home, or perhaps just a flight from boredom. It is not by making a catalogue of such 'reasons' that one can hope to understand the phenomenon of migration any more than an attempt to describe the manifold motives leading people to want to buy a commodity would constitute an analysis of demand. Nothing is easier than to draw up a list of factors labelled 'push' and 'pull' and then write a descriptive account in terms of these sets of influences. Such an approach, however, will not throw much light on the deeper problems posed by migration as part of the process of economic expansion.[11]

Writing from a different historical tradition, Samir Amin has similarly observed that the

problem is to elucidate the reasons for the basic choice: that of the overall strategy, because it is there that the ultimate cause of migration lies. The rational choice of the migrant is nothing but the immediate apparent cause: a platitude which leads nowhere.[12]

In an important theoretical contribution to the seminar Colin Murray took this point even further. Criticising attempts by social scientists to resolve the problem of structure and motivation by distinguishing 'between an underlying economic pressure to migrate, which operates at the level of structure, and contingent social circumstances, which operate at the level of motivation', Murray maintains that the study of migration is 'the study of structural transformation', which can only be understood through an analysis of particular historical processes of differentiation and integration; in this analysis the economic cannot be hived off from the political and social, with the former labelled 'structure' and the latter 'contingent'.[13]

As organisers of the seminar and editors we have sought to encourage contributors to approach their material in this light, while avoiding the over-mechanical concepts implicit in Amin's notion of 'strategy'. Specific examples of the treatment of the structure/motivation problem are to be found in the contributions of Donald Denoon and Colin Newbury, while three other contributors to this volume in particular tackle aspects of the problems of structure and population as well as motivation by closely analysing three very different supplier societies: David Souden on early modern England, Adrian Graves on the south-west Pacific 'labour reserve', and Peter Richardson on the northern provinces of China. Souden in particular addresses himself to the demographic issues. Thus he argues that in the early stages of English emigration to the newly established colonies of the New World, there was 'considerable outward impetus'; this was not simply, as some have argued, that 'early modern Englishmen were conditioned to movement and that the Atlantic crossing was one more stage in a migratory career, but that similar (demographic and economic) forces were impelling much movement within England as well as outside'. Without the efflux of labour from England, he maintains, the necessity for demographic reversal in England would undoubtedly have occurred earlier than it did.[14]

Richardson is also concerned to show the connections between population pressure and outward migration — again not in any simplistic sense, but in relation to the existing forces of production in the northern Chinese provinces of Shantung, Chihli, and Honan, from which the vast majority of indentured labourers for the Transvaal gold mining industry were drawn. Overpopulation came in the context of natural and man-made disasters after 1900 meanth that the continuation of the emigration outlet was economy; according to Richardson 'the intensification of the disasters after 1900 meant that the continuation of the emigration outlet was imperative for continued socio-economic stability in north China.'[15] Both Richardson and Souden show the differential impact of these pressures on rural society. In England Souden suggests that it was not necessarily the poor who left as indentured servants in the seventeenth and eighteenth centuries — a finding which has been used, misleadingly in our view, by some to undermine structural interpretations of migration.[16] In the Chinese case Richardson suggests that the migrants were drawn from 'the lowest strata of the rural economy' of north China: members of poor peasant families, rural wage labourers, urban casual labourers, and the entirely destitute.[17] The difference between the two examples is perhaps in part to be explained in terms of the closer control of recruitment in the Chinese case by state and local authorities.

Like Richardson, Graves is concerned with the complex, yet concrete, material origins of migrant labour. His analysis of Pacific Island migration concentrates on the way in which the communal agricultural economy of the islands was transformed into a labour reserve for the sugar plantations and colonial labour markets of the region. Contesting the views of the 'revisionists' who have concentrated on the individual initiatives of the migrants or the (undoubted) brutalities of the trade, Graves stresses the 'interactive and disruptive effects of expansive, intrusive capitalism' on the subsistence economy of the islands with its finely-honed system of production, and redistribution through exchange. Unlike the situation described by Souden and Richardson, in the south-west Pacific, as in nineteenth-century southern Africa, there was no readily available supply of landless labourers waiting for the opening up of a colonial labour market. The processes of proletarianisation resulted from the penetration of traders, settlers, missionaries, and foreign navies and were exacerbated by natural disaster.[18] In many ways the picture drawn by Graves parallels recent work on the early stages of labour migration in southern and central Africa,[19] though clearly the specifics of social organisation of the pre-capitalist societies in the two regions are very different.

For all their concentration on the transformation in the supplier countries, Souden, Richardson, and Graves leave little doubt that the flow of labour is intrinsically related to colonial demand. In the case of the south-west Pacific the connection is clear: the labour force was literally created in response to the demand; in the case of the Chinese, too, the mechanisms of recruitment show very clearly the way in which China's 'surplus population' was tapped; even in the English case, however, Souden is able to show that supply was related to demand. 'In depression, there were many who wished to emigrate for whom there was no demand; in boom times merchants were able to dupe many to go [to the New World colonies] by promises of work . . . Demand called the tune since booms and slumps in staple trades determined the intensity with which indentured servants were sought.'[20]

This crucial relationship between migration and the development of the modern international economy was one that presented itself insistently to the seminar over the years and it can be seen clearly in almost all the chapters in this collection dealing with areas as diverse as the United States, Surinam, Chile, Mauritius, Guyana, and South Africa, to name but a few at random. To those familiar with the pioneering researches of Brinley Thomas, the association of the phenomenon of migration with inter-national capitalism will come as no surprise. As early as 1958 he noted that from the 1840s until the First World War:

The long swings in the economic development of the United Kingdom and the United States were inverse to one another; and that this coincided with a one-way traffic of capital and labour across the Atlantic . . . . The inverse relation was true not only of Great Britain and the United States, but also of Great Britain and the other debtor countries — Australia, Canada, and Argentina.[21]

Two of our contributors in particular, Newbury and Denoon, in pieces which are in themselves comparative, and which deal respectively with New Zealand, Northern Nigeria, and Australian New Guinea on the one hand, and with six regions of European settlement in the temperate zone (in Australasia, southern Africa, and southern South America) carry Thomas' analysis further. They show the contribution that differing forms of migration made to specific and widely dispersed forms of capitalism, identified by the boundaries of the present-day nation state. Paradoxically, the increased 'nationalisation of the globe' was accompanied by the increased internationalisation of capital and of labour, and was indeed dependent and consequent on this process.[22]

Writing from a very different tradition to that of Brinley Thomas, Philip Corrigan has recently made a very similar point:

It may well be that the major form of labour's contribution to the making and remaking of capitalism as a world market system is large-scale circulation. We shall never grasp 'the facts' if we fail to appreciate labour as it is itself treated (in practice, in accounts, in State policies) as a commodity which is circulated.[23]

If the expansion of capital internationally saw the circulation of labour as a commodity, the second point which needs to be made in this regard is the multiplicity of forms which it took: again this is illustrated in the comparative piece by Newbury but also emerges clearly from all the chapters. Newbury further elaborates his critique of the settler/indentured labour distinction current in much comparative writing on international labour migration. He suggests that:

a more useful distinction in migrant categories lies between those whose conditions of work and levels of skills allowed them to enjoy a measure of vertical mobility, and those whose entry into such economies was partial, peripheral and without political influence on the organisation of the state.[24]

Newbury's point about migrant categories is a clue to one of the most fruitful and recurrent themes of our meetings: the extent to which the extension of capitalism and its attendant circulation of capital and labour contributed directly to the widespread reintroduction of forms of constrained or bonded labour. As the papers by Emmer, Graves, Legassick and de Clercq, Richardson, Tinker, Denoon, and Newbury all indicate, indenture was a widespread response of colonial governments and capitalists to a variety of situations where relatively abundant supplies of cheap land, alternative and competitive sources of wage labour, or relatively low capital investment made free labour an impractical base upon which capital accumulation could proceed. Souden shows very clearly the persistence with which indentured service remained part of the labour migration within the confines of the British empire, in the case of Barbados actually pre-dating slavery.[25] Charlotte Erickson's contribution, however, suggests the difficulty of sustaining forms of bonded labour in societies where abundant land is readily available outside the control of the importing society — one reason for the failure of indentured service to survive for long in post-independence north America. There alternatives such as contract labour only provided for particular industrial and managerial skills but were not the chief means of obtaining skilled or unskilled labour.[26] (Joy Parr's work on the indentured migration to Canada of the children of the poor through such philanthropic agencies as Dr Barnado's suggests another way round the dilemma found by colonial employers.[27]) In short, as Philip Corrigan pointed out in the article already cited, far from the extension of capitalism being synonymous with the introduction of 'free' labour or a free market in labour, in many colonial and post-colonial settings constraint and bondage became the very basis upon which capitalism developed: Corrigan terms these forms of unfree labour 'capitalist monuments' rather than the 'feudal relics' they are so often perceived to be.[28]

This issue is closely related to another which also received prominent treatment in the seminar: the distinction between voluntary and involuntary migration, or between free and bonded labour. Both Newbury and Denoon treat this question at some length in their papers, and as their conclusions echo many that were voiced in the course of our discussions, they are worth repeating here. In reviewing the predominant form of labour migration identified in his six settler countries of Argentina, Chile, Uruguay, New Zealand, Australia, and South Africa, Denoon concludes:

While white migrants did indeed make individual choices in response to employment opportunities, they did so in a highly structured context. In effect, the government of our societies delegated to market forces the provision of white immigrants; when market forces were inadequate governments intervened. The distinction between 'voluntary' and 'involuntary' migration is not as sharp as it may seem. Any reliance upon voluntarism to explain the quantity, quality and fluctuations of labour migration is unfounded.[29]

Similarly, Newbury concludes:

. . . it may be objected that the category of 'settler' implies a freedom of mobility and location which was absent from plantation and industrial labourers in the imperial tropics. Such a distinction ignores the large proportion of colonial state assistance for white settlers as well as indentured labour in the nineteenth century, and the constraints on choice apparent in the market mechanisms of passage-brokers, limited capital and personal savings, and sheer ignorance of conditions of settlement and employment in overseas territories in North

America, Australia, and Africa. It ignores, too, the large amount of rural-urban migration and settlement within the imperial tropics not subject to administrative control.[30]

A more important distinction, then, than that between 'settler' and migrant worker is that between different kinds of workers, skilled or unskilled. A great deal depended too on the specific type of production involved. Six papers in this volume deal with the inter-relationship of particular commodities and immigrant labour; five deal with unskilled migrants and one, that of Gillian Burke, with the metalliferous miners of Cornwall who had their own very special set of skills.[31]

Burke's discussion of the Cornish diaspora has a very different flavour from that of the other five papers in this category, in part because it illuminates the position of workers who had a relatively scarce skill at a time when changing technology increased the demand for hard rock miners. As a result this group of international 'tramping artisans' came in the course of the nineteenth century to play a central role in the development and exploitation of mineral deposits around the world which provided the raw material upon which new industrial techniques were built. As they did so, they developed a peculiar migratory pattern, which was fully undermined only at the end of the century when the demand for new types of mining skills was making the more fully trained and scientifically informed American engineers the new international skilled migrants of the mining world.[32]

In the nineteenth century, however, the greatest demand was for un-skilled migrant labour and came from plantations, especially sugar plantations in the tropics and sub-tropics, and from mines and railways around the world. It is unfortunate that we were unable to include an exploration of the international brigades of railway workers in this collection. In the case of sugar, which we consider at some length, the demand for vast quantities of labour, either in the new colonies of white settlement such as Queensland, or from former slave-owning societies such as Surinam, Guyana, or Mauritius (to name only those represented in this volume) was almost exclusively met by the introduction of indentured labour, a correlation that gave this form of commodity production an unenviable reputation for exploitation, building as it did on the previous correlation of sugar and slavery. The papers by Graves, Emmer, and Tinker all suggest that the predominant form of sugar production in the nineteenth century was largely responsible for the necessary connection between indenture and immigration. Without penal sanction to civil contract, the necessary regularity of labour supply could not be ensured either to meet the requisite scale of production or to continue its labour intensive character. According to Legassick and de Clercq a similar necessity of guaranteeing labour supplies for the gold mines of South Africa in the face of inadequate local supply and persistent production demands lay behind the extension of the 'international indentured labour system', for a short period, as Peter Richardson's paper records, as far afield as north China, and, over a more protracted period, to southern Mozambique.

Yet if the message of these papers is that the form of labour service was remarkably similar for the unskilled in similar types of commodity production in widely differing colonial settings, the reserves of labour which met this demand varied enormously. The submission of African producers from Mozambique, Indian agricultural labourers, Pacific Islanders, and impoverished Chinese peasants to the common bondage of indenture, whatever the difference of contract, illustrates the interaction between expansive capitalism and the great range of alternative modes of production which characterised international migration at this time. The insights into the nature of 'labour reserves' pioneered especially in the southern African literature[33] should not be confined, however, to our understanding of the sources of 'unfree', unskilled labour. As Gillian Burke's piece illustrates quite clearly, Cornwall functioned as a major labour reserve for the provision of skilled labour in a manner directly comparable with that played by India, China, the Pacific Islands, or the subsistence societies of central and southern Africa, even if these reserves were exploited in a variety of ways, ranging from direct coercion and manipulation in southern Africa and the Pacific, through treaty-port capitalism in China, to studious official neglect in the case of Cornwall.

The exploitation of these far-flung reserves of labour also necessitated the introduction of local intermediaries to facilitate the process of interaction between these radically different forms of social organisation, and in many cases required the introduction of a new functionary in the business of moving people, the contractor. As Eric Hobsbawm has remarked, 'Where there is a large demand for labour (or land) on the one side, a population ignorant of conditions in the receiving country on the other and a long distance between, the agent or contractor will flourish.'[34] Graves' piece on Pacific Island labour in Queensland contains a particularly instructive study of the role of these intermediaries and functionaries, the so-called passage masters of the South-west Pacific.[35] Their strategic position in the chain of interests involved in the importation of labour opened up new sources of wealth and prestige within 'traditional' society which directly parallels the functions of many African chiefs or Chinese and Indian headmen in their dealings with labour recruiters. In this context the absence of a study of the minutiae of moving subsidised emigrants to a colony of settlement is unfortunate, for the shipping companies and their agents probably fulfilled a directly comparable role, as Newbury suggests. Some of this can be gleaned, however, from the valuable information in Erickson's paper about the procedure of recruiting for contract labour in the United States in the nineteenth century.[36]

Closely connected to the growth of shipping agencies and recruiting contractors is another equally important feature of migration, particularly in the nineteenth century: the role of technology in transforming the transport of migrants. Although this received attention in the seminar, it is unfortunate that we have been unable to secure a contribution on the subject for this collection for, as Ashworth and many others after him have commented, 'the railway and the steamship transformed the physical problem of movement'.[37]

Recruiting and shipping agencies in the colonies of white settlement were, as Newbury and Denoon remind us, frequently linked with the colonial state, and this brings into focus another range of questions which featured prominently in our discussions and which run through a number of the contributions in this collection. The first of these concerns the role of the state. Several issues are, in fact, subsumed under this heading and we are unable to do them full justice here. The importance of identifying precisely the particular locus of state instrumentality was stressed continously. This can be followed in Pieter Emmer's discussion of the introduction of Indian labour into Surinam, following the abolition of slavery in the Dutch colony. Here the distinct role of the Indian state as a mobilising agent for colonial capitalism and the concurrent role of the colonial state in Surinam as an arbiter of the local labour market and a dependent importer of labour for particular industries can be identified. A not dissimiliar set of preoccupations recurs in Tinker's account of the transitions in the British sugar islands from 'slavery to nationalisation'. Graves' paper also draws attention to the function of the state as controller and regulator of the conditions of the emigrant trade between the source country and the colonial labour market, while Erickson draws attention to the judicial function of government in administering anti-immigrant legislation — a subject which was elaborated by Robin Cohen in an analysis (not included in this volume) of contemporary United States policy towards migrant labour from the Caribbean and Mexico.[38] Contrary to nineteenth century *laisser faire* ideology, in all these situations the colonial state, and at times also the British state, intervened actively to shape and control the labour market.

Perhaps the clearest exposition of the multifarious role of the state in the processes of migration can be seen in two contrasting pieces in this volume, by Newbury and by Legassick and de Clercq. Newbury draws attention to the comprehensive state intervention in the differing contexts of New Zealand, Nigeria, and New Guinea. In identifying the comparative poverty of capital investment in these regions in contrast to the more developed economies of north America and Australia, he argues that:

in these circumstances of comparative disadvantage . . . the role of colonial governments, whether representing settler interests or installed as simple autarchies of the 'Crown Colony' type to uphold the interests of the metropole and a balance of local polities, is correspondingly increased.[39]

Legassick and de Clercq go even further in their analysis of the conditions governing the accumulation of capital in southern Africa. They identify three distinct but inter-related functions of the state in this context: the promotion of a supply of labour from within the boundaries of the colonial state by such means as increased monetary taxation on subsistence producers and restrictions on land tenure; the regulation and reinforcement of recruiting procedures in conditions where measures promoting an internal supply of labour were insufficient to match the demand; and, lastly, by intervention in the resultant division of labour, to both perpetuate and extend it while protecting the dominant classes from the contradictory effects of such a policy.[40]

The broad sweep of their remarks raises several issues which are also touched on by other contributors to this volume, but which warrant further exploration. Thus the relationship between international and internal migration is of concern to Erickson in her discussion of the difficulties of sustaining forms of contract labour in societies where abundant land is readily available outside the control of the colonial state — a feature also of South Africa's pre-industrial economy, and a major factor behind the conquest of African societies there in the late nineteenth century.[41] Such considerations are not only relevant, therefore, to societies with a high incidence of constrained labour, whether or not there is an abundance of land, but are also significant in settler societies generally associated with a predominance of 'free' emigration.

Thus, as Marx pointed out in his critique of Wakefield's theory of colonisation, if the availability of land is not to undermine the capitalist development of the colonies, the price of land must be high enough to prevent labourers from becoming independent landowners until others have followed to take their place:

This [Wakefield's] sufficient price for the land is nothing but a euphemistic circumlocution for the ransom which the worker must pay to the capitalist in return for permission to retire from the wage-labour market to the land.[42]

A recurring theme in this collection and in our seminar discussion relates to the political advantages of a system of migrant labour for dominant classes in both the supplying and the recipient countries. Both Souden and Burke in the British context and Graves and Richardson in a Third World context point to the significance of emigration as a 'safety valve'.[43] For societies undergoing socio-economic and demographic dislocation, the ability to disgorge their 'surplus population' contributed powerfully to the maintenance of social order. Burke takes this point furthest in her examination of the much vaunted tradition of worker docility in Cornwall and the failure of trade union organisation there until the twentieth century. Her view that migrant labour constituted an 'escape hatch' when conditions in Cornwall worsened is strengthened by the timing of working class discontent there — periods when the 'escape hatch' was closed; and by the evidence of considerable militancy on the part of Cornish miners who found themselves in Australia, South Africa, and the United States.[44]

For the host countries, too, as Legassick and de Clercq point out, there are considerable advantages in a system of migrant labour. Even after the proletarianisation of a sufficient number of Africans within the boundaries of the Union/Republic, the mining industry recruited the bulk of its labour force from outside, and there are many other examples of situations in which capitalist enterprises 'deliberately sought migrant labour rather than use available local workers'.[45] In addition to Legassick and de Clercq, Denoon's papers discusses some of the advantages: a migrant labour system not infrequently lends itself to the division of the working class along ethnic/racial or national lines, which gives actual and ideological power to dominant social groups. This is most clearly seen in the divided working class in South Africa, and in the way the state there has manipulated boundaries of ethnic groups in order to define and redefine those who had access to the labour market and on what terms. For the host country the creation of a rightless population with the attendant possibilities of control which derive from such juridical status can be of crucial importance: here again South Africa provides the most blatant, but by no means the only, example.[46]

There is a further consideration in this context and that is the nature of militancy and resistance, as well as class consciousness, which emigrant groups display in such rightless and dependent situations. It is frequently held that their resistance is defined by the structural position in the labour processes of the industries they are employed in, and has a largely defensive character.[47] At the same time this structural dependency makes such migrants particularly useful as strike-breakers.[48] There is some confirmatory evidence of this in the frequently held stereotype of the Cornish miner yet Burke's evidence is rather more complex and contradictory. In this case we are dealing with a fully proletarianised, highly skilled, working class: even in the case of the unskilled migrant, however, we should not assume universal docility. Much depended on the organisation of the workplace, and the 'moral economy' of the society the migrant left behind. David Hemson has shown, for example, that in Durban the dockworkers, who were daily paid migrants, were the most militant and class-conscious sector of the workforce,[49] while recently Ernesto Laclau has suggested that, although migrants to the city inevitably bring with them 'the symbols and ideological values of the society from which they come', these may in fact express 'exactly the opposite of traditionalism: a refusal to accept capitalist legality'.[50] The experience of migrant labour may also lead returnees to the rural areas to reject the legality of existing social authority there.[51] Certainly the transforming effect of migrant labour on rural society has received a great deal of attention in the African literature on migration,[52] and is represented in this volume by Graves' analysis of its impact on societies on the Pacific Islands. The whole subject however warrants further exploration and is not adequately represented here.

III

It is, of course, inevitable in a collection of this nature that certain areas have remained under- or un-explored. Nor would we want in any way to claim that the volume represents the coherent and distilled essence of a research school of migration theory, working from a common perspective. Although we tried to direct the attention of contributors to, and participants in, the seminar to what we considered key areas, we have not tried to impose a uniform approach. The diverse approaches are to some extent inevitable given the context in which the seminar came into being. It is hardly to be expected that a seminar and a subsequent collection of essays which owed their rationale to a long tradition of unsatisfactory empirical and theoretical work on the subject should, in the space of four years, succeed where others with greater experience and resources at their command have failed.

The generally unsatisfactory state of migration theory and historical studies dealing with migration is still clearly reflected in this volume. There is certainly no consensus about either theories of labour migration or the methodology that would derive from such theories, whatever the perceived inadequacy of the current literature. The problem is perhaps less easily recognisable in this volume because of the sheer diversity of the material published: the methodological and theoretical differences are probably only immediately apparent to other specialists familiar with the debates surrounding issues tackled in particular essays. Only on occasion are differences of opinion made explicit and obvious between the different contributors. Nor is this surprising. Historians tend to work in a tradition of empirical research in which it is unusual for them to spell out their ideological or philosophical vantage point. Yet it is from this conceptual framework, however unconscious, that their more specific analysis and conclusions are drawn.[53]

When this seminar was first proposed it was suggested that one possible way forward amid the confusion of competing explanatory models was to adopt what Marx termed in the *Grundrisse* the method of political economy which rejected 'a chaotic conception of the whole' and worked instead on the basis of a 'rich totality of many relations and determinations',[54] political, economic, social, and demographic. This can, however, only be done through the study of historical particularity. In this context a point made strongly by William Freund in his presentation to the seminar is worth repeating:

Only when analysis of migration is given historical specifity can we transcend the 'debate' of push or pull and undigested quantitative roll-calls of migrants which underlie an unsatisfactory sociological literature on the subject.[55]

Colin Murray, himself an anthropologist, made a not dissimilar point to the seminar. After a careful discussion of the way labour migration has been handled in the African anthropological and sociological literature, he concluded:

The study of migration is the study of processes of structural transformation. Recognition of this implies its corollary: a commitment to historical particularity — the processes by which societies X and Y have been incorporated and transformed — rather than to functionalist generalization — the attributes of societies X and Y, respectively, predispose them to respond to generalized pressure by exhibiting different rates of migration.[56]

It is by the combination of the methodology of political economy with historical specifity, we would suggest, that something of conceptual significance can be extracted from a comparative study of labour migration of the type we have undertaken. Yet it is important also to stress the limits of this claim. We are not arguing for what Guy Standing has called 'an attempt to do the impossible: to provide a general framework for a materialist approach to migration research'.[57] By directing attention, however, towards the nature of the demand for labour in relation to capital accumulation, the structure of both supplying and host country in relation to its social and property relations, and the impact of migrant labour on these relationships at the economic, political, social, and ideological levels, we believe that the complexity of the phenomenon of labour migration and of the labour migrant can be understood in a manner that has both comparative and historical value. For all their obvious lacunae and limitations, the essays in this collection represent a first step in this direction.

1

ENGLISH INDENTURED SERVANTS AND THE TRANSATLANTIC COLONIAL ECONOMY

DAVID SOUDEN

WILLIAM DOUGHTY expressed his home thoughts from Barbados in 1667, writing to his brother Robert in their family home in Norfolk; he hoped he might soon 'clare mee of this isle to w[hi]ch is Easy to giit on but hard to get of [f] many so find it by experience'.[1] Doughty was a plantation accountant, he had '. . . . tried other places in these remote parts to have Raysed my Fortune for Benefit my selfe & children . . .', but his prospects were not bright:

And as for my continuance here cann doe noe good, for that Every tradesman that buy and sell under ye Notion & Collour of a merchant tho not knoweinge in booke keepeinge & accounts as every Merchant ought yet are growne soe riche by Trade, as they cann bring upp their owne children or other Young Ladds to write a faire hand wch satisfye them in keepeinge bookes and drawing out accounts for them.[2]

He eventually got back to England, leaving an island increasingly dominated by white sugar planters and their Negro slaves, in which work opportunities for whites were mainly confined to craft, overseeing, and mercantile positions. The opportunities for self-advancement which had obtained in the early years of white settlement in this part of the Caribbean were blocked.[3]

Doughty was one of the hundreds of thousands of Englishmen and women who crossed the Atlantic to the plantation colonies in the course of the seventeenth and early eighteenth centuries; he was one of the relatively few who made their way back. Given his social position, from a gentle family, and crossing with trading goods to sell, he would have been in the minority who crossed at their own expense and who were free. At least some of those who usurped his position, and very many of his co-islanders, would have crossed the Atlantic under indenture.

Barbados, other English possessions in the West Indies, the plantation tobacco economies of Virginia and Maryland, and the later plantations of the Carolinas and Georgia, received considerable white labour supplies in the seventeenth and eighteenth centuries in the form of indentured servants. In exchange for their rights to offer their labour freely after a defined period, most commonly four years, indentured servants were given passage across the Atlantic, board and lodging during the term of the indenture, and, at least in theory, payment in land, money, or in kind at its expiry.[4]

One of the consistent features of colonial and imperial organisation of migrant labour, the indenture system provided a means of retaining labour in the medium term, a means of exchanging labour performance for future economic or labour prospects, and an institutional framework to facilitate the movement of people. A number of major flows of labour migrants have operated through indenturing in the modern period as well as in earlier centuries.[5] Much of the colonial peopling of England's New World plantation colonies — or at least the white portion thereof — was achieved through indenturing. As in the case of slavery, commentators have often been tempted to regard indentured servitude as an institution which, because of its longevity, remained essentially unchanged for extended periods. The major purpose of this paper is to examine the course of change within the institution of English indentured servitude through the seventeenth and into the eighteenth century. A changing English supply of labour and changing, differential colonial demand for labour shaped that institution, its meteoric rise and its equally impressive decline.[6]

The scale and timing of movement

Writing in the 1670s, Carew Reynel registered his disapproval of the scale of emigration from England in preceding decades:

The country complains of small vend of commodities, which proceeds especially from want of people; for our people were consumed mightily in these late years, some three hundred thousand were killed in the last Civil War; and about two hundred thousand more have been wasted in repeopling Ireland; and two hundred thousand lost in the great sickness, and as many more gone to plantations.[7]

The figures Reynel provided are very broad estimates (he wildly overestimated the contemporary population of Barbados, for example) but nevertheless they do suggest the large degree of English emigratory activity towards her seventeenth-century colonies. One of the greatest difficulties in assessing that movement has been to estimate the size of those flows and to estimate the proportion of those flows represented by indentured servants.

Recent advances in estimation procedures have provided more refined evidence on the global scale of transatlantic movement. Henry Gemery's estimates, deriving from colonial population totals and demographic series, suggest a total of some 380,000 British migrants crossing the Atlantic in the years 1630-1700.[8] Well over half of that number crossed during the three decades between 1630 and 1660, with some 69,000 in the 1630s, about the same number in the 1640s, and 72,000 in the 1650s. Thereafter, numbers fell somewhat: 42,000 in the 1660s, 52,000 in the 1670s, 43,000 in the 1680s, and 30,000 in the final decade of the series.[9] Of all these migrants, a proportion approaching two-thirds are estimated to have moved to the West Indies, little more than a tenth to New England and other northern and middle colonies on the American mainland, and the remainder to southern colonies — and hence in particular to the Chesapeake colonies of Virginia and Maryland. Moreover, each region had a distinctive chronology of immigration. The attractiveness of the Caribbean was especially notable in the years to 1660, with two-thirds of its immigration occurring then; the southern plantations received most numbers in the period 1650-80, while movement further north peaked in the 1630s with the Great Migration to New England, and in the 1660s and 1680s with the capture of colonies from the Dutch and foundation of Pennsylvania. The 1690s undoubtedly saw net out-migration from these northern areas.

The mental picture most carry with them of the seventeenth century English emigrant is that of the Pilgrim Father, of the divine bound for New England. Whatever their importance for subsequent historiography, self-esteem, and as a seed population for that region's substantial level of natural increase, this group was in the aggregate relatively insignificant. In the 1630s, when that movement was particularly concentrated, just as many went to Virginia — and probably four times as many to the West Indies.[10]

Without doubt the size and timing of these various emigrant streams vary in direct relationship with the share of indentured servant labour, destined predominantly for plantation work, in those streams.

An independent set of estimates for outward movement from England — although net movement and for all destinations — is presented in Wrigley and Schofield's recent volume on England's population history.[11] These results are problematic, in that they are the residual element in a much wider investigation, represent the net balance between inward flows (especially from the Celtic countries of the British Isles) and outward flows, and encompass all destinations and those dying in war or at sea. Nevertheless they represent a considerable advance on previous knowledge, and are readily open to interpretation.

These estimates likewise suggest a rapid rise in the level of emigration from the 1620s to the 1650s and 1660s, and an equally rapid fall thereafter. The low point in the late seventeenth century was followed by a rise to a plateau which lasted for some two-thirds of the eighteenth century, with a noticeable drop in the latter years of that century. This procedure has produced estimates of some 100,000 net emigrants in the 1640s, 100,000 in the 1660s, 40,000 in the 1680s, 50,000 in the 1700s, and 33,000 in the 1780s. For comparison with Gemery, the years 1630-1700 thus saw about half a million individuals 'lost' to the English demographic system.[12] At its peak in the 1650s, this represents a net loss at the rate of 2.4 per 1,000 per annum — a figure noticeably higher than that obtaining in the mid-nineteenth century.

As the quotation from Reynel indicated, and as other contemporaries noted, Ireland received many English settlers and traders in the seventeenth century. Given such discrepancies, these two series match each other gratifying well: transatlantic migration may be seen to have been a substantial proportion of all observable movement, the general trends in movement would appear to have moved together and to have turned at the same time.[13]

The scale of wastage among these migrants was considerable: the 210,000 which Gemery estimates left for the colonies between 1630 and 1660 served to raise colonial populations by some 100,000 only, an expression of the swingeing mortality levels in the Caribbean and the southern colonies.[14]

The indentured

If it is difficult to ascertain with any great degree of accuracy the size of the migrant flow to the colonies, it is even more of a problem to estimate the size of the indentured component within that. Indentured service was extremely rare in the northern colonies and only represented a small share in that stream.[15] Most commentators are agreed that at the very least a half of the emigrants to colonies in the south and the Caribbean in the seventeenth century travelled under indenture. Henry Gemery's estimates would indicate that Bristol and London annual shipments of indentured servants accounted for between a quarter and a half of the annual level of aggregate emigration which his data suggest for the third quarter of the century; Lois Carr and Russell Menard estimate the indentured servant component in Maryland immigration during 1634-81 to have been in the range 70-85 per cent of the total.[16]

The origins of indentured servitude are, if not obscure, by no means entirely clear. The institution had obvious ancestors at home, however. Labour retention in exchange for security was a primary feature of the employment patterns of the young and unmarried in early modern England. Servants in husbandry, domestic servants, and apprentices formed a large proportion of that section of the population.[17] Given the initial expenditure on indentured servants bound for the colonies, principally the cost of the passage across the Atlantic, retaining labour for periods longer than the year's hiring customary in service at home would be needed in order to recoup the investment made.[18]

For the most part servants were indentured for four years: men with special skills often received shorter indenture terms, youngsters longer.[19] Males dominated the institution; most seventeenth century evidence shows there to have been three or four men indentured to every woman. Servants were most commonly young adults — lists of indentures show those aged between 15 and 24 to represent some 60 to 75 per cent of the total.[20] Occupational ascriptions for the indentured, where they were recorded, present a seemingly bewildering occupational mix, although concentrated in agricultural, impoverished textile working, and skilled craft groups.[21]

Contemporaries who expressed their written thoughts about indentured servants in the colonies divided between those who castigated the indentured as indigent and vagrant, and those who stressed their superior qualities and the reasonable nature of their work — both expressions of vested interest in the debates which ranged over the colonies and their contribution to the home economy.

At mid-seventeenth century the propaganda war raged. George Gardyner painted a picture of deluded settlers and of hardship, and believed that trade with America '. . . . is prejudiciall in that it carrieth away daily such men as might serve their country . . . .' 'Tis dishonourable, in that we are upbraided by all other Nations that know that trade for selling our own Countrymen for the Commodities of those places.'[22] His descriptions of the horrors are countered by the blandishments of tracts advertising the delights of the colonies: 'Young youths from 16 years and upwards, for Apprentices and Servants for some years, then to have Land given them, and cattel to set them up. Thousands of these kinds of young boyes and maydens wanting.'[23] John Hammond advised his readers that 'The labour servants are put to, is not so hard nor of such continuance as Husbandmen nor Handecraftmen are kept at in England.'[24]

To penetrate the polemic on working conditions is difficult. In the heat and harsh mortality environment, conditions must have been difficult, and occasionally impossible. Richard Ligon claimed, for example, that English servants in Barbados were excessively ill-treated, but then proceeded to show in his descriptions of plantation life how, with a few exceptions of cruel and exploitative masters, the servants' lot was not unduly severe.[25] Historians until recently have tended to side with one view or the other. We shall have occasion to examine the validity of some of the statements later; certainly, shifts in the timing and volume of migration are likely to have produced changes in the treatment and consideration of servants.

England was not alone in possessing a colonial plantation empire, staple crops being worked by white servants. The French and Dutch empires were closest in character to the English, especially in the Caribbean. Neither, however, appear to have had quite the same extent of labour migration: the French possessions were not as large as the English on islands and mainland combined, while the Dutch were considerably more involved in trading and shipping than they were in colonisation.[26] Thus, for example, there were over six thousand *engagés* leaving La Rochelle for the French Antilles in the period 1634-1715, and another twelve hundred in 1715-72.[27] Emigration from France to the islands and Canada stood at a reasonably high level in the eighteenth century: 26,000 or 27,000 from the Pyrenees, for example, left Bordeaux in the years 1713 to 1789.[28] There are indications therefore that the trends in the seventeenth-century European colonial empires move in sympathy, but that eighteenth-century developments were more variegated.

What were the circumstances which impelled the English in particular to move overseas, what were the opportunities which lured them?

Supply and the 'margin of migration'

One of the major contentions of this article is that emigration activity for our period must be viewed within the context of general levels of physical mobility in the English economy. For the most part historians have been unwilling to work on both internal and external migration in tandem — a product of the objectives for which their researches have been designed, and of the documentation available. Recent work on migration activity within early modern England provides a clearer view than that available hitherto of the scale of, and variation in, mobility at a variety of levels.[29]

This was a society characterised by a high degree of localised movement, movement conditioned by agricultural and domestic service, apprenticeship, spatial exogamy, and neo-local residence of married couples, landholding and -markets, and by variable labour demand. Welded to this was longer-range movement, into London, and other towns and cities, and into areas which were better able to sustain growing numbers. Rapid population growth in the second half of the sixteenth century and the first half of the seventeenth pressed heavily on finite economic resources, and there is much evidence for considerable structural difficulty within the economy. Areas which were better able to absorb the increase, although by no means easily, were not only urban environments but also pastoral and woodland localities, where part-time industry was often used to help secure a living.

With demographic and economic disparities within the country, there were not only intra-regional migration flows but inter-regional flows as well, predominantly away from the more marginal north and west towards the wealthier south and east.

However, with stagnant, at one point falling, numbers in the population in the period from the mid-seventeenth to the early eighteenth century, and with rising real wages (and incomes),[30] so the pressures of numbers which had produced the large-scale 'subsistence' character of movement in pre-Civil War England were diminished. The volume of rural movement appears to have contracted quite considerably: fewer people were making significant moves, and were moving less often. Men, in particular, were moving shorter distances. Males in the professions and distributive trades, and women in general, provide a significant exception. Women in the countryside moved as often and usually as far as they had done previously, and moved further and in greater numbers into towns.

The structural necessities which had produced so much movement were considerably reduced; soon commentators were complaining of the paucity of numbers and the insufficient size of the home labour force.[31]

There is nothing so much wanting in England as people; and all sorts of people, the industrious and laborious sort, and handicraftmen, are wanted to till and improve our land, and help to manufacture the staple commodites of the kingdom; which would add greatly to the riches thereof.[32]

The broad similarities between these two forms of English migratory activity, internal and external, are suggestive. Emigration built up from insignificant levels to a mid-century peak and then fell a way thereafter quite rapidly; the volume and flows of internal movement were high to the mid-seventeenth century and then contracted, becoming much less 'subsistence-derived' in character.

In essence therefore, an important part of emigration may represent an extension of the 'margin of migration', another expedient in migration strategies to attempt to overcome economic disadvantage. Such was directly expressed by Sir Henry Blunt to the House of Lords Committee investigating the decay of rents and trade in 1669. 'Ireland takes many away, some the fens and some the plantations', he declared.[33] The fens represented a pastoral destination for internal migrants wishing to secure an economic toehold;[34] Ireland and the staple colonies represented some of the alternatives. All were known as high-risk mortality environments.

So on the one hand emigration may be viewed as representing the end of a chain of such options for movement, involving the possibility of movement to town or pastoral location, movement out of such areas to a major port city, and, finding limited opportunity there, taking ship for an overseas destination. On the other hand, many movements represented the result of a series of cost-benefit calculations: movement overseas would mean discounting future penalties against the short- and medium-term economic gains in much the same way as did movement into towns and unhealthy marshy areas.

This discussion, when coupled with that in the previous section on the nature and composition of the indenture system, raises the likelihood that we may be able to disaggregate the flows. There were always 'higher-status' emigrants under indenture: planters' or merchants' apprentices, the fictitiously indentured intended to procure land rights, men possessing specialist craft, literacy, or accountancy skills. If an interpretation of emigration which, in its supply side, stressed the changing character of internal movement and a 'margin of migration', were to hold, then we might expect the 'higher status' emigrants to be proportionately less important when the flow was at its greatest, more important when subsistence pressures were less acute.

The limited character of direct sources on indentured servants does nevertheless provide some indication that this may well have been the case. Registrations of indentured servants at Bristol, from 1654 to 1686, cover the period of the peak and decline in indenturing.[35] Investigation of these archives has suggested that, rather than being a general cross-section of society, emigrants in the years 1654-60 (when details entered in the registrations were fullest) came disproportionately from towns and from pastoral-industrial regions. This was in contrast to other documented groups of immigrants to Bristol.[36] In his investigation of emigrants from Wiltshire, Anthony Salerno found that some of the areas from which indentured servants came, pastoral areas in the main, were also places from which New England-bound emigrants of the 1630s had stemmed.[37] These were also areas which showed low mobility of the resident population — but also had a high incident of longer-distance out-migration.[38] In 1684-85, when personal detail on indentured servants was again full, the pastoral bias is much less prominent, the urban bias if anything more.[39]

Meanwhile, analysis of servant registrations for London departures in this later period shows a much more considerable urban bias. Although a slight majority of these emigrants had been resident in the metropolis itself, two-thirds of the rest had come from other towns.[40]

Information on occupational structures is problematical. Controversy has been engaged, for example, over the problems of the definition and proportions of 'yeomen' in the servant stream, and whether or not that indicated an upward social bias.[41] Nevertheless, that too suggests some movement over time towards more skilled and higher status occupations, while study of the London servants shows them to have possessed considerable levels of literacy compared with the general population.[42] Certainly colonial demand for those with skills as a proportion of all servants increased over time: the fact that planters' pleading often went unheeded suggests that the willingness of Englishmen to emigrate had diminished considerably.

Males were always in the majority among the indentured: if females survived in the colonies they were in considerable demand as wives. But the plantation colonies suffered from a chronic shortage of women, thereby delaying the onset of natural increase. If economic opportunities at home were growing for women, in terms of wages and occupation, as the evidence above on urban immigration might suggest,[43] then it might be reasonable to expect that women would be less willing to venture overseas in large numbers. Again, evidence on the sex ratios among indentured servants might seem to confirm this, being higher by the eighteenth century than they had been in the seventeenth.[44]

The thesis advanced here, therefore, is that demographic and economic conditions at home produced, for the first phase of emigration, considerable outward impetus. There are suggestive parallels between levels and varieties of internal and external movement. This is not to suggest that the significance of internal movement has necessarily been overlooked by historians, although it has on occasion been mis-specified. It is not simply that early modern Englishmen were conditioned to movement and that the Atlantic crossing was one more stage in a migratory career, but that similar forces were impelling much movement within England as well as outside. In the second half of the seventeenth century the English population restricted nuptiality as a response to the previous rapid growth of numbers and hence pressure on resources. In those decades after mid-century, when emigration was beginning to fall although not as rapidly as was the general population, the efflux helped put on the brakes — one of the few periods in which emigration may be seen to have had significant effects on the home population.[45]

Thus considerable colonial demand for labour provided large-scale opportunity for emigration, and available evidence seems to suggest that much of that movement at its peak may have been 'subsistence'-derived. Sir Josiah Child was certain that economic conditions at home could not have sustained all the population:

That very many People now go, and have gone from this Kingdom, almost every year for these sixty years past, and have and do settle in our foreign Plantations is most certain. But the question will be, whether if England had no foreign plantations for these people to be transported unto, they could or would have lived at home with us? I am of opinion that they neither could nor would.[46]

Colonial demand

The preceding discussion has placed considerable emphasis on the supply side in the indentured servant equation. Despite Child, however, the existence of plantation colonies with variable but often rapacious labour demands provided the principal reason for the volume of the efflux — without it, the necessity for demographic reversal in England would undoubtedly have occurred earlier than it did.

The attention of most historians of the English New World colonies has been concentrated on the mainland, the tobacco economy of the Chesa-peake.[47] We have already seen that, in terms of total migration flows, the Caribbean islands represented the most important destination area, especially so in the first thirty or forty years of mass emigration. Thereafter the southern plantation colonies took the primary position. This suggests that we need explanations for two phenomena. Why was the Carribbean so important in the first phase, and why did it then drop out? And how important were factors in colonial demand schedules for servants in producing the prolonged demise of the institution?

The state of the archives, and the divorce between island and mainland history which was one result of the American Revolution, has meant that we still know remarkably little about the islands in their earlier years of settlement. St Christopher and Barbados, the earliest-developed of the islands, were first colonised in 1624 and 1627 respectively, and very many moved there. We know most about the development of West Indian society after the establishment of sugar production on a hugely profitable scale, which began fully in Barbados around 1643. What happened in between, so as to bring in so many?

The growing of tobacco in Virginia had produced an unprecedented boom: the home market for tobacco had been primed by South American countraband, and its introduction in English colonies from 1617 produced fortunes for many. Tobacco production proved highly profitable because the price was initially so high in Europe: it not only proved highly remunerative on the mainland, but also in the islands.[48] An official of the Virginia Company in 1619 boasted of a settler 'by his owne labour' making £200 in one year from tobacco, and that 'Our principall wealth . . . . consisteth in servants . . . . if they escape [the hazards of the first year] they prove very hardy, and sound able men.'[49] The rapid expansion of cultivation on mainland and island not only brought settlers and merchants to cash in on the boom, but also created huge demands for field labour. Undoubtedly in the earliest years demand could not be met except by expedients which tapped 'sub-standard' resources of labour — from 1618 and into the 1620s, the London Bridewell shipped many of its young vagrant poor out to the colonies.[50] Nevertheless, indentured traffic rapidly became institutionalised: there were individual merchants in the ports who specialised in trading to the colonies, including servants in their cargoes, plus individuals who occasionally found willing servants to send to specific planters in the colonies. In the cargo of the ship *Abraham,* for example, trading to Barbados in 1636-37 from London, servants were sent out along with other commodities. Four merchants sent over between six and twelve servants each, while another ten sent one or two servants each. Similarly, on the *Tristram and Jeane* on its way to Virginia in 1637, three merchants sent across five, six, and seven servants respectively, while another eleven despatched two servants, and twenty-eight one servant apiece.[51]

Progress in the tobacco and in the servant trade was by no means uniform. Very rapidly, the tobacco economies moved into a boom-bust cycle, as over-production periodically forced down prices. Inelastic demand in the short run within European economies meant that, although generally falling prices eventually expanded the market, immediate impasses were easily reached. Slumps usually entailed a temporary cessation of colonial demand for indentured labour, along with attempts at restricting production and schemes to extend the range of commodities produced.[52] Thus the first Virginia slump came in 1629, with recovery coming in the mid-1630s. Again and again, as European demand for colonial tobacco increased, so the price rose, new investment was attracted and credit was easier, the demand for labour grew and the margin of cultivation was extended. Such rapid expansion soon exceeded demand — prices fell thereby reducing investment and demand for immigrants. As the base for demand widened with lower prices (and consumers were hooked) so the process would begin again. Hence, in times of depression, there may have been willing potential emigrants for whom there was no demand, while during a boom there was considerably more scope for the unscrupulous to dupe emigrants or for the merchants who despatched indentured servants. A number of court cases which alleged fraud in servant trading, for example, concern boom years.[53]

The break between the two regions, Caribbean and mainland, came in the 1640s. The depressions brought with them attempts at diversification of the forms of stable production, which were most successful in Barbados. Experimentation with cotton, ginger, and especially indigo proved successful to some degree. Interruptions in supplies to Europe meant that indigo production was a success; and when indigo prices fell interruptions in Brazilian sugar supply, as a result of the Dutch Wars, produced the opportunity for a full-scale switch to sugar. The Barbadian change was swift; the position of the other island and the mainland colonies in tobacco production was correspondingly improved as a competitor was removed from the field.

Indigo and sugar both required large labour forces and higher capitalisation, which the initial huge profits even from inefficient production had been able to provide. Their Brazilian trade blocked, the Dutch traders offered slaves at generous terms to the Barbadians; heavy investment sorted the planters out, with the big men buying up the little. So in the first phase of the sugar boom white indentured immigration was large-scale, but was soon curtailed as the Negro slave presence became overwhelming. Barbados deserted its white servants.[54]

The other islands did not change as quickly. So much trade and investment had previously been directed towards Barbados which was militarily the more secure. Sugar eased their tobacco problems, while the first sugar boom would never be repeated, so that other islands could change but slowly towards slave labour and sugar production. They continued to recruit white labour, and the indenture trade was largely redirected towards them.[55]

Meanwhile, the expansion of cultivation on the mainland, and stagnant or falling profit levels, meant that demand for white servants continued to increase. The transfer to slave labour there was slow. Newly settled areas tended to be established by migration from older-established regions, especially in the boom periods, and often by freed indentured servants. Once established there, new importations of indentured servants were needed.[56] Thus as areas expanded or diversified, and as profitability rose and fell, so the timing and direction of immigration shifted. Paul Clemens notes that for Talbot and Kent Counties in Maryland, for example, indentured servant immigration was only especially significant in the periods 1675-85 and 1697-1701, boom years after the initial settlement. The onset of natural increase in the later seventeenth century meant that more labour would be native-born.[57]

The early eighteenth century saw relatively little importation of indentured servants from England, even to the newer colonies — Delaware, Pennsylvania, South Carolina — where so much opportunity was taken up through internal migration.

Colonial planters, especially on the mainland, were experiencing considerable and increasing difficulties in the latter third of the seventeenth century in attracting servants under indenture. For reasons we have seen, white English servants felt better able to resist the lure of the colonies. From the 1670s Chesapeake planters bought slaves as well as servants in some numbers, but were unwilling to pay the extra for a full-scale slave labour force until circumstances forced them to do so. Price evidence suggests that they experienced considerable difficulties in the first instance, but eventually came to prefer a Negro labour force.[58]

Sugar and tobacco planters continued to require some white servants, even with large numbers of slaves, men with skills who could act as craftsmen, supervisors, overseers, or accountants. This is seen earliest in the islands, but is increasingly obvious for the mainland in the later seventeenth and the eighteenth centuries. And eventually slaves were trained to perform these tasks.[59] Indentured servitude was not dead: English indentured servants did continue to come to the colonies in the eighteenth century, but in nothing like the same numbers or proportions. Convict labour and continental 'redemptioners' were of greater importance.[60] The attempt to use white indentured labour in the plantations of Georgia during the trusteeship, instead of Negro slaves, proved to be a signal failure.[61]

The preceding sections have considered the conditions of English labour supply and the variegated nature of colonial labour demand. Striking changes in the home demographic and economic environment in the seventeenth and early eighteenth centuries undoubtedly produced a rapidly changing pool of available labour ready and willing to be tapped for employment in the colonies. Suggestive parallels between internal and external migration indicate the possibility that potential emigrants would be more willing to present themselves in large numbers in the first fifty or sixty years of the movement, and considerably less willing thereafter. Various features in the home economy — wages, urban employment, labour force participation — are reflected in aspects of the servant trade.

However, the considerable size of the outward stream from England would not have been possible without considerable demand for labour in the colonies. That demand called the tune, since the booms and slumps in staple trades determined the intensity with which indentured servants were sought (and new free settlers attracted). That demand could cease almost overnight on occasions when, as in Barbados, comparative advantage moved in favour of Negro chattel slaves and against white servants. The evidence suggests that, as the potential and willing supply contracted, so planters found life considerably more difficult: the existence of a slave labour supply based on the unwillingness of the transatlantic migrants undoubtedly meant that the increases in labour demand, particularly during the boom periods, never forced the price of white labour to levels which might have considerably augmented their supply.[62]

Knowing as little as we do about the individuals who crossed the Atlantic under indenture, and often relying on the biased reports of commentators with vested interests, it is difficult to provide a valid description of the internal composition of the flow. The evidence above suggests that at all times there was a component in the traffic to the colonies indentured for mercantile business rather than labouring; there were always those with specially needed skills; demand for their skills grew over time and they were more assiduously courted. Above that there was a large body of people, recruited predominantly for their labouring potential, which varied considerably in size and therefore significantly altered the dimensions of the flow. The often derogatory comments of contemporaries may thus be seen in a subtly altered context. Elite descriptions of the poor and those seeking subsistence were rarely complimentary, and apprehensiveness about them acute.[63] Rather than taking descriptions of the mass of emigrants such as 'vicious and destitute of means to live at home'[64] simply at their face value, we should perhaps recognise the level of rhetoric employed in descriptions of the poor and their attributes in general.[65]

Without doubt very many of those who left England represent the large 'underbelly' of the poorer elements in England's towns and cities. Equally undoubtedly, there were significant numbers attracted by great potential economic benefits. Attempts to encapsulate such an enormous group within a single, narrow description are surely misguided. All the available evidence now suggests indentured emigrants to have been a highly variegated population — and to have been at their most heterogenous at the height of the outflow.

The object of this essay has been to demonstrate the extent to which indentured servitude was intimately linked with colonial economic expansion in an earlier period, as other contributors show it to be for the nineteenth and early twentieth centuries. The main thrust of the argument has been to stress the rapidly changing character of transatlantic migration within a little-changing institutional framework. For the system to operate smoothly, enough people had to be willing to go, enough willing to purchase their labour: the rise and fall of the system is attributable to changes on both sides. Opportunity opened and closed with often amazing speed; at varying points between the third quarter of the seventeenth century and the second quarter of the eighteenth the current importance of indentured servitude for colonial labour supply, demographic and economic growth, and for the partial alleviation of home demographic pressures, was effectively ended..

The scale of English emigration in this period was staggering, the degree of that movement largely determined by the rhythm of the staple economies. Except in the earliest years these emigrants rarely achieved significant economic opportunity for themselves, while large numbers died early. 'Easy to get on, but hard to get off, many so find it by experience.'

2

WHY DID CONTRACT LABOUR NOT WORK IN THE NINETEENTH-CENTURY UNITED STATES?

CHARLOTTE ERICKSON

THE British colonies in the mainland of North America in the seventeenth and eighteenth centuries relied to a notable degree upon institutions of forced or unfree labour to acquire a population and a labour force. Antedating slavery, though later superseded by it in parts of the south, was the institution of indentured service. This form of servitude, unlike slavery in that the term of service was specified and the condition could not be inherited, was a means by which poor British, Irish, and European emigrants secured passages to America, and rural and industrial householders in America obtained workers.

J.F. Jameson pointed out many years ago that the beginnings of anti-slavery and anti-slave trade agitation during the decade of the Declaration of Independence were not accompanied by a similar movement to abolish white servitude.[1] Yet probably by 1819, and certainly by 1831, the institution of indentured service had disappeared. Efforts spanning most of the nineteenth century to revive it in the more limited form of contract labour never met with much success. Contract labour was insignificant in the building of transport projects and in the expansion of mining, industry, and agriculture during that century. Indentured service was not abolished by legislation, as was slavery. It was not introduced in the wake of emancipation in 1863, even under the guise of apprenticeship, as it was in other parts of the western hemisphere.[2] While debt peonage, and even involuntary servitude, could be found in parts of the American south at the end of the nineteenth century, it was not the dominant labour system even in that unhappy region. The planters failed dismally in their attempts to substitute European contract labour for the freed blacks.

Free or hired labour was, of course, also used in colonial America. During the nineteenth century it displaced first indentured service, then slavery, and finally the vestiges of child apprenticeship.[3] To attribute these developments simply to modernisation or some other such broad concept would be to overlook that at times and in certain places in the United States during the nineteenth century circumstances of the labour market were such as produced the recruitment and contracting of migrant labour in other parts of the world at that time.

These circumstances might be summarised as follows: first of all, certain types of economic activity were associated with the use of migrant labour. These were chiefly extractive industries, specially mining, and certain types of commercial agriculture which were labour intensive and in which economies of scale could be obtained. Equally, the construction of roads, canals, and railways and other public works often required concentrations of considerable numbers of unskilled labourers.

Whether or not the exploitation of economic opportunities in such fields encouraged the search for migrant labour also depended on conditions in the local labour market. Where suitable local labour was difficult or impossible to recruit, the labour supply price might be inelastic or too high, and information too imperfect, to permit the development of such an extractive industry. If the cost of labour formed a large share of the total cost of production, as it did in mining and in plantation agriculture, and if the substitution of capital for labour was impossible because of high interest rates or technological obstacles, production without some form of migrant and semi-servile labour seemed impossible, particularly in that the entrepreneur or firm often had no control over the price of the product.

Such labour markets could be expected when work-sites were isolated and a local population thin or absent. Even where a local population seemed to present a potential labour force, there might be social obstacles to its entering a new activity. One specific obstacle of this kind occurred when land was sufficiently abundant for free labourers to have access to it and to subsist at an acceptable standard of life on family labour without becoming wage labourers, at least not full-time.

A third general circumstance in which migrant labour might be specially recruited was to provide skills, either managerial or manual, needed for industrial undertakings which otherwise appeared to be viable.

The American economy in the nineteenth century exhibited all three of these types of need for migrant or cheap labour. The rapid growth of the indigenous population, together with a massive voluntary and self-financed immigration, satisfied most labour needs in the course of that economic expansion. Nevertheless, one can single out a number of instances of the kinds outlined above in which labour at a viable price did not appear to be available and in which special efforts were made to recruit and attract workers below the prevailing wage. Yet, with the single exception of Chinese labour used in western mining and railway building from the 1850s until further Chinese immigration was prohibited in 1882, none of these attempts to secure foreign labour on contract was notably successful. Railways were built through uninhabited prairies in the 1850s, through mountains, desert, and plains to reach the Pacific after 1867; mines were opened out in the distant upper peninsula of Michigan, as well as in the Rocky Mountain states; southern cotton growing regained its productivity if not its prosperity after emancipation, all without resorting to the types of recruitment and contracts discussed elsewhere in this volume.

To explore the question why contract labour did not work in nineteenth century America, it is appropriate to begin by examining the decline and disappearance of indentured labour during the first third of that century.

At the time of the American Revolution indentured service was a long-established institution supported by custom, by English common law, and by a mass of colonial statutes and legal opinions. For immigrants there were two main routes into servitude. British immigrants from the seventeenth century onwards bound themselves, or were bound by parents or guardians, before a magistrate to a master or owner of a vessel in return for passage, provisions, and outfitting. Even children were thus bound for a period of years if they were immigrants, although by the late eighteenth century masters were frequently required to provide them with a few weeks' schooling a year.[4]

Among German, Swiss, and many Irish immigrants, no such contract or indenture had been drawn before departure. These immigrants secured their passages by signing a note acknowledging a debt to the captain of the vessel. If they, or their relatives or friends, were unable to redeem that debt within a specified time after landing, they could be sold as indentured servants according to the 'custom of the country' or the particular colony. These redemptioners thereafter stood in exactly the same position with respect to their masters as did servants bound in Britain.[5]

There were, of course, other ways to lose one's freedom. Any people brought to America from Britain against their will, as well as convicts increasingly transported to America in the eighteenth century, acquired the same legal standing once they were sold. There were also ways in which native-born whites might become indentured servants, by falling into debt, for example.

Immigrant servants were sold by ships' masters, sometimes on the vessels as they lay at anchor, sometimes at auctions. An innovation took place about the middle of the eighteenth century in Pennsylvania when 'soul-drivers' began retailing servants, whom they bought in lots of fifty or so and sold off as they marched them around the countryside.[6] For the most part servants were used in small units and in small numbers by employers who would have been hard put to find coin with which to pay wages. In turn, the want of coin limited the mobility of servants.

Once purchased, the servant found that this master had a property interest in him, could sell him with service unexpired, or pass him on to heirs. The laws on runaways were generally more severe in the American colonies than in England, doubling or more the time a servant had been away and adding that to his unexpired period.[7] Although he was bound because of a debt and his labour was the means of satisfying that debt, he did not normally receive a wage from which to repay his master for his expenditure in acquiring him. In this respect indentured service differed from contract labour. In addition, the bound servant sacrificed personal freedom, such as the right to marry or change masters for the period of his indenture. Periods of bonding varied not only according to the size of the debt but also according to estimates of the immigrant's productivity. The young were bound for longer periods than adults; skilled workers could obtain shorter terms of service. Literacy attracted little, if any, premium in the eighteenth century, however.[8]

While the importation of servants for both industrial and agricultural work continued throughout the colonial period, by its end slavery had very largely replaced indentured labour for tobacco growing in the Chesapeake region. Virginia was no longer a market for servants. Maryland did continue to employ them, but hers consisted more and more of convicts during the twenty years before the Revolution.[9] Pennsylvania had become the principal market for the German and Irish redemptioners who, by the 1770s, outnumbered indentured servants from Britain.

After the outbreak of war interrupted the trade in servants, the exigencies of the colonial armies led some of their governments to use servants as soldiers. At least two of the ex-colonies compensated masters for the loss of unexpired time.[10] At the close of seven years of war in 1783, there must have been relatively few servants still in bondage.

The coming of peace brought an immediate resumption of the traffic, above all in Pennsylvania. The British consul in Philadelphia estimated that between 1783 and 1789, 25,716 redemptioners and servants had been imported into Pennsylvania, a great majority of them Irish 'and a very few

Scotch'.[11] New York in 1788 and Pennsylvania in 1785 passed legislation which departed little if at all from colonial practice except in matters of administration. The aim, at least in part, was to remove any uncertainty about property rights in servants. Those aspects of the law designed to protect servants aboard ship and limit the debts which might be added to those contracted before embarkation, or prevent the separate sale of husband and wife, had colonial precedents.[12]

The subsequent demise of indentured servitude (unlike the abolition of the slave trade) had little to do with the ideology or sentiments of the Revolutionary generation itself. One writer has found one instance, in 1784, in which a public subscription was proposed to free a boatload of servants from their debts on the grounds that the system was 'contrary to... the idea of liberty this country has so happily established'.[13] Indentured servants continued to arrive in Pennsylvania though no longer in Maryland and Virginia. The records of arrivals in Philadelphia, examined years ago, showed that two-thirds of all immigrants to Philadelphia from 1786 to 1804 were redemptioners.[14] Runaway servants continued to be sought partly through press advertisements until the 1820s, although in decreasing numbers. Servants advertised for sale in the *American Daily Advertiser* declined in numbers from 1793 until none appeared in 1824.[15] The Register of German redemptioners in Pennsylvania was not closed until 1831. Yet the last ships with servants who proved unsaleable appear to have arrived in 1819.[16]

To some extent it is still true that 'the history of the system in the nineteenth century remains deeply shrouded in uncertainty', as William Miller confessed to leaving it in 1940.[17] Most students of the subject have attributed its decline to changes in law which affected the system indirectly. The assertion by M.A. Jones that the traffic in servants was 'killed off' by British legislation in 1785 banning artisan emigration to the USA, a law which prohibited British ships from carrying bound labour, flies in the face of evidence of some continuance of the trade even during the long period of warfare and the frustrations British customs officers experienced in trying to enforce such legislation.[18]

Other pieces of legislation better fit the timing of the decline. Consistent with a tradition reaching back into Colonial times, Pennsylvania in 1810 and 1818 passed statutes giving servants further protection in an attempt to give the force of law to customary practices. Maryland also did so in 1817.[19]

Many years earlier Phineas Bond had recommended regulation as a means of cutting immigration:

The price of the passage renders the profit of the voyage very precarious ... any obstructions therefore which may lessen the profit or increase the risque would effectually abolish this trade — these obstructions may grow out of regulations calculated to meet the convenience of emigrants in their voyage and to correct the abuses committed in this traffic.[20]

What he had in mind were Passenger Acts such as were passed by Parliament in 1803 and 1817 and by the American Congress in 1819. Even if not perfectly enforced, this legislation tightened regulations just at the time, after a quarter of a century of war, that an attempt was made to revive the traditional trade in servants. It remains to be demonstrated, however, that the British requirement of one passenger for every five tons on a vessel bound for the USA meant that 'no contractor could profitably transport servants to America', though it does seem possible.[21] The American law limiting passengers to two for every five tons hit immigrants from the German states, as did the increasing investigation of shipping and passport regulation in Holland and Switzerland. McCormac calls these early Passenger Acts 'a death blow' to the institution of servitude. Another blow, according to Richard Morris, was the decision in Indiana courts in 1821 that indentures were unenforceable because of a provision in the State Constitution based on the Northwest Ordinance prohibiting involuntary servitude in the Northwest Territory.[22]

Even more renowned as a 'death-blow' was the abolition of imprisonment for debt. K. F. Geiser was the first writer to regard the fruits of this agitation by prison reformers and working men's associations of the 1830s as the main reason for the disappearance of indentured service. Most of these laws were passed in the ten years after the first federal statute abolishing imprisonment for debt in cases appearing in federal courts was passed in 1832 — somewhat late to offer it as an explanation. Yet Geiser cites a Pennsylvania Act of 8 February 1819 which stated that 'no female shall be arrested or imprisoned, for or by reason of any debt contracted after the passage of this act'.[23]

Legislation in several states at first limited and then abolished imprisonment for debt and in so doing removed an important legal underpinning for indentured service. In most of the states of the Confederacy after emancipation, laws permitting imprisonment for debt and the working off of such debts through labour continued to make it possible to coerce Negroes in times of labour shortage into involuntary servitude or peonage.[24] Thus in the north, legislation was passed which made the trade in, and keeping of, indentured servants more costly and servitude unenforceable, while in another part of the country, where slavery existed at that time, the same sorts of common law and statutory prohibitions against enticement of employees, contract-breaking, vagrancy, and debt lasted, with some spurious revisions, well into the twentieth century.

The reforms which undermined indentured service in the northern and western states probably reflected changes in their economies as well as in the supply of immigrant labour. The cost of transport fell sharply from the close of the Napoleonic Wars onwards to reach low levels of three pounds sterling or less on timber ships to Canada by the late 1820s.[25] (It is not clear why such ships could not have been used for the purpose of transporting servants.) As more immigrants were able to afford to finance their own emigration, the supply of self-financed immigrants rose secularly from 1816 onwards. Furthermore, the growth of banks in the United States after independence, as well as the favourable balance of payments obtained during the wars, may have eased the problem of paying wages for north-eastern employers both rural and urban, nearly all of whom still operated in small economic units and in an uncertain economic climate in which bound labour probably seemed more of a burden than did wage-earners. Perhaps the simplest explanation is that the supply of servants was small and intermittent during twenty-five years of war, and Americans adapted to this.

In any case, there is evidence that European indentured servants were proving increasingly difficult to retain in service against their will in the last years of the eighteenth century. Richard Morris has noted the great disparity between numbers of runaway servants and the few fugitives who came before the courts in New Jersey and Pennsylvania.[26] Employers appear to have been prepared to pay a little more for German servants whose want of English made it more difficult for them to manage as runaways.[27] The Irish were notorious runaways. In the 1780s 'soul-drivers' found it impossible to keep servants from slipping away as they were taken round the countryside in search of purchasers.[28] A local historian attributed the incidence of dealers' losses in 1785 to the opposition of public opinion to their activities.

Such problems with retaining indentured servants, in spite of the backing of the law and courts, were present even before Independence. In the last of the thirteen colonies to be founded, Georgia, where slavery was at first prohibited, most of the single men among German servants were reported in 1750 as 'sculking about the outsettlements of South Carolina from whence it is almost impossible to recover them'.[29] It was not always possible to employ servants fully the year round. George

Washington's overseer on his plantation in western Virginia thought he saw an opportunity to secure additional work for his servants, as he explained in a letter to Washington in 1774:

> Mr Simson has built a Fort at the place where they are building of your Mill by the Esistence of his Neabours and part of your Carpenters and I have been there Severell times and have Encuraged him all I can to Stand his Ground and I have Severell times offered him all the Carpenters and all the Sarvents but he would not take aney of the Sarvents and but four of the best of the Carpenters his Reason for not taking of the Sarvents as there Wase a great dale of Companey att the Fort and drink Midling plenty it would be out of his power to govern them and he Said they would Run away from him …[30]

Similar problems bedevilled attempts to use European contract labour on construction projects in the nineteenth century. Contract labourers, as distinct from indentured servants, were being introduced during the same generation of war that saw indentured service decline. Contract labour, while not registered in the courts, was similar to indentured service because the immigrant signed a contract to work for a period of time, usually with the obligation of repaying transport costs from wages. In these early years contracts were sometimes as long as indentures, from two to even five or six years. Geiser thought he saw the origins of ordinary wage labour in a case in 1784 when a husband and wife rebound themselves to an employer, having completed a period of servitude.[31] However, other writers have identified similar cases going back to the time of Peter Kalm's travels in the 1750s. Closer to such a transition might be the interesting indenture of 1803 cited by McCormac. As he explains:

> Free-willers usually signed no indenture, but when they did, the term was necessarily the same as that of the 'custom' servants. If they were without money and indebted for their passage they were not in a position to demand any shorter term than was provided by law for servants without indentures. On the other hand, they could not be forced to sign for a longer term, for, by refusing to sign any indenture whatever, they could be compelled to serve only four or five years according to the 'custom' at the time they were transported. In exceptional cases, they were required to serve long enough only to pay the expense of the voyage. In an indenture made in 1803 in Baltimore a certain Adam Hoy contracts to serve Charles L Boehme for two years, eleven months and twenty days in 'Consideration of the Sum of Eighty Dollars and sixty-four cents … paid by Charles L Boehme to James Brays for (my) his passage from Amsterdam to the City of Baltimore'.[32]

'When servants were scarce', continues McCormac, 'indentures were sometimes made for as short a term as one year without any diminution of the freedom dues'. Although British skilled workers had clearly been willing to indenture themselves in the eighteenth century, a transition or shift from indentured labour to contract labour, where the worker had more independence and obtained wages during his service, may have come about as a consequence of the American search for some of the particular new skills and empirical knowledge of innovations in machinery and metallurgy being developed with such ingenuity and commercial sense in England and Scotland at this time.

Contract labour developed mainly in connection with this search for a new kind of skilled worker, for overseers, machine makers, and metal workers, mainly in England.[33] Undertaken in the face of British prohibitions on the emigration of artisans not lifted until 1824, this recruitment and contracting was often quite costly to the American employer. The practice of contracting with selected key skilled workers was to continue throughout the century, although it was prohibited by federal law in 1885. In importing such contract labour, employers preferred to use their own contacts abroad, rather than intermediaries, to identify suitable workers and make arrangements. Relatives of partners or employees, the firm's mercantile contacts, and, later, exporters of machinery might be trusted with such delicate negotiations. The numbers involved for any one firm were never very large but even in these cases contracted labourers were often enticed away or simply left for other jobs or to take up land before their debts were paid.[34]

Before mass immigration began in the late 1840s, the construction of public works such as roads, canals, and finally railways presented another sort of labour supply problem, in which quantities of unskilled labourers might be needed temporarily in any one location. George Washington considered recruiting and purchasing German redemptioners to help build the new capital city in the early 1790s.[35] A very late reference to indentured adults appeared in October 1829, when it was reported that labourers had recently arrived in Washington from England who had 'entered into indentures' to serve the Chesapeake and Ohio Canal Company for four months for the expense of their passage. These men had refused outright to comply with their engagements on the grounds that they could not 'make themselves slaves'. The Company succeeded in bringing them on a writ of *habeas corpus* before a judge, who remanded them to prison.[36]

This case was probably exceptional.[37] Long before the Great Famine, the Irish were finding their way to transport construction sites without having become contract labourers. When a railway was projected from Albany to Jacksonville in Georgia in 1834, the chief promoter, A. J. Brisbane, was able to induce some of his countrymen to come to Irwin County without investing in their transport but merely on the basis of a promise to pay them either in shares or in wages. In this case it was the entrepreneur who fled from the scene when he ran into financial troubles.[38] Irish workers came to Illinois in the late 1830s without contracts, to help in the construction of the Illinois-Michigan Canal, another case in which the Company could not have honoured any contracts with workmen. Some of these immigrants at least found their way to La Salle County at the instance of two of the subcontractors who were natives of County Cork.[39]

As Albert Fishlow has demonstrated, most of the ante-bellum railway construction took place in areas where potential traffic (and therefore some labour) was present.[40] These roads were not so developmental as used to be suggested. Immigrants with limited means found their way to the western regions of settlement, partly because they were assured through private information in letters like this from a Scotsman in Ohio in 1829 that work on transport projects could be obtained:

This is an excellent country for a poor man with a large family, if he is industrious, and has a plantation, he may have plenty of the food of the earth, the every thing that he is liable to is two or three Dollars of a tax, and to be a civil citizen; if a farmer wants a servant for three or four months (which is not often the case in this part), he gives from $9 to $10 per month, at canals and such works as that, a digger, or common hand, gets about $13 per month and his board, quarriers from $16 or $17 per month and their board, stone cutters are paid by the piece, they clear upwards of $1 per day ...[41]

A few major projects of the 1850s involved more isolated sites away from a local farming population that might be supplemented by some immigrant labour, largely through the wages offered. One of these was the canal at Sault Ste Marie which was to open up the Lake Superior copper and iron resources. In this bleak northern site, where the General Agent could echo the words of an Irish workman who lamented that 'the sun will get warm one of these days, when I can get away from here',[42] the summer of 1854 brought cholera and dysentery as well, carrying off to their final rest both bosses and workmen as they strained to complete the construction of the canal.[43] During the winter of 1854-55 'the sudden exodus of nearly 1500 men from the work' on the last steamer 'was aggravated by the immediate setting in of a very severe winter'.[44] The

Company obtained workmen through their own agents, who were paid a commission for each man recruited in upstate New York and New York City and forwarded to Sault Ste Marie. The Ship Canal Company officers themselves arranged directly with the Michigan Central Railroad for their transport and to pay these costs as well as 'all meals taken by the men on the way'.[45] No debts were contracted by the men so forwarded, and they left both voluntarily and by death. Men hired in New York were 'generally too weak & small for such heavy work and many of them never take a tool in hand'. The head of the Company's land office in Detroit reported: 'I have been strongly impressed with the belief I could get selected men in this country enough to carry the work through and have sent many from here, but as the cry from the work site is for men! men! perhaps you had better continue to forward more from New York'.[46]

This was the kind of site against which immigrants were warned in guidebooks and newspapers which cautioned that firms would attempt to recruit a surplus of labour in order to keep down wages.[47] Records survive which give some details about the combination of inducements and force used by this company to try to retain an adequate workforce. The General Agent attributed the insubordination of the men to drunkenness and pointed to 'the famishing legion of Saut groggery keepers (some 50 or more)'. The Company tried to enforce temperance. 'We now charge and collect from each man $5.00 for coming into his boarding house drunk — 75 cents per day for board when idle for any cause but genuine (anti rum) sickness besides reductions of wages from 20 to 50% on bad cases …'.[48] The Agent had earlier found in the provision of board a means of coercing the men, at least temporarily, in spite of the want of contracts or indentures. In August 1853 the men had struck for a ten-hour day:

I refused mildly but firmly to change the Co. terms whatever — stopped their monthly pay and *removed* the deposits of food and bed clothing from the shanties before the succeeding meal.

Before the expiration of twenty four hours symptoms of repentance were evident, and by persuasion without irritating them eighty men returned to work the next morning, whom I tested for a hour or two, and then gave them their breakfast. The rest soon followed suit and before another day all or nearly all had returned to work.[49]

Normally the Company claimed to be supplying board to three-quarters of its workers at a saving to them of 50 per cent over going rates and to be providing those with families with flour and other provisions at lower prices than local merchants asked.[50]

During the same years the Illinois Central Railroad was being laid in part through unsettled prairies.[51] The means used to bring in immigrant labour were similar in most respects to those employed by the St Mary's Falls Ship Canal Company. The railway company paid its own agents in New York and New Orleans during the early years of construction, 1852-53, to forward immigrants. The agent in New York had 'arrangements with all the through lines to bring men here at $4.50 each', though in this case the men themselves appear to have had to find their own travel money.[52] Advertisement and assistance with travel arrangements appear to have been sufficient to induce Irish and German workers landing in New Orleans and New York to make their way to construction sites. 'I have never authorized him [the agent Phelps] to employ men for the company or to contract that the Co. would pay them — but simply to induce men to Illinois by stating that work was plenty here and by stating the rate of wages that was paid in the state.'[53] By the autumn of 1853 the work force totalled about ten thousand men. From 1854 onwards the Illinois Central no longer needed to make known its needs farther afield than Missouri and Ohio.[54] Although their labour supply problems did not cease until the road was completed, that they were not alleviated by using indebted or contracted labour is clear from the company papers. Competition for workers through wages prevailed, not only between roads being built as far apart as Illinois and Missouri, but also among the many contractors who built various portions of the line. From between 75 cents and a dollar a day, the pay for common labour in Illinois when construction commenced, wages reached $1.50 a day by 1854. An attempt by the Chief Engineer of the Illinois Central to get several lines and contractors to agree to fix wages failed utterly. In the summer of 1853 Roswell Mason learned that 'Mr Lee of the Chicago & Mississippi is understood to be willing to pay $1.50 because they have but little work left to do and must have men'. 'Men are on strike nearly half the time', he opined, 'for wages or for time or for whiskey ... There is not half men enough in the country to do the work now in progress and those that are here do not half work.'[55] In 1856 one of his contractors wrote that he was already having to pay $1.50 for unskilled labour and wanted to finish in four months. 'In order to accomplish it I shall raise the wages so as to secure men if they are to be found ...'[56]

These were difficult circumstances in which to trust the market for labour, especially in view of the wretched fever and ague-ridden, damp work-sites. Yet I find no evidence of anything which might be called forced labour on these particular difficult sites in the northern part of the

Union before the Civil War. Neither indentured nor contract labour was involved, although slave labour was sometimes used in the construction of railways in the south. Even there Irish workers were said to be preferred because their deaths or illness constituted no loss to their employers.

From the time of the last shipload of indentured servants for whom a market could not be found, probably in 1819, until the Civil War, firms which recruited immigrant labour did so through their own agents without the use of intermediaries. Labour migration, other than voluntary self-financed emigration, was not important in quantitative terms. The introduction of contract labour from the 1790s onwards served needs for particular industrial and managerial skills, but was not the chief means of securing skilled industrial workers, much less unskilled labour.

*

The Civil War seemed to present a new situation. Some northern undertakings experienced real labour shortages; everywhere wages rose.[57] For the first time since the decline of indentured service an attempt was made to offer a service as intermediaries between immigrants and potential employers. This time it was not the shippers who sought to organise the traffic in immigrant labour but a number of incorporated firms which set out to provide a more specialised service of providing European workers with particular skills to order to American industry and mines, on contracts under which the workmen were committed to repay travel expenses.

The most conspicuous of these firms, the American Emigrant Company, incorporated in the state of Connecticut, but also supported by a group of ironmasters around Henry Carey of Philadelphia, secured an Act of Congress in 1864 to encourage the importation of contract labour. The Company used this piece of legislation in its recruitment efforts in Britain, northern Europe, and Scandinavia to give the impression that it had a semi-official status and that it operated by the authority of the Federal Congress.

Many United States consuls abroad sought to act as agents for such labour recruiting firms, either to supplement their poor pay or under the impression that the Act of Congress sanctioned these companies and gave contracts they made with immigrants standing in federal law. Writing to the American consul in Liverpool to recommend the American Emigrant Company and its directors, the Reverend Henry Ward Beecher described it as 'a real one [society], on a business basis, as a Labor-Brokerage, and conducted by men of standing and pecuniary respectability', among them his brother-in-law, John Hooker, and a former Senator, Francis Gillette.[58] Dudley also received letters from British citizens asking to be appointed as recruiting agents to fulfil the terms of the Act. One of these wrote from Newcastle-upon-Tyne enquiring about the nature of aid proposed: 'to what class of workmen — If a passage would be given *on credit* to *families* of *workers* — and single men'.[59]

The American Emigrant Company and its less well-known rivals sought to act as brokers in securing labour for northern industry, and counted on employers to provide the working capital needed to pay for transporting workers to the job. It left those employers with the problem of securing repayment from the wages of such contract labourers. After the war a number of southern states also sought to secure European workers for cotton cultivation through similar firms of labour brokers, since many planters and others clearly believed that blacks would never be efficient workers as freed men.[60]

By 1866 it was clear that the effort to revitalise and extend a contract labour system for workers recruited in Europe by means of such labour brokers was a failure. The companies which had attempted to fulfil this function reverted to land sales (the American Emigrant Company originated as a land company), or simply became passenger agencies providing travel information and services, such as selling tickets or exchanging money, for prospective immigrants. In 1867 a Federal Act against peonage reached the statute books. In 1868 the contract labour law, by then a dead letter, was repealed. Then in 1885, in response to agitation from trade unionists, Congress passed an Act to prohibit the importation of contract labour, with little opposition.[61]

A few people were deported each year under this Act, although the law was to be amended time and again, largely because it did not fit the circumstances. American federal law required immigrants to show that they were not coming to any specific job but at the same time to establish that they were not likely to become public charges. The irrelevance of these experiments to curbing immigration is suggested by the fact that immigration continued to increase whenever the number of jobs rose. Immigration continued to grow to reach more than a million arrivals a year during six of the years of the decade before the outbreak of World War I, which brought this relatively free and spontaneous labour migration to a stop.

The scale of this voluntary, largely family-financed immigration (much of it through the cash earnings of earlier immigrants, a method not possible for indentured workers) and the temporary willingness of recent immigrants, under the spur of necessity and ambition, to take disagreeable jobs spurned by natives, is a proximate answer to the question why contract labour did not work in America. But why did the well-organised effort to provide skilled immigrant labour by specialised intermediaries or labour brokers, under the nominal blessing of the federal government, fail so abysmally? And how was the labour market organised, especially in relation to isolated projects and thinly populated regions such as the transcontinental railways and western mines, without the migration of some kind of unfree labour?

*

To explain the failure of those labour brokers who tried to organise the labour market on both sides of the Atlantic, one must recognise first of all that the European workers whom they sought, above all skilled workers, had access to information which enabled them to appraise the claims of the recruiting agents. The American Emigrant Company met opposition in most European countries in which it attempted to contract workers. Only in Britain did its agents operate with much freedom of speech and movement. Since the Company began these activities during wartime, European governments warned migrants that its real purpose was army recruitment.

Press criticism and rumour-mongering had their counterpart in the immigrant agents' advertising campaign in pamphlets, broadsheets, and newspapers. Prospective migrants, their friends, and families who could read, or heard about, the one had access to the other. The incidence of literacy in the working populations of Scandinavia, Britain, and the German states, where recruitment was concentrated, was sufficient to make the publication of cases of contract labourers whose expectations were not fulfilled a considerable deterrent.

Trade unions in England and Scotland at first welcomed agents of the American Emigrant Company, especially during strikes such as occurred in the iron industry of Staffordshire and the North-east in 1865.[62] But this strange honeymoon did not last long. In due course the American unions most concerned, above all those in the iron industry, organised the publication of regular reports on the state of the labour market and industrial disputes in the journals of their British counterparts.[63]

The American Emigrant Company equally had difficulty in securing the confidence, and even more the financial support, of the other parties for whom they proposed to act as intermediaries — American employers. Some thought their charges too high and questioned the ability of non-specialists to select appropriate workers. The insurmountable problem came to be the impossibility of guaranteeing that workers imported at considerable expense would remain in the employment of the importing firm. If contract labourers found higher wages nearby where they had no debts to repay, or the housing inadequate, or that they had been lured into an industrial dispute, they left. This was in part the consequence of recruiting in old emigrant regions where migrants were likely to have contacts in the free labour force of the host country.[64] Sometimes immigrants clearly used the contract simply as a means of getting across the ocean and into the interior to join friends and relatives. As a last resort, European consuls and immigrant welfare agencies might help immigrants who claimed to have been, felt themselves to be, or were intentionally deceived.

The many cases of contract-breaking do not fall short of the known cases of actual importation of contract labour.[65] The difficulties with keeping contract labourers appeared even in relatively isolated areas, such as the copper mining region of northern Michigan which was not surrounded by arable lands, as the lead mines of Wisconsin and Illinois had been when they were opened up before the Civil War.[66] The young mining firms of the Lake Superior region found high wages an insufficient inducement to secure workers for enterprises being started during the Civil War. Several companies joined together to subscribe $90,000 to recruit contract labour in Norway and Sweden through American consuls in Bergen and Stockholm. The immigrants were to obtain loans for their own travel costs plus one-third of the costs of families, the loans to be repaid by having one-half of their monthly pay deducted (they were to earn $260 a year) for a period of two years after which they would be 'free to do as they pleased'. One contemporary recalled that most of these Scandinavian miners refused to work for the companies on arrival. 'They could not be made to work. They boldly and defiantly resisted all efforts to make them fulfil their written contracts.'[67]

The directors of the American Emigrant Company concluded that the lack of any law enforcing the validity of such debts was the obstacle to their success. In 1865 and 1866 they pressed for a federal law stipulating that the amount to be repaid should be doubled if a contract labourer quit before his debt was extinguished, and also that an employer should be able to impound the wages of the migrant if he took another job. Failing that, the new employer should be required either to assume the debt or to dismiss the workman. These bills, which bore certain similarities to the laws concerning runaway servants in an earlier period, when length of service was doubled or more since there were no wages, failed to be passed on both occasions. The American Emigrant Company did secure such a law in the state of Connecticut, where it was incorporated. Even where legislation was secured, employers had to incur additional expense in tracing absconded workers.[68] They do not appear to have used the courts or the police to try to enforce labour contracts. Employers were not well organised, the first trade association for tariff lobbying being founded only at the time of the Civil War. On the whole they were competing with each other for labour, though no cases of enticement against other employers seem to have been brought in the north. In turn, immigrants found around them a diversifying economy with no formal barriers to employment and a large economy which offered possibilities of moving from place to place, or dropping off the train on the way to a destination previously arranged.

For skilled labour not otherwise available employers reverted to the pre-war method of private recruitment through their own contacts. Then it often sufficed to place advertisements in the press to secure applicants. A Cornish-born mine manager in the Lake Superior region by the name of John Daniell advertised for engine men in the Newcastle *Chronicle* and elsewhere in the 1870s and 1880s. As he explained, the reason for seeking immigrant workers was this:

There are plenty of men here but direct hoisting is new in the region, and Engineers not accustomed to the work are slow starting and landing cages. We are putting up a new plant, and I feel like trying a man or two from a district noted for able Enginemen . . . .[69]

Of several applications received, one came from Michael Harrison of Spennymoor, County Durham:

Sir I see in the New Castle Chronicle that you want two steady men to run direct hoisting Engines well Sir I am a Enginemen and has been to all kinds of Collery Engines and I think I could sut you I am a total Abstainer well I have never tasted drink and am 28 years old. I enclose a coppey of a character for 3½ year and I had one for 8½ year but lost it if you have got men for the Engines if you could give me work an eaney think eles I would come and I have a Brothe or two that would come. The way that I lost my charriter is I gave it away at a Emigration Office at London as i am traying to get out to Australia but if you hav not got men and you can give me work and the wages sutes i would rathe com to you hapen that you will let me know as soon as you can and if you will give me eaney assistean out . . . .[70]

In reply, Daniell noted that the pay would be £10 to £12 per month:

I offer you the privilege of coming because you are an abstainer. And if you are competent and industrious can assure you steady employment. We can do nothing towards paying your expenses, but if you give us satisfaction, at the end of a year would pay you £10 to reimburse your outlay . . . .[71]

The occasions on which employers tried to use the Federal Act to secure unskilled labour were usually disastrous. The Southern Pacific Railway claimed to have lost $40,000 on 250 Swedish immigrants acquired from the American Emigrant Aid and Homestead Company on contracts to work off passage advances.[72]

The attempts by some southern state governments to secure immigrants either direct from Europe or from New York City were equally unsuccessful. Even before the Radical Reconstruction governments overturned some of these state emigration bureaus, or converted them into agencies for assisting Negro migration,[73] the impossibility of securing European immigrants in place of Negroes was apparent. Europeans had the same objections to Mississippi as they had to South Carolina: hot climate, bad housing, poor roads, lack of schools, and low wages.[74] The most successful recruitment society in South Carolina, according to Woodie, furnished field labourers and mechanics at $25 for a single labourer and $60 for a family. They were obtained in New York City and the fee (which the worker was to repay from his wages) covered transport, a contingency expense, and a $5.00 contribution which the Society agreed to set aside in a fund to secure the planter from loss if the immigrant failed to turn up after his passage money had been advanced or left the employer before the loan was repaid.[75] The Germans who came under these arrangements 'amidst so much flourish' became dissatisfied with the food of bacon and corn bread. It is worth quoting at length from this classic article:

A party of Italians haughtily rejected a yearly wage of one hundred dollars and a weekly ration allowance of corn meal and bacon. A planter on Beach Island had the following experience: Unable to secure sufficient Negro labourers for his lands, he imported fifteen white immigrants from New York, paying their transportation. The men contracted to work for twelve and one-half dollars a month and the women for eight dollars. When they became dissatisfied with the usual diet of corn bread, he gave them rye and wheat. Not content with their wages, they demanded and received an increase at the end of the first month. When they demanded another increase at the end of the second month, the planter was glad to dispense with their services . . . . Such experiences led the more thoughtful champions of the interests of the white farmers to believe that immigrants were not satisfactory substitutes for the negroes.[76]

How, then, was the migration of unskilled labour organised? How did employers or contractors secure workers for isolated sites or temporary work? How did information about labour markets scattered throughout a continent by the end of the century reach the immigrant who had no extended kin network in the states or whose family had been unable to secure work for him?

In fulfilling this function with respect to unskilled labour, brokers or intermediary service agencies, such as the American Emigrant Company attempted to be, became established and succeeded. Where the labour required could be described mainly in terms of quantity, so many hands, rather than in differentiated qualitative skills, such intermediaries were already feasible even in this early phase of industrial development. Not all employers nor all immigrants used the private labour agencies, but they served to improve labour markets and the success of both parties. These private labour agencies, often called 'intelligence offices' or 'information bureaus', did not sign up contract labour either in European countries or in the immigrant receiving cities in America in which they were located. An intelligence office had been established in Philadelphia as early as 1813 to help place both indentured servants and free labour. Intelligence offices also appeared in New York and Boston during the 1850s, but they served only local labour markets, the demand for servants, laundresses, and clerks.[77] In undertaking to supply the needs of firms outside these local urban markets, these firms were innovating. They emerged just as the skilled labour bureaus seeking contract labour were collapsing, at the end of the Civil War, and as massive railway building resumed.

After they came upon the scene it was no longer necessary for railway contractors to undertake this function themselves or through agents employed by the railway company. Labour bureaus appeared not only in the main immigrant receiving port of New York but also in inland immigrant distribution centres, notably Chicago. A Swedish immigrant newspaper explained the system as it operated in Chicago as early as 1870:

. . . . when it has been decided to build a track, entrepreneur-auctions for certain sections of track are advertised . . . .

When a person obtains a contract, he has to procure workers for himself. He then usually travels to one of the larger cities, especially those through which the emigrant stream goes. Here are always found good labour bureaus or intelligence offices, and the railway contractors always turn to one of these bureaus to obtain the necessary work personel.

There is now such a shortage of workers that the contractors usually pay a not insignificant fee to the labour bureau for each worker, and sometimes even give these workers free travel to work places or at least pay the cost of part of the journey. In such cases the workers usually escape from having to pay anything themselves for obtaining work.[78]

By the next big cyclical upswing in railway building in the 1880s, private labour agencies in New York and Chicago were the dominant means of distributing immigrants who did not have work arranged. Although there was at first a wide variation in the honesty of the men operating such agencies, their abuses were widely publicised in the immigrant press.

When such agencies supplied considerable numbers of workers who spoke little or no English, they frequently supplied an interpreter as well. If the railway contractors would not employ the interpreter directly, he would seek to get a return on his effort in other ways, by boarding and lodging the workers in the construction camp or by taking a cut of their wages. In fulfilling these quite essential functions for recent immigrants, the *padrone* system got started not only among Italian workers but among other recent groups as well. Clearly the *padrone* interpreter/banker/boarding-house keeper had abundant opportunities to exploit the new-comer. After the system had received much adverse publicity in the 1890s, the states of both New York (April 1904) and Illinois (June 1909) passed legislation designed to protect labourers from exploitation by such bosses.[79] Repeated efforts by Congressional committees to prove that *padrone* imported workers on contract failed to turn up much evidence. One non-English-speaking witness by the name of Chiesa, who confessed to having had his passage paid by a *padrone,* recognised that he could not be forced to pay the debt or to remain in the employ of the man who brought him out.[80] The decline of the system of the independent boss/interpreter (something the Illinois Central sought to avoid in the 1850s) was to a substantial degree brought about by railway and construction officials terminating 'padrone services, replacing bosses with certified labor agents'.[81]

The decline of the *padrone,* if his power had ever been extensive or long-term, may be witnessed from his point of view in a recently published letter from one V. Palumbo to the Central Superintendent of the Florida East Coast Railway building southward in 1901. Claiming that 'I have always been against the padrone system', Palumbo wrote that he was willing to accept a commission for each man forwarded from New York in order to defray his expenses. When the General Superintendent demurred at this, Palumbo declared himself willing to 'renounce the Dollar Commission; but you must fulfil the contracts which I shall enter with the men . . . . and I shall endeavour to make a living by myself, in Florida looking over the interests of these people as indeed I am responsible to them in case of any eventuality . . . . if you stop to accept labourers you will ruin me in many ways . . . .[82]

By 1905, when the Florida East Coast Railway began construction south of Miami to reach Key West, a vast and treacherous engineering project over water and mosquito-infested swamp in hurricane country, it turned to the Italian-German Labour Exchange in New York for workers. Its advertisements now offered to put interpreters who brought fifty or more men on the company payroll at $60.00 a month. However, problems of labour turnover and contract-breaking, when it had forwarded transport costs to be recouped from wages, repeated the experiences of others before it. According to a man who worked in the office of the Chief Construction Engineers, 40,000 workers had to be recruited in distant cities for a construction force which never exceeded 5,000. Some men took transport south simply to get out out of New York City for the winter, and many refused point-blank to work when they saw the working and living conditions on one of these sites. After the first year or so the Company gave up recruiting men *en masse* through New York labour exchanges.[83]

An early response to the expansion of labour exchanges dealing in unskilled labour was the establishment of state systems. Ohio set up the first of these in 1890. Seventeen other northern and western states followed suit. Although organised labour had frequently asked for such bodies, the unions opposed them unless they could man their offices themselves because they feared public labour exchanges might become sources of strike-breakers.[84] Usually underfinanced, these state labour exchanges tended to serve local markets for domestic servants. They were unable to supply skilled labour because trade unions themselves served as labour exchanges for organised workers.[85]

The public exchanges did not fulfil their original aim of curbing private labour exchanges. The head of the Illinois system noted in 1911 that there were more private agencies at that time then when the state went into the business in 1899; and the volume of private work had also increased. Unable to compete successfully, the state of Illinois sought to control the activities of private bureaus through licensing and regulation.[86] Fraudulent agencies were prosecuted. In Illinois in 1904 alone 361 suits were brought and convictions obtained in nearly every case, registration fees recovered for the workers and licences revoked.[87] By 1911 the chief inspector of private agencies in Illinois, William H. Cruden, wrote that private agencies could not be eliminated. The best hope was to regulate them more completely to reduce their number by increasing requirements and by licensing only the better class of agents.[88]

Why could the public exchanges not drive the private ones from the field? According to their assessment, the main reason was underfinancing. As the head of the Illinois system explained, many privately managed agencies catered to a particular business and had years of experience in special lines. Most of their work was in placing unskilled men in contract and railway work. The private agencies were better equipped to send large numbers of men to other states. The men must be located, collected, often lodged and fed, and transport advanced. Interpreters were provided in the pay of the labour agency. In his efforts to urge the state of Illinois to make more generous appropriations, he mistakenly reported that the British Parliament had provided finance for all these services.[89]

These private labour agencies succeeding in fulfilling the function of providing unskilled labour, most of it immigrant, for transport projects. It all happened before there were any very large employers in American mining, manufacturing, or railway contracting. No widespread and persistent use of contract labour, or of workers in debt for advances, appears to have been necessary for their work. Peonage was not only made difficult by legislation in northern and western states, but it was also clearly resisted by European workers themselves from whatever part of the continent they came. Even when state laws did permit involuntary servitude by enforcing contracts involving debt and by harsh vagrancy laws in the southern states, the law was used more effectively to exploit native blacks than it could be used against Europeans.

Where Chinese indentured and contract labour was employed in western mines and railway camps, the immigrants were controlled by the powerful Chinese companies to whom their debts were owed and isolated from the fluidity of the American economy which made escape so easy, as European immigrants soon discovered. No indentured Chinaman could get a ticket home unless his debt was discharged.[90] American law was not required to enforce this system. The author of an article in the *Merchant's Magazine* in 1870 argued 'no contract which could be made with Asiatics at home could be practically enforced here . . . . shippers would in the end have to rely entirely on the good will of their labourers to return their money. The investment is too uninviting to divert much capital from other employment.'[91] He might have had knowledge of attempts to import European contract labour but had less insight into the Chinese system of control, which was already well developed before the Chinese came to California.

3

THE CORNISH DIASPORA OF
THE NINETEENTH CENTURY

GILL BURKE

THROUGHOUT the nineteenth century there were massive migrations from Britain to the colonies and ex-colonies of the Empire from rural and urban areas. Cornwall contributed to these migrations at both a general and a particular level. In general, the agricultural population took ship to settle in the new worlds. In particular, workers in the tin and copper mines took ship also, but apparently not with settlement as their main aim. The metalliferous mining industry of Cornwall was one of extreme antiquity; industrialisation took place relatively early in the eighteenth century, and by the nineteenth century thousands of men and women were employed in deep, hard rock mines which were run on the Cost Book system[1] of investment. Ownership of the mining companies was diffuse and complex; it was spread between shareholding 'adventurers', landlords who owned the mineral rights, and the tin smelters who exercised powerful control as price setters for tin ore. By the mid-nineteenth century Cornwall was supplying almost one-third of the world's tin and copper. Thirty years later the development of overseas ore deposits had rendered Cornwall's output negligible, a decline marked in Cornwall by abandoned and closed mines and 'clemmed' (starving) mineworkers.

This decline was not the sole cause of labour migration from Cornwall, however, and in this paper I will examine the various forms that Cornish mine labour migration took during the century. Much of the historical literature on labour migration has been characterised by parochialism and filio-pietism and has rightly been criticised for this.[2] Nickolinakos has powerfully and persuasively argued for the need for a general theory of migration despite the difficulty of developing such a theory beyond the broadest generality.[3] Most often it is argued that all labour migration falls into two main categories. That is, migration because of 'push' factors at home — particularly the 'push' of poverty, starvation, and trade depression; or migration because of the 'pull' of higher wages and 'bright lights' abroad.

Undoubtedly, push factors operated for very many of the migrants from Europe during the nineteenth century. As Hobsbawm comments, people migrated 'overwhelmingly for economic reasons, that is to say because they were poor.[4] Erickson has suggested that 'dark forebodings' about the future of Britain, plus hopes of economic advancement, also took many migrants from Britain to the United States in the early part of the nineteenth century.[5] The notion of the pull of the 'bright lights' has recently been challenged, however,[6] particularly the implication that the labourer exercised free choice in going or staying. Corrigan, arguing that labour was unfree, with no choice between working or starving, has developed a 'coercion model' of labour migration which he suggests was an important part of capitalist relations.[7]

An examination of the migration patterns of the Cornish mine work force during the nineteenth century is saved from parochialism in part because of the part such migrations played in the development of capitalist organisation of world metalliferous mining and investment, and in part because of the possible contribution such an examination can make towards the development of theoretical perspectives. Migration by workers in the mining industry from and to Cornwall during the nineteenth century, while similar in some ways and on some occasions to migrations from other parts of Britain, also differed in important ways. Often, it is true, the Cornish mineworkers were 'pushed' by poverty at home, not least because of the indebtedness that made poverty a structural part of Cornish mining organisation. In the depressions of the 1840s, the 1860s, the 1870s, and the 1890s there was clearly little choice between leaving or starving. At other times it might be said that perhaps they were 'pulled' abroad by the bright lights of mining frontier towns, but this would seem to miss the complexity of Cornish mining migration.

Throughout the nineteenth century the Cornish provided a highly mobile, highly skilled workforce whose expertise made a significant contribution to the world development of metalliferous mining, a contribution that can still be traced today in the use of Cornish mining terms such as 'stope', 'winze', 'rise', and 'adit' by mining engineers and metalliferous miners throughout the world. In addition the established practice of migration, in good times and bad, had important consequences for social and economic relations within Cornwall, particularly for the development of trade unionism within Cornish mining. In this paper, therefore, both the nature and the type of Cornish mining migration, and the relationship of migration to labour relations both within Cornwall and overseas will be discussed.

I

There were three main areas of migration by the Cornish: to North America from the 1830s, to Australia from the late 1850s, and to South Africa from the 1880s. These continents provided the greatest concentration of mining activity, and considerable Cornish settlements grew up there over time. Rowe has estimated that at least four or five thousand of the settlers of the Wisconsin region had emigrated there from Cornwall in the years between the ending of the Black Hawk war in 1832 and the discovery of gold in California in the 1840s — at which time many of them removed to the goldfields.[8] In Montana from the 1880s the racial feud between Cornish and Irish was a fundamental part of the war of the copper kings — Marcus Daly employed only Irishmen at Anaconda, while William Clark employed only Cornishmen.[9] These came either directly from Cornwall or indirectly from the Comstock or California.[10] In Australia, Blainey has drawn attention to the numerous 'cousin Jacks' at the gold mines of Ballarat and Bendigo in Victoria and at the silver, lead, and zinc mines of Broken Hill, New South Wales,[11] while during the 1860s the copper fields of Moonta and Wallaroo in South Australia became known as 'Little Cornwall'.[12] In South Africa, prior to the outbreak of the Anglo-Boer war, it was estimated that 25 per cent of the white mine workforce on the Rand came from Cornwall.[13]

In addition to these foci of mining migration, however, the Cornish migrations were both more diffuse and of earlier beginning. From the late eighteenth century Cornish miners had been exporting themselves, initially into England and Wales but also abroad. By the early nineteenth century there were Cornish miners working in the copper mines of Angelsey and the lead mines of Shropshire,[14] while migration between mines in different parts of Cornwall was also clearly established:

> Oh I'm a miner stout and bold,
> Long time I've worked down underground
> To raise both tin and copper too
> For the honour of our miners.
> Now brother miners I bid you adieu
> I'll go no more to work with you
> But scour the country through and through
> And still be a rambing miner[15]

The difficulty of travel within Cornwall and into England, later eased by the opening of the Saltash railway bridge in 1859, apparently made it almost as easy to cross the Atlantic as to cross the Tamar. Certainly it was possible to book right through to Houghton, Michigan, from the general stores in St Just.[16]

In the 1820s English mining companies were taking Cornish miners and Cornish equipment to Central and South America, especially to the silver mines of Mexico.[17] These were recruited by the John Taylor Company, were bound by contract, and had part of their wages remitted home. Perhaps the most famous migrant at that time was the engineer Richard Trevithick, who, in 1828, was maintaining the pumps at the San Judas Socavon in Peru.[18] Absent for eleven years, he returned destitute to Cornwall, having borrowed the fare from Robert Stevenson.[19] At Hayle he was given a tumultuous reception, 'welcomed home by all the neighbourhood with the ringing of bells'.[20] As Trevithick had not written or sent any money home the whole time he was away, it is perhaps fortunate that his wife's comments on his arrival have not been recorded. Cornish miners were to continue to be found in Central and South America throughout the century, in Mexico and Peru but also in Brazil, Chile, and Bolivia,[21] while by the 1890s they were also to be found in Central and West Africa and India.[22]

As Blainey has pointed out, the development of any particular mineral deposit during the nineteenth century cannot be seen as purely coincidental but was closely related to wider economic factors.[23] Thus it was not unusual for the initial opening up of an orebody overseas to coincide with a depression in the Cornish industry which released skilled labour for overseas expansion and development. But, in addition to this, at all times there was a steady passage of miners from Cornwall taking their skills to participate in less significant fields, like Brazil, or to reviving areas such as Nevada after the first boom, or to continually growing districts such as Butte where there was almost constant demand. In addition there was a demand for Cornishmen as prospectors and as consultant experts. This fondness for Cornish consultancy was most marked among British investors in North American mines[24] and continued even after the loss of the chance to purchase the (subsequently) rich Batemans Eureka in the 1870s.[25] As technological changes and increasingly capital intensive working began to change the nature of metalliferous mining, the skills and expertise of the Cornish began to come into question, and the risk of investing on the strength of a Cornishmen's report was increasingly stressed. In 1881 *The Economist* termed this:

. . . . a most risky of investments . . . . A company is formed, two or three mining captains are readily obtained, some picked up lumps of ore are assayed . . . . and an allotment made to a small sprinkling of gulled investors.[26]

The dispersion of migrant miners throughout the world and throughout the various metalliferous fields of the foci continents suggests that even in hard times their migration was purposive. They were not simply fleeing poverty at home but, rather, were setting their faces purposefully towards mining frontiers where their skills would be required. This was often in conflict with the recruiting policies of developing British colonies where stress was placed on the need for migrants to have agricultural skills:

The majority of the immigrants are natives of Cornwall and it appears they have all been more or less accustomed to work in mines. From what has been seen and heard of these people it is apprehended that, taking account of their previous habits and occupations they are not the descriptions of persons who are likely to prove useful in the colony.[27]

Such a migration pattern meant that on the majority of occasions the Cornish miner did not benefit from assisted passage schemes. Thus, unless he was going out under contract, the miner had to pay his own fare. While this frequently led to further indebtedness at home, it added greatly to the miner's autonomy and freedom of movement. It separated him from those who were simply fleeing from poverty perforce. Robert Louis Stevenson's description of the Cornish on their way to America in the 1880s caught this autonomy very well:

There were no emigrants direct from Europe — save one German family, and a knot of Cornish miners who kept grimly to themselves, one reading the New Testament all day long through steel rimmed spectacles, the rest discussing privately the secrets of their old world mysterious race. Lady Hester Stanhope believed she could make something of the Cornish — for my part I can make nothing of them at all . . . . A division of races, older and more original than Babel, keeps this closed esoteric family apart from neighbouring Englishmen. Not even a Red Indian seems more foreign in my eyes.[28]

This freedom of movement and the autonomy it gave had important implications for the Cornish miners' relations with other workmen, as will be discussed below.

Although it was their skills as hard rock miners that made Cornishmen in demand, this did not prevent them participating, like many others, in the 'rushes' that followed discovery of alluvial deposits of minerals — the gold rushes of California and Victoria and to Griqualand West for diamonds. Unlike many others, however, the Cornish miner was more likely to remain at the field as panning dried up and as holes in the ground began to deepen. At that point he might send word back to his 'cousins' in Cornwall to come and join him. The varying development of mineral deposits, and the spread of these alongside major mining areas, all helped to determine the type of migration undertaken by the Cornish miner.

II

I would suggest that there were two kinds of mining migration from Cornwall. The first was that of the 'single roving miner' who, if married, left wife and family in Cornwall and who (married or single) returned as often as possible to Cornwall either to work or *en route* for somewhere else. The second type was emigration pure and simple, with the miner and his family leaving Cornwall never to return. This type characterised the periods of deep depression within the Cornish industry, most particularly the late 1860s and late 1870s; indeed, during the decade of the 1870s, one third of the population of Cornwall — men, women, and children, migrated in this way. For these there was little or no autonomy and freedom of movement. They had their passages paid either through the Poor Law or through various Assisted Passage schemes such as the County Distress Committee fund established in Cornwall to coordinate charitable relief during that depression.[29] Yet there was no clear-cut relationship between depression in Cornish mining and family migration. The period of deepest crisis and depression in Cornwall, the 1890s, was marked by migration of single men not families.

Although it was the single roving miner that was most characteristic and the most significant form of Cornish labour migration, such mobility did not preclude settlement abroad. Passage money might be sent back to enable families to come to Mexico, Michigan, or Moonta, or the miner himself might return to fetch them: '. . . . and indeed, this is one of the most pleasing traits in the miner's character'.[30] Likewise, young men would often return to Cornwall to find a bride, and would subsequently either go back overseas with her or, more often, leave her to keep the home in Cornwall.[31] The 'three lives' system of leaseholding allowed this type of migration perhaps more easily than did other renting systems elsewhere.

It is a quite common thing for them to stay away for 20 years without ever returning and very often after being married only a few months. In the majority of cases they send money home and write the most affectionate and interested letters. They are an extraordinary people . . . .[32]

Inevitably returning to Cornwall was infrequent. For every miner who returned home to work, visit, or marry there was another who rarely if ever returned. Yet it seemed that for most miners the intention was ultimately to return to Cornwall with sufficient to give up mining for a small farm or shop, or to become an innkeeper. Some few did achieve this, but more did not.[33] Inevitably, too, many lost touch with wives or relatives at home. Thus some returned to find parents dead or wives remarried — a favourite theme for popular novelists at the time.[34] In any case returning to Cornwall was expensive, and often miners apparently preferred to use their money to get to another mining area. Thus miners went from Mexico to Calfornia, from California to Nevada, from Nevada to Michigan or Montana, or South America, or Australia, following the development of mineral deposits as fishermen follow shoals of fish.

The *Report on the Health of Cornish Miners* of 1904, illustrates this migration pattern clearly.[35] The Appendix to the Report gave the history of all miners who had died in the Redruth, Camborne, and Illogan districts during 1900, 1901, 1902. Of the 342 deaths examined, 216 or 64 per cent had worked in one or more mines abroad, while among the 126 men who had only worked in Cornwall all save five had worked in more than two mines. Almost certainly there was under-reporting of some miners' work patterns when details had to be obtained from the work-house rather than from the miner's widow or close family. All those men who had worked abroad had been to more than one country, most had been to several, as the following examples show:[36]

Case No 58	age 58	Condurrow (Cornwall) some years
		Durham 15 years
		Montana 2 years
		Tolcarne (Cornwall) 2 years
		South Africa 5 years
Case No 93	age 46	Dolcoath some years
		Peru 3 years
		California 8 years
		South Africa 1½ years
		South Africa 4 years
Case No 112	age 57	St Day Mines first
		Dolcoath some years
		California 7 or 8 years
		Mysore, India

Obviously such a wide ranging pattern was less typical of the younger men. These had, in the main, gone chiefly to South Africa. One such miner, aged 26 when he died of miners' phthisis, had worked in the 'Cornish mines until 19 yrs of age — then left for South Africa, worked as engine driver there until the war commenced, removed to Australia;

returned to Africa; came home very ill'.[37]

Indeed, South Africa dominated the Report. Of the men who had worked abroad more than half of them had spent some time there. Fewer had been to North America (68 men, 31 per cent) and only six had been to Australia which by that time had ceased to be a focus for the single roving miner and had become a place of settlement. The wide dispersion pattern remained however: 11 men had been to Central America, 15 to South America, and 19 to the Mysore gold mines in India. Six had worked in coal pits (in Wales, Durham, and Pittsburgh), four had been to West Africa and one each to Italy, Ceylon, Germany, Demerara, Cumberland, and the Straits Settlement.[38] Not all these last were hard rock mines so presumably the men went out in a management capacity.

Such mobility between Cornwall and other countries, coupled with the way in which migrants were classified in the returns of both Britain and the receiving countries, makes the actual extent of the Cornish diaspora extremely difficult to quantify. Isolated though they may have been, the Cornish figured in the returns as 'English', and, when classified by occupation, the metalliferous miners were often not distinguished from coal miners and both were often subsumed under the heading 'mechanic'. Furthermore, at the time of mass migration during the depressions, it was not solely the underground mineworkers who left. The extent of mine closures during these times made it imperative that other mineworkers migrated also. The masons, smiths, and carpenters previously employed at the mines had almost as little hope of work in Cornwall as the miners themselves. These skilled men formed part of the Cornish mine labour migrations, but their migration patterns and the numbers involved are even more difficult to quantify, since they are categorised in the returns by their original craft. Thus, although there are clear indications that migration from Cornwall was considerable, and passing references build up a qualitative picture — 'Probably Cornwall contributed a sensible contingent of the 42,990 miners of British or Irish origin who emigrated from the United Kingdom in the course of the ten years 1881-1891'[39] — the full extent would appear to have been underestimated. Ross Duncan, for example, in his case study of emigration to New South Wales from Cornwall and Gloucestershire, omits from his calculations all those who had what he terms 'pre-industrial' skills, e.g. carpenters.[40]

It is too crude to suggest that these Cornishmen who went from mine to mine throughout the nineteenth century were forced to do so by the prospect of starvation, except at the most general level. It is true that the Cornish were poor. Earnings were lower than those of most colliers and diet was correspondingly poor. Both wages and food were better overseas. But the high degree of autonomy with which they came and went suggests more than simply the coercion of starved labour. In addition, the relationship between these migrant miners and Cornwall remained sustained and complex. A man might return and take work at a Cornish mine after an absence of many years, only to find a deduction made from his first month's earnings to cover an 'advance' owed from years before.[41] At least one Cornish newspaper ran a 'News from Foreign Mining Camps' column from the 1890s to the outbreak of the First World War. This carried gossip culled from correspondents the world over: news of weddings, deaths, visits home, labour disputes, new mineral strikes, etc:

James Stevens, head Timberman at the Tamarah Shaft of the Calumet and Hecla mine, and his son-in-law Fred Jeffry, were amongst those who took advantage of the cessation of work in the Copper Country to pay a visit to friends in the iron Ranges and in the course of their journey visited Thomas Chenhall, a brother-in-law of Mr Stevens.[42]

This autonomy of the Cornish mineworkers was sustainable not least because they had a particular and specific skill. None the less, such autonomy and mobility should not necessarily be interpreted as suggesting that these Cornish were 'free' labour; it seems rather that their migration pattern justified, possibly more than any other group of industrial workers, Marx's description of migrants as 'the light infantry of capital'.[43] That is, a segment of the labour force which could be flexibly deployed wherever there was a need for labour to enable commodity production to expand. It was in this way that the Cornish mineworkers played a crucial part in the expansion of world metal production during the nineteenth century, and it was this that also played a crucial part in determining relations of production within Cornwall.

III

There has been general agreement among writers, both today and in the past, that the Cornish miners were far from the forefront of labour struggle and that in Cornwall strikes, industrial unrest, and political activity were conspicuous by their infrequency if not by their complete absence. The Webbs were unable to find any evidence of trade unionism when they investigated during the 1890s[44] and a similar lack of evidence had been noted by earlier commentators: 'No one has heard of disagreements between Cornish miners and their employers — no combinations or unions exist on the one side or the other.'[45] The cause of this apparent lack of militancy has been variously ascribed. Rowse, for example, in 1969 appeared to attribute it to some deep innate Celtic virtue.[46] Other twentieth-century writers have adopted a more multi-causal approach while differing in the stress they put on various factors. Thus Hamilton Jenkin attributed much of the miners' behaviour as he saw it to their indentification of interest with the mine companies and their ability to 'face facts'.[47] Todd and Harris, on the other hand, saw occupational isolation and the influence of Methodism as of more importance: 'Methodism unmasked the folly of ever expecting that the New Jerusalem could be found in Cornwall.'[48] Both Rowe and Rule support this view of the controlling role of Methodism, although neither give it predominance as a causal factor. Rule quotes a writer who, in 1865, commented: 'We have few turbulent demagogues in Cornwall. A miner who has any rhetorical powers and strong lungs prefers the pulpit to the platform.'[49] (Interestingly enough, among coal miners, whom commentators see as the antithesis of the Cornish miner, these or similar features are often cited as being the causes of militancy or radicalism;[50] but what is significant here is not that apparently similar causes were ascribed for apparently contradictory behaviour, but that both causal conjectures are open to question.)[51]

The factor that is often given most prominence in explanations of Cornish labour relations is the Tribute system of work organisation. Under Tribute a miner would bid for the pitch to mine, in competition against his fellows, and received a percentage payment of the value of the subsequent ore, thus appearing to be a self-employed contractor selling the proceeds of his labour rather than his labour itself. Rule suggests that, despite other explanatory factors, Tribute was of paramount importance in explaining the weakness of Cornish trade unionism during the period he studied, prior to 1870.[52]

Yet while it may be true that the Tribute system offers an explanation of events in the early part of the nineteenth century, it cannot be said that this holds true of the later part. Indeed, I have argued elsewhere that to focus primarily on Tribute is misleading, not least because the majority of the mine workforce were not Tributers, and because this ignores the relationship of the Cornish metalliferous mining industry as a whole with the rest of the world, in particular the growing links of investment and ownership.[53] Above all, by focusing on one aspect of work organisation in Cornwall, it overlooks the role played by labour migration, and ignores the role played by Cornish mineworkers in labour organisation overseas, a role which suggests that they were far from being 'anti-union' as such.

Cornishmen were prominent among the founders and officers of the Miners' Union on the Rand,[54] in the Australian Miners' Union,[55] and in the Federation of Western Miners in the USA.[56] It was not until 1917, however, that trade union organisations arrived in Cornwall. I would suggest that the patterns of Cornish mine labour migration had much to do with this late development. This is not to suggest a 'safety valve' theory with migration acting to prevent social unrest or the development of class consciousness at home — indeed I would suggest that class consciousness was on occasion quite clearly expressed in nineteenth century Cornwall — but rather that the existence of an established habit of migration provided an escape route during a period of change within the home industry where otherwise the development of clear class antagonisms might have been expected to occur.

This period of change was closely linked to the expansion of world metal production in which the Cornish miners played such a part. Its beginnings can be traced to the period of Free Trade with the lifting of tariffs on imported ores during the 1840s. The establishing of the Amsterdam metal market at the time, and the increase of imported tin ore from the Straits, undermined Cornwall's position as price setter for that metal, but the home industry survived the initial crisis relatively unaltered. Not until the drastic falls in the price of copper during the 1860s and of tin during the 1870s was change forced upon a reluctant industry. The further fall in the tin price during the 1890s, to its lowest point of the century in 1895, saw Cornwall finally moved from its position of premier producer of the world's copper and tin to one of residual importance. At this time the Cornish industry was completely restructured, from cost book to limited liability company, and from what Samuel has termed 'handicraft relations' to full capitalist relations of production.[57]

It was during this period of change and reconstruction of the Cornish mining industry that the beginnings of recognisable labour organisation occurred in Cornwall. But it was also during this time that the large-scale migrations occurred — the 'family' migrations during the late 1860s and again during the late 1870s, and the migrations of 'single roving miners' during the 1890s. The closure of the mines, and the massive shedding of labour from those mines that stayed open, provided powerful 'push' factors while ensuring that embryonic labour organisation withered. It was not surprising that the Webbs found no signs of trade unionism in Cornwall during the 1890s — most of the men were away, and those that remained behind and in work vented their frustrations in arson and sabotage below ground rather than in strikes and formal organisation.

From the 1850s onwards there were sporadic but large-scale spontaneous combinations at individual mines. As Rule has pointed out, these were not marked by class hatred, nor by attempts to form unions, but were of similar character to earlier recorded disputes.[58] They were speedily crushed, but contained elements which were to crystallise in 1866 with the first real attempt at unionism — the founding of the Miners Mutual Benefit Association (MMBA) among the workers in the mines of East Cornwall and Devon. Almost all these mines were major copper producers and thus the level of men's earnings had been drastically affected by the fall in price of copper, but the widespread membership and the apparent enthusiasm with which several thousand men joined the MMBA cannot be solely attributed to this. Drakewalls mine, at Gunnislake, for example, was a tin producer, yet there the Association was strong. The officers of the Association claimed '20,000 out of the 45,000 miners in Devon and Cornwall',[59] yet even half that number would have been a substantial membership. Certainly the mine companies saw the Association as a major threat for no sooner had the formation of the Association been announced, its rules published, and subscriptions collected, than they moved to a lock out that lasted almost two months. The March setting day (when pitches were agreed) at Devon Great Consuls mine took place in the presence of 150 soldiers of the 66th Regiment, 129 Police, and 150 Special Constables together with three local magistrates and the local Director of the Mine,[60] yet only four pitches were taken up and the assembled miners stayed firm to the Association.

The speakers at the mass meetings of the MMBA — held in the open air and opened with a hymn[61] — laid great stress on the fact that as members of the Association they were fighting for their rights as free-born Englishmen, and for 'Liberty'.[62] Yet, despite this rather eighteenth century style, there is evidence to suggest that the MMBA leadership itself clearly saw the class antagonisms implicit in the lock out: 'They had the crushing weight of capital against them. The weight of capital was worse than king-craft, and worst than any priest-craft for the poor sons of men.'[63] Furthermore there was a recognition of the relationship of migration abroad to struggle at home. 'Liberty' could be found in a foreign land, and a possible bargaining counter existed in the use of migration as a threat:

The best way to make the higher classes feel this would be for every miner to cast his wife and family upon the support of the parish (cries of 'yes', 'hear, hear' 'we shall be obliged to do it'). Every man could leave a place when he liked, and if the

Agents persisted in putting down the Association, the men should remove to another land and leave their families for others to maintain ('hear, hear')[64]

However, the migration of the single roving miner could only be a threat in times of high labour demand. In 1866 it was no threat at all as the price of copper continued to fall. By the end of the decade most of the East Cornwall mines had closed. Many were never to reopen. Later commentators were to remark on the number of families kept alive by remittances from men who went overseas during this time[65] in addition to the thousands who, with their families, left Cornwall for good.

The MMBA was crushed as much by the fall in the price of copper as by the swift action of the employers. After this attempt at unionisation, industrial action was spasmodic and took various forms, strikes, riots, and political agitation for reform of working conditions (following the enfranchisement of most of the mineworkers in 1884). In 1900 the votes of the 'Rand Miners' newly returned from South Africa following the outbreak of the Anglo-Boer war in 1899 played a decisive part in the defeat of the Conservative sitting member for the Mining Division. But there was no further attempt to form a trade union of Cornish miners within Cornwall during the nineteenth and early twentieth centuries. There were two clear reasons for this. The first was the collapse of the industry that began in the 1860s. Labour organisation could not be sustained on a falling market and subsequent industrial action mirrored the peaks and troughs of the industry within the context of its overall decline. Secondly, the long established practice of migration offered an alternative to attempting to 'build the New Jerusalem' in Cornwall. Migration was not solely coincidental with the depressions in the Cornish industry, since throughout most of the nineteenth century the Cornish miner had a skill in world demand. Changes at home and abroad changed the nature of that demand and effectively de-skilled the Cornish miners but migration, either temporary or permanent, continued to offer an escape route for a considerable while. So it was that large-scale labour organisation did not become established in Cornwall until the outbreak of war in 1914 when migration was no longer possible.

During the war years the antagonisms between mine labour and capital in Cornwall became clearly expressed and conflict of interest could no longer be masked. There were a series of long and bitter disputes, including a three-month lock-out at Levant mine in 1918. These involved both underground and surface workers, and were concerned with both wage levels and union recognition. During this period the majority of mineworkers in Cornwall joined either the Dockers' or the Workers' Unions, whose officials had first become involved in Cornwall during the strike of the china clay workers in 1913. In their turn the mine companies combined to form the Cornish Mines Employers Federation. Both sides were represented on the Joint Industrial Council for the Tin Mining Industry established in 1919, but this did not initially achieve much success in raising wage levels for the mine workers, which by now were among the lowest in the country.[66] By 1920 a general strike by all Cornish mineworkers seemed imminent, and was only averted by a last ditch wage offer from the Employers.

The crisis in the industry was heightened by the post-war decontrol of food prices, and there were riots in several parts of Cornwall in which farmers who had raised the price of their butter, milk, and eggs had their produce smashed as they brought it to market. The Unions organised protest demonstrations at which clear class antagonisms were expressed:

Mr Behenna (WU organiser) said. . . . There were thousands of babies dying in the country and at inquests the coroners returned verdicts of 'natural causes'. A truer verdict would be 'capitalism'. . . .

Mr J.H. Bennets (WU) said. . . . the Government were to blame for the present plight. Instead of treating all classes alike they had only studied one class — the capitalist. A bigger output was urged, but how could men on a C3 diet do A1 work?. . . .

Mr Robinson (Carnmarth) stated that he had six children but was only in receipt of 7/- per shift. . . . he wanted to see butter brought to the alleys of the workers as well as to Albany Road and the people in the principal streets of Redruth.[67]

By this time, however, the mine companies were experiencing the consequences of years of profit taking at the expense of underground development, culminating in the short-term demands of the war economy. When the price of tin fell yet again, with the onset of the post-war depression, it was not surprising that the mines, with no reserves to fall back on, were in crisis. As the Cornish capitalists rationalised their assets and turned to their more profitable ventures overseas, all save two of the remaining Cornish mines closed, thus rendering hundreds unemployed and labour organisation academic. By this time there were few overseas opportunities for the migrating Cornish miner; the escape route had closed.

IV

In addition to an apparent reputation for non-militancy, the Cornish miners also gained, during the nineteenth century, a reputation as strike breakers, particularly in the coal-fields of the north of England, but also overseas. In 1864 the (mainly Irish) Miners League of Storey County was broken with the use of Cornish labour: '. . . . who are aliens and who come here only to hoard their gains and carry them back to their native land.'[68] In Butte, Montana, where the Cornish/Irish antagonism was perhaps the most bitter, Cornish miners frequently blacklegged:

> Oh fellow worker, Cousin Jack
> On you we're keeping tab
> Your first name may be Tussie
> But your middle name is SCAB[69]

Rowe suggests it was anti-Irish feeling that kept the Butte Cornish out of the International Workers of the World, during the strike there in 1917.[70] Such prejudice was not one-sided. Rowe quotes the howls of protest when a Cornishman was proposed for the IWW Committee of Grievances, whose membership was meant to represent all the ethnic groups at Butte.[71]

Such evidence would seem to substantiate the view of the Cornish miners as individualist non-militants, yet I would argue that this was not in fact the case. In the USA, despite racial antagonism, the Cornish 'became the leaders of mining labour movement in the West.'[72] In South Australia similarly, the miners earned for Moonta and Wallaroo (nicknamed 'Australia's little Cornwall') a reputation as 'a red hot Labour centre'[73] and many Cornish miners rose to prominence in the Australian Labor Movement, with one, John Verran, becoming first Labor Prime Minister of South Australia.[74] I would suggest that Cornish blacklegging needs to be re-examined not only with regard to the apparently more predominant union-supporting behaviour of Cornishmen abroad, but also with regard to the migration pattern of the 'single roving miner'.

The method of recruiting Cornish miners as strike breakers was apparently quite straightforward: an advertisement would be placed in the Cornish local newspapers offering work. Indeed, the papers frequently carried such advertisements from all over the world, and requests for blacklegs did not differ greatly in wording or format save that they specified that men were wanted 'on contract' and would have their fares paid to the mine. During the late 1860s and early 1870s there were several such advertisements placed by English coal-mine owners from Lancashire and Durham. In both these areas there were labour disputes, although the advertisements made no mention of this. It does not appear that very many men went north, that is compared to the numbers who went abroad, and a possible explanation may lie in the Cornish miners contempt for coal-mining, regarded as mere unskilled hewing. In fact, as Harris has pointed out, coal-mining did contain a body of skills and 'knacks' and a hierarchy of skills existed between borers, sinkers, hewers, and drawers.[75] Most of these skills would, however, have been familiar to the Cornish, except possibly that of testing for fire-dampt, and in the early 1870s the Cornish miner had additional skills to offer. For the collier, as Harrison has noted, the main problem was that his skills were expendable. The work could be done and coal produced — less well perhaps and with more accidents, but produced nonetheless — by the unskilled labour of agricultural workers. This tension, between 'honourable men' and 'degraded slaves' Harrison suggests, was what determined the nature of coal-mining trade unionism between 1850 and 1888.[76] In Cornwall there does not appear to have been any such tension. On only two occasions was any attempt made to introduce unskilled labour into Cornish mines and then on a very limited scale. In contrast to the coal-fields where demand for labour grew, it was technological innovation — particularly the introduction of rock drills after 1875, decreased demand for labour, and the growth of professional trained mining experts, that de-skilled the Cornish miner and moved him from honourable man to degraded slave. In the early 1870s, although deskilling was about to begin, a Cornish miner stood to gain more by working in a metal mine overseas than in a coal-mine in Britain. With an established pattern of autonomous migration, only those men who were unable to raise the fare to Nevada or elsewhere would be likely to 'take the bosses' shilling' and go north on contract, with their fares paid, to the coalfields.

This view is underlined by an examination of the Burnley coal strike of 1874, not least because one of the first actions of the striking colliers' union (the Amalgamated Association of Miners) was to pay the fares of the incomers back to Cornwall again. Indeed, the Secretary of the AAM, Thomas Halliday, together with seven officers of the Association, faced arrest and imprisonment on a conspiracy charge for financially aiding the Cornish miners.[77] It seems hard to believe that, isolated though Cornwall was, the miners involved had no idea they were to be strike-breakers, although this is what some of them claimed.[78] Others became persuaded of the justice of the colliers' cause. As four Callington miners stated in a letter home:

We consider it our duty as honourable men to inform you that we have been into Lancashire, and have worked in the coal mines in the neighbourhood of Burnley, but we did not find that ease and comfort which we expected to find, but we found hard work and not seven shillings per eight hours for one or two years which we understood we were to have; but when we were there a short time only our wages were reduced . . . . Although we had been working in the places of the men who were locked out by the employers, the poor men treated us with the greatest kindness and respect, and enabled us to reach home in safety . . . . The poor men are locked out because they wish to belong to a Miners' Association known as the Amalgamated Association of Miners. They also desire to get coal by weight not by measure or the box. It is right that they should be united with their fellow miners as by the power of combination they would be able to claim demand and obtain their rights according to the Statute Law of this Realm. Fellow men — do not engage with any Agent just now; better days are in store for us. The Amalgamated Association is a noble institution, and it will be our moral redemption in days to come. It is ready to take us in with open arms, to aid in bettering our condition . . . .[79]

The AAM was certainly only too ready to take the Cornish miners in 'with open arms' in that it did not limit itself to being a trade union solely for the Lancashire coalfields. In 1873 it numbered men from Wales, Bristol, the Forest of Dean, and Cannock Chase among its 23,676 members as well as having strong links through the *Examiner* system of local papers with the Potteries and with tin plate, iron, and agricultural workers.[80] The policy of the AAM, resolved in 1872, was the regulation of wages and the use of arbitration to prevent strikes but that strikes, when they did occur, should be funded from levies on the rest of the membership.[81] It was from this fund that the AAM officers paid the fares back to Cornwall of many erstwhile strike-breakers.

It would appear that the AAM was actively campaigning for members among the Cornishmen rather than simply endeavouring to remove troublemakers from Burnley. Officers of the Association visited Cornwall in January 1874, holding public meetings and writing at length in the local press.[82] They urged the justice of the Association's cause and called on Cornish miners to join them rather than accept the coal companies' offers of work. Their approach was in marked contrast to that of the Durham miners, who the following May also sent representatives to Cornwall stating: 'We therefore ask all strangers to keep from Durham until we have settled with our employers as we intend to resist the proposed reduction in wages.'[83] The Durham union was, in contrast to the AAM, a union purely of colliers, but the AAM itself, despite its broad base could not sustain the pressure of concerted demands for wage reductions from coal companies that occurred with the fall in the price of coal. Thus, although it was claimed that many hundreds of Cornishmen had joined the

AAM,[84] their membership was of short duration. The optimism of the Callington men was not realised; 'better days' were not at hand for labour in Cornwall; rather, the metal mining industry also moved into depression, with wage reductions, mine closures, and mass unemployment. The migrations of the late 1870s once again eclipsed those of the single roving miner as families, aided by the Country Distress Committee, sailed away. Some 60,000 people left Cornwall during the decade 1871-81. None the less, the example of the Burnley miners' strike was not unique, and it seems reasonable to suggest that the autonomy of the single roving miner does provide insight into the strike-breaking phenomenon. Both extreme financial straits and family migration limited this autonomy of mobility.

A similar example can be found in 1913, when three Cornishmen, newly arrived in Michigan and believed to have come as strike-breakers in the long strike at Calumet and Hecla, were shot dead by members of the Western Federation of Miners. The reporting of the killings in the Cornish press, together with a discreetly worded advertisement from the Calumet and Hecla company for mine labour, elicited a letter from some Cornish miners in Arizona, not unlike that of the Callington men thirty-nine years before:

. . . . it is our purpose to inform miners of Cornwall what the miners are fighting for in the Copper Country . . . . That the struggle is a righteous one has been admitted all over the United States, and the working classes of every trade and calling have supported it morally and financially and are continuing to do so . . . . Thus far the mining companies have not been able to find competent miners to fill the place of the strikers. Consequently they have resorted to advertising in foreign papers that are published in mining districts for men to come and bring their families, as they are well aware that it will cost any miner all he has financially to go to Michigan, and after he gets there he will have to work to sustain them . . . .[85]

In conclusion, I would reiterate that there was an important relationship between long-established patterns of labour migration, and the form of labour relations that occurred within Cornwall. Possibly migration acted as a safety valve for men despairing of change in Cornwall, certainly there was most frequently the coercion of poverty, but the migration of the Cornish mineworkers to the metalliferous mining fields of the world was one whose complexities transcended both safety valve and coercion theory, not least because they migrated as miners to a mine (any mine, anywhere) rather than to a 'new world'. The Cornish diaspora poses a challenge to individualist perspectives on labour migration. Rather, examination suggests that migration was determined by international development and investment with concommitant shifts in international demand for labour. Furthermore, the history of the Cornish miner and the Cornish mining industry during the nineteenth century poses a challenge to those who interpret labour migration in terms of betterment. The Cornish mining economy was inextricably linked to the economies of the metalliferous mining fields of the world in a dialectic relationship whereby the expansion of the latter inevitably meant ruin for the former. That this expansion and change in world mineral production was assisted — indeed in many cases largely made possible — by the labour of the Cornish miners, while the consequences in terms of social dislocation, poverty, disease, and death subsequently borne by Cornishmen and women both at home and abroad[86] underlines these challenges with bitter irony.

4

INTO SERVITUDE: INDIAN LABOUR IN THE SUGAR INDUSTRY, 1833-1970

HUGH TINKER

WHEN the Moyne Commission visited the Caribbean in 1939 in the wake of strikes and violence on the sugar estates, they discovered that in important respects the world of sugar had changed little since the days of slavery. The basic unit of production, the field worker, was still treated as a work animal, and sweat and sinew were supplemented, technologically, only by the hoe and the slashing blade, the cutlass. The sugar workers were still treated as a people apart, to be isolated from the other elements in the colony. The estate was organised on rigid, hierarchical lines, with coercion rather than reward as the main incentive towards effort. The repressive resources of the colony were held in reserve to reinforce the estate system of discipline. Between the almost servile non-white estate labour force and the white management was interposed a 'buffer' group, drawn from those who — in socio-economic if not always strictly in racial terms — were the descendants of the 'free coloureds'. Finally, the finished product, the sugar, was destined for a market thousands of miles away in the metropole. Sugar was a colonial product dependent on the colonial power for its value, and out of this dependence stemmed the dependent status of the sugar workers.

Much has changed since the Moyne Report appeared.[1] Yet in fundamentals the condition of the sugar worker remains the same. During the last hundred and fifty years the sugar colonies have witnessed three dramatic 'liberations': the abolition of slavery (1834-38), the abolition of indenture (1916-20), and the abolition of colonial overlordship (1962-70). Each liberation has been hailed as the means of transforming the condition of the sugar worker, a new start in freedom. Yet each time the transformation has ended in something like 'A New System of Slavery'.[2] Perpetuation of the old conditions has not been affected by the changes in the overall system of economic control. The original resident owners, the old plantocracy, gave way to metropolitan-based companies, amalgamations of estates with vastly bigger factories, and refineries in Britain. These in turn are giving way to the assimilation of the industry into public ownership, that of the newly independent sugar states. Yet important elements of the slave system still persist. If all this sets a puzzle for old-fashioned *laissez-faire* liberals, it is not altogether explicable to the modern Marxist. The present paper seeks to do little more than present an outline narrative of events and trends. Knowledge may lead to understanding. Most of the evidence is drawn from Mauritius and Guyana — spatially so far apart, yet in experience so close — with some additional reference to Trinidad and Fiji.

The legacy of slavery

Adam Smith observed in *The Wealth of Nations*: 'The work done by slaves though it appears to cost only their maintenance is in the end the dearest of any.' This was very true of the estates, where planters had to maintain a permanent, all-the-year-round work-force to support what was (and is) a seasonal industry. Work was spread out by means of the *task,* a specified amount of work to be completed in a specified time by a gang under a taskmaster or *slave-driver.* At crop-time the gang worked round the clock; during the rest of the year they had little more than maintenance tasks. Because they were driven so hard, the death-rate was high. Tasking was enforced by cruel punishments, inflicted by the driver or by order of the overseer (in charge of several gangs). To ensure slaves did not escape, they were locked up at night in barracoons. Even more important, the slave was forbidden to move off the estate, unless (exceptionally) his master had given him a pass or 'ticket'. Any white could stop any black on the highway or in town and demand to see his ticket. If unable to produce one he would be arrested and jailed or otherwise punished. Elsa V. Goveia observes: 'Each of the plantations . . . . was itself a small world and the field slave was trapped . . . . like a fly in a spider's web.'[3]

A few slaves did escape to the hills. These were hunted down like wild animals. The urge to escape was explained by the theory that the blacks had a propensity to wander off. *Marronage* (the state of the 'Maroons') derived from a Spanish term, *cimarron,* meaning a tame animal that had escaped and become wild. Hence there was almost a moral imperative to capture the Maroon and punish him for his deviance.

By enforcing restriction and isolation the planters were able to ensure that any protest or revolt could be confined within the estate. The nightmare of a general slave rising was always in the planter's mind.

Protest would be savagely repressed to ensure that it was stifled immediately. A militia of poor white or coloured men was often available to reinforce the individual planter's authority, while there were British troops on call in emergency. As the colonial legislature was largely dominated by the plantocracy (even in the newly annexed Crown Colonies), the planters could be certain that in any dispute the colonial power was behind them.

During the last phase of slavery the pressure of humanitarians in Britain brought about the regulation of the system and the reduction of estate punishments to a standard norm. Protectors of Slaves were appointed in four Crown Colonies (British Guiana, Trinidad, St Lucia, and Mauritius) and these were officials despatched from Britain. The Protector, however, found himself totally isolated amid white planter society. The official sent to Mauritius 'was insulted, abused, harassed at every turn, and eventually recalled'.[4] In some respects, because slavery was now within the web of law and government regulation, colonial officialdom could more effectively be induced to support the planter's cause.

During the last days of slavery and during the apprenticeship interlude, the planters tried to exact even greater effort from their blacks and treated them with even greater harshness. This was specially true of Mauritius and Guiana, where the French and Dutch planters bitterly resented the alien interference of their unwanted British mentors. Hence, when released from apprenticeship, the great majority of the ex-slaves quit the plantation for ever. The only alternatives were the cultivation of small plots, fishing, hunting, and petty huckstering. The pursuit of these occupations tended to make the Negroes adjust to a style of individualism and free enterprise: in a way, to regard themselves as small capitalists. In Guiana some went off prospecting and mining, and many were the stories told about the 'Pork Knockers' who set out with a bag of provisions and returned from the wild as rich men. Those blacks who remained on the estates soon found that the planters wanted to go on treating them as slaves: in particular, the planters resented having to pay wages, and delayed paying out for months on end. 'Busha Don't Pay' became the Negro's verdict on the planter, and increasingly blacks would only work to a new version of the task. They made a contract, as a gang, to do a specified amoung of digging, planting, or harvesting, and thus emerged not as workers but as contractors.

Even before the termination of slavery the Mauritius planters were turning away from Africa and looking towards India for their labour. Were not the Indians diligent, docile, obedient: everything that the blacks were not? The first cargoes of Indians — 'coolies', as they were invariably called — were exploited atrociously, and, following revelations about the Gladstone estates in Guiana the Government of India abruptly banned any further export of labourers. It was, however, part of the thesis of the British humanitarians that 'Free Labour' would be more efficient than slaves. Pressure developed to permit the resumption of the export of 'free' Indian labour. Elaborate provisions were made to ensure that the recruits were protected from their ignorance of conditions in the sugar colonies. Arguing that emigration presented great opportunities to the rural poor of India, officials in the Colonial Office, India House, the Secretariat at Calcutta, and the various colonial governments, put together a package labelled indenture.

The framework of indenture

The new feature of this system was supposed to be that the labourer arrived in the sugar colony as a free agent and then freely entered into a contract of indenture with an individual planter. The labourer was taken from his place of domicile by the agent of a commercial firm, but once arrived at the emigration depot in Calcutta or Madras he, or she, was in the care of a British official, the Emigration Agent. The regulations laid down that when quotas were made up for embarkation there must be 40 females (married or unmarried) to every 100 males. On board ship the recruits were under the care of a Surgeon Superintendent, appointed by the British government, and there were strict rules for their welfare.[5] We cannot linger over the various ways in which these apparently watertight safeguards were inadequate to ensure that conditions were fully observed (notably in the constant failure to meet the 40 to 100 female to male ratio).[6] We shall begin at the moment when those of the coolies who were 'landed alive' entered the immigration depot (which, in Port Louis, was the old slave depot) and were handed over to the official known as Protector of Immigrants or Immigration Agent-General. Under the agreed terms, the Protector was to have been appointed by the Government of India, but in all cases he was a local, colonial official, responsive to the pressures of the local plantocracy.

Originally, the immigrants were to sign indenture agreements for one year; they might then re-engage on new terms or claim a free return passage to India. Quite rapidly, under planter pressure, the period of indenture was extended to five years: there were constant demands that the period should be ten years. Many Chinese coolies going to Cuba and other non-British colonies were bound under ten-year contracts, with no provision for a return passage. The Colonial Office resisted initial ten-year indentures, though it accepted second indentures for five-year periods as normal. The Colonial Office also resisted the efforts of planters to whittle away the right to return (although in some cases conceding that the labourer must pay part of the return fare).

The free choice provision was ignored; drafts were assigned to plantations and, where a draft proved to include trouble-makers, these would be separated and consigned to other, distant estates. The five years of service was interpreted as five years given to the satisfaction of the planter; absences through sickness or any other cause did not count, so that a sickly coolie might find himself bound for six, or seven years. The coolies described themselves as *bound*, and they were portrayed in folk art with hands bound behind their backs. Those out of indenture were known as *khula*, 'opened' from bondage.

Rates of pay were laid down: normally the equivalent of Rs5 (50p) per month in Mauritius, with rations provided. In the Caribbean the rate was supposed to be 5s (25p) per week, without rations. Any absence, whether for sickness or any other reason, led to an automatic loss of pay. In addition, failure to complete a task incurred the loss of a day's pay. In Mauritius the penalties were doubled under the notorious 'Double Cut' system. As with their black workers, the planters invariably allowed pay to fall into arrears: it was normal for the coolies to be two or three months in arrears.

The indentured workers were housed in the barracoons vacated by the slaves. Gradually, as these fell down, coolie lines were built, providing minute separate quarters for three or four men apiece.[7] In place of the former black slave-drivers there were now Indian coolie-drivers (*sirdars* in Mauritius). These men had better quarters, and they were almost the only estate workers having wives and living a family life. The few other females were mainly living under the temporary protection of one or sometimes three or four males (in addition to cooking, washing, and other domestic duties, these females had to labour in the canefield). As under slavery, the estate workers were rigidly confined within the estates. None might venture beyond without a pass. Absence without a pass incurred a fine or imprisonment, in addition to loss of pay and added indenture time. In Mauritius, even when freed from indenture, an Indian had to carry a *livret* or passbook with his photograph. If a free Indian wished to move from one district to another he had first to register at the district police station. Loss of a *livret* led to a swingeing fine. The rationale of all this was that, like the Negro, the Indian was prone to *marronage* and had to be restrained from his vagabond instincts.

Estate discipline was maintained by the whip and the stocks. The power of the planter was reinforced by a penal code, specially enacted for the indentured people, which made industrial indiscipline — absence from work, or, above all, challenges to estate authority or strikes — an offence punishable by a magistrate, by fine or imprisonment. In theory these stipendiary magistrates were also obliged to move against planters who did not conform to the industrial law. It was a courageous magistrate who actually enforced this side of the law. Thus (at random), in Mauritius in 1893, 78 complaints by workers against employers (mainly for assault or non-payment of wages) resulted in a fine; in the same year employers' complaints led to 6,754 convictions against male workers and 722 against females, many resulting in jail sentences. Right at the end of indenture, an official enquiry established that in 1907-08 the percentage of indentured labourers convicted under the labour laws in that year was: Guiana, 20%; Fiji, 20%; Trinidad, 16%; and Mauritius, 3%.[8]

Under these repressive conditions, protest by workers was almost always spontaneous and sporadic. Such protests were almost always against deprivation of existing rights or reduction in pay: hardly ever organised to obtain improvements. When protest was beyond the employer's power to control he invariably invoked the aid of magistrate and police. The magistrates were almost all white (British, or in Mauritius domiciled Frenchmen, *Francos*), as were the police superintendents and inspectors. The constables were almost all Negro Creoles. Hence an industrial confrontation also assumed the role of racial conflict.

The racial division between blacks and 'East Indians' remained almost complete. The Negro regarded plantation labour as coolie work, and in evidence to the West India Commission of 1897 it was related that the indentured Indians were generally called 'Coolie Slaves'.[9] This racial gap did not narrow significantly as the Indian population became creolised. In Mauritius the period of mass immigration ended about 1880. Migration to Guiana peaked in the 1870s and thereafter continued, at a more modest level, until World War I. Substantial immigration to Fiji did not begin until the 1880s and then persisted at a high level until World War I. Migration to Trinidad never attained the same levels, although the island was a popular destination for some emigrants. This was because at an early stage the colonial government instituted land grants in lieu of a free return passage. The Trinidad Indians thus began to include a number of small landowners who combined seasonal work on the big plantations with the cultivation of sugar on their own plots. In Mauritius also a class of small agriculturalists began to emerge, largely from among former *sirdars* or foremen, and at a later stage the same phenomenon began in Fiji. Guiana saw little of this; estate land was confined to the coastal strip, and reclaiming new land brought often insoluble problems of drainage. Those East Indians who became farmers largely took up paddy cultivation; rice production in Guiana became an entirely Indian sector of the economy.

The trend towards sugar culture by farmers outside the white-owned estates was in conformity with the general development of the sugar industry. There was a process of consolidation: the two hundred estates in Mauritius in the 1850s had been reduced to fifty early in the twentieth century and to twenty-one by the 1950s. The big estates had large, modernised factories where the cane was processed into crystalline sugar. The Indian farmers had no choice but to take their cane to the nearest factory, for delay in processing the cane after reaping soon leads to a fall in the extraction rate. Hence the small farmers were as much in the power of the estates as the actual employees. The resident estate work-force was substantially reduced, thus effecting a massive reduction in the payroll. Increasingly, the Indians lived in ramshackle villages just off the estate limits, or survived by casual odd jobs. Nevertheless, the planters still demanded that the structure of indentured immigration remain in operation. Their object was to ensure that there was always a surplus of labour so that wage-rates could be kept depressed. In the early twentieth century, rates were generally somewhat lower than they had been fifty or sixty years before.

Resistance to the system

From time to time, as an occasional revelation of ruthless exploitation was carried back to India, the British-Indian government was moved to protest. These protests filtered through the Whitehall machinery and then out to the sugar colonies. They led to little more than cosmetic reform. The Government of India possessed only one real sanction: to suspend emigration, and there was always hesitation because of its supposed advantages to the Indian poor.

Humanitarian agencies in London, notably the Anti-Slavery Society and the Aborigines Protection Society, attempted to monitor the system and to make representations in Whitehall. They never tried, however, to challenge the whole system, arguing only for reform. In the sugar colonies the leaders of the Indian communities were business men and owners of small estates: they were part of the buffering mechanism. Hardly ever did an Indian of stature stand up as an opponent of the system; if he did, he was denounced as an agitator and isolated and excluded, as happened to Manilal Doctor in Mauritius and later in Fiji.[10]

When a powerful movement for abolition at last developed it acquired muscle because the Indian nationalists — led by Gandhi — championed the cause, and the Government of India deemed it expedient to adopt the role of champion also. Abolition was brought forward by the appalling story uncovered by C.F. Andrews as emissary of the Indian National Congress, in his investigations in Fiji.[11] It was also assisted by the shipping crisis in mid-World War I which made it impossible to continue the coolie traffic. New recruitment was stopped in 1916 and on 2 January 1920 indenture was abolished throughout the British sugar colonies.

After indenture

As when slavery was abolished, the employers were determined that the former conditions would, so far as possible, be preserved. They were utterly determined that wages would be kept down, despite the massive post-war rise in the cost of living. The first major protest occurred in Fiji, where Suva-Rewa sugar workers came out on strike, led by the wife of Manilal, Jayunkvar. The whole apparatus of colonial power was mobilised to break the strike. Troops were brought from Australia and New Zealand, the navy was called in, rigid restrictions on movement were imposed, and the Manilal family were deported. The strike was broken but a second strike-wave erupted in 1921, led by a *sadhu,* Bashishth Muni. This eventually involved almost all the Fiji Indian workers, not only those in sugar, but the colonial government was able to break it in the end.[12] A major consequence was that the image of the 'docile' Indian was shattered; Europeans, and also the chiefly leaders of the Fijians, saw them as threatening potential domination of the islands. A more conscious alliance between colonial government, white business interests, and the chiefs now became the cornerstone of political development in Fiji.

Industrial protest elsewhere did not attain the same proportions, although there was a rash of disputes in Guiana in 1924, culminating in a confrontation between strikers and police on the Ruimveldt Estate in which thirteen Indians were killed. There were primitive attempts at unionisation. Hubert Critchlow founded the British Guiana Labour Union (BGLU) in 1919, but its activities were little more than nominal. The employers ensured that no workers dared to join the union, on pain of instant dismissal.[13] Sidney Webb, Lord Passfield, issued a circular as

Colonial Secretary encouraging the formation of trade unions (September 1930). The administration in Trinidad and Guiana responded by enacting legislation permitting unions; Fiji and Mauritius remained without a trade union law. Nevertheless, two organisations which were virtually unions emerged in Fiji in the 1930s: the *Kisan Sangh,* representing the tenant farmers, and the *Mazdur Sangh* for the labourers. In Mauritius a creole doctor, J.M. Curé, established the *Parti travailliste,* intended as a political party and also as a labour organisation to mobilise the sugar workers. In Guiana the BGLU was replaced by a more effective body, the Man-Power Citizens' Association (MPCA), whose organisers were both Indians and blacks. The new union recruited 10,000 members, but the employers, led by the giant Booker combine, refused to recognise the MPCA.

In the metropole the subject of the Indians in the sugar colonies was even more out of sight and out of mind than during the indenture period. The Government of India no longer felt any direct obligation to look after their interests. Indian nationalism was too much wrapped up in the coming struggle for independence to remember the overseas Indians. The Anti-Slavery Society also felt less involved in their fate. The Colonial Office was content to issue bland circulars urging that the Indians should integrate into creole society. In the colonies the formal safeguard provided by the local Protector of Immigrants was no longer available even as a formality. The efforts of the emerging Indian colonial middle class were directed to gaining a foothold in the local administration, the Bar, schools and colleges, and to a limited extent in the lower levels of the hierarchy of the sugar industry. The workers had to depend on their own efforts to gain any improvement.

Wage-rates in the 1930s reflected the conditions of a hundred years before. In Mauritius, a fieldhand was still paid Rs 10 (70p) per month plus rations. In Trinidad, the rate was 35 cents per day (about £1.50 per month), and in Guiana it was less. Unrest first began in 1935 among Caribbean blacks (angry at the invasion of 'their' country, Ethiopia), and spread to the Indian sugar workers. The first Guiana strike was on Plantation Leonora, which had a long history of bad labour relations. From Essequibo to the Corentyne coast the strikes extended, and on the vast Rose Hall estate the workers defied the police, hoisting the red flag, beating drums, and waving cutlasses.

The Governor appointed a commission of inquiry but rejected the demand of the East Indian Association to be represented. The Indians refused to give evidence, following the example of Gandhi, but they were compulsorily subpoenaed. The only member of the commission independent of the sugar interest, the manager of the Bauxite Mining Company, made some pertinent points, remarking: 'The only difference between the indentured labourer and the labourer of today is that the indentured labourer could have been prosecuted for not turning out to work: but the free labourer of today is entirely dependent on the estate.' The reply was that any worker who gave trouble would be fired and would never be employed on another estate.[14] The commission reported that conditions in the industry were worse then they had been ten years before; they urged the government to set up a board to regulate conditions of work and wages. Otherwise, the highly organised Sugar Producers' Association would continue to impose its own arbitrary terms upon the workers.

The response of the Guiana administration was quite tepid; all that was conceded was a wholly inadequate system of government inspection. Meanwhile, trouble flared up in Trinidad and the Colonial Secretary decided to send out a commission of inquiry, the Moyne Commission. In their report (whose publication was delayed till 1945) the Commission declared:

The discontent that underlies the disturbances of recent years is a phenomenon of a different character (from before) representing no longer a mere blind protest against a worsening of conditions but a positive demand for the creation of new conditions that will render possible a better, less restricted life.

Far away in the Indian Ocean, Mauritius went through the same cycle of repression and revolt. In August 1937 a series of strikes began and sputtered on. The Governor urged the employers' association (the Chamber of Agriculture) to negotiate, but they replied that the strikes were the work of 'agitators' and 'intimidators' and declared a lock-out. The government appointed a commission of inquiry (again without Indian membership), which was strongly critical of conditions. They described the workers as underpaid and underfed: wages ought to be raised, at least by 10 per cent. The small cane farmers were at the mercy of the factories: the prevailing set-up was described as 'evil'. They recommended that unions be recognised and a proper labour department created.[15]

As a result, twenty-five unions were registered during 1938 within the framework of a new Industrial Associations Ordinance. In August 1938 there were more strikes. There was also a new Governor, Sir Bede Clifford, and he set out to break these strikes, deporting the front spokesmen to a remote island and sentencing lesser strike leaders to long jail sentences. Within a few months the nascent trade unions had crumbled: only two of the original twenty-five survived.

Under wartime conditions the cost of living rose steeply in Mauritius, while wages lagged behind. A minimum wages board was established in 1941 to compel employers to compensate for inflation (being themselves compensated under Commonwealth purchasing agreements). On many estates wages fell below the legal minimum of Rs 20 (£1.40) per month. In 1943 bands of labourers undertook hunger marches to Port Louis, but their protests were ascribed to trouble-making agitators. Failing to impress the labour department, they resorted to strike action. The police were sent in to arrest the leaders and on one estate, Belle Vue Harel, there was shooting; three were killed and sixteen badly wounded. The usual commission of inquiry was set up and the usual criticisms were produced: they found that conditions had not improved and might well have deteriorated. The job of the labour department was conceived as 'to keep labour quiet'. The report was considered too damning to be published. The year 1943 also witnessed a prolonged struggle in Fiji between the workers and the cane farmers against the colossal Colonial Sugar Refining Company, backed by the government. Demands for better prices for cane were resisted and the 1943 crop largely remained unharvested. In the end the farmers gave in and accepted their defeat; the company served notice on fifty-six of the farmers that it would never again purchase their crop.[16]

Towards self-government

The years after World War II saw rapid political change in the British sugar colonies but only a limited modification of the economic pattern. In the 1950s the sugar colonies experienced a dramatic extension of the franchise and the emergence of political elites, which took over the administration structure although remaining outside the economic structure: the real position of power. These new political leaders owed their position to the support of the workers, and in their rhetoric they assumed a radical, populist stance. Only in Guiana did Cheddi Jagan, with his People's Progressive party, attempt to bring about a change in the economic structure, based upon a powerful, recognised trade union movement. His Guiana Agricultural Workers' Union (GAWU) replaced the MPCA, which had over the years become more and more a bosses' union. Because of his openly Marxist stance, the British government (under pressure from the United States) dismissed his ministry and sought to create an alternative political force under the leadership of Forbes Burnham. This is not the place to record the political struggle in Guyana which led to Burnham-type independence (1966). More sedately, the other sugar colonies passed down the same road: Trinidad (1962), Mauritius (1968), and Fiji (1970). All proceeded to handle the great sugar corporations with extreme care: their revenues depended on sugar, and on the prosperity of the industry largely depended employment for their people. The tactics of the sugar combines varied. In Guyana (having ensured that Jagan could be removed by suggesting the introduction of proportional representation). Bookers settled down to adjusting gracefully to the new order. Happy gestures (such as donating the site for a new university campus) were combined with a practical programme of training an indigenous management to take over from the expatriates. So skilfully was this accomplished that the new managers (mostly the grandsons of indentured coolies) began to take on the attitudes of paternal authority which had stamped their white predecessors.

Only in Mauritius did the ruling white elite, the *Francos,* organise for a long siege. The *Francos* had successfully resisted British penetration of the industry. Such apparently British firms as the Rogers group remain under *Franco* control (Rogers actually owns a London subsidiary, L.G. Adam & Company).[17] Only the ubiquitous Tiny Rowlands has managed to dent *Franco* hegemony (Lonhro own two Mauritian estates). The big Franco corporations, such as the Weal group, have buttressed their position by transferring investments to South Africa while largely capturing the profitably burgeoning tourist industry through ownership of new luxury hotels and other assets.

The Lomé agreement signed by the EEC with Africa, Caribbean, and southern Oceanic states served to provide a guaranteed market at stable prices (about £180 per ton). With this guarantee, three countries — Trinidad, Guyana, and Fiji — proceeded to nationalise their sugar industries. The departing corporations received compensation (Bookers were already diversifying into the Middle East and Africa) and some residual tie-up arrangements remained. The government of Mauritius hesitated to join this movement. One sugar estate was nationalised, but this unsatisfactory experiment served to deter further nationalisation. The *Francos* grasped that Lomé meant increased profits and they expanded production.[18]

Taking stock

It is time to consider whether the propositions laid down at the beginning of this paper are still valid. The field labourer still remains the man with the hoe or the cutlass. The main difference from the days of slavery and indenture is that employment is seasonal, not permanent. The incidence of unemployment is high, and is concentrated among the younger age groups. In Trinidad, among those aged 15-19 it runs at 35 per cent, and for those aged 20-24 at 20 per cent; the Mauritius figures for the same groups are 55 per cent and 26 per cent respectively. Until recently wages on the estates have remained low: in Mauritius, an average of Rs 20-25 per week (£1.50-£1.80); although since 1974 they have risen considerably, to about Rs 60 (£4.60), during the same period the cost of living has probably risen faster. Because the wages bill represents about 60 per cent of the cost of production, there is now reason to expect that employers in Mauritius will switch over to large-scale mechanisation, such as long ago transformed the Australian (Queensland) sugar industry. This would bring the unemployment figures to the point of crisis.

The Indian sugar workers still remain a people set apart. Their physical isolation in Mauritius, and even more in Guyana, is virtually complete. Blacks live in black villages and Indians live in Indian villages. But whereas the blacks form the main element in the urban work-force of Port Louis and Georgetown, the labouring Indians have only a minor place in the urban economy. They remain a rural lumpenproletariat (an 'underclass' in more recent terminology) whose way of life has changed little since indenture days. Apart from going to the cinema, their only leisure activity remains the rumshop (it is stated that the incidence of alcoholism in Guyana is the highest in the world).[19]

Despite the widespread organisation of trade unions over the last twenty years, the sugar estate remains a rigidly hierarchical structure where bosses and workers are separated by an unbridgeable gulf. This is probably best illustrated by describing the six-months strike in Guyana in 1977 which effectively paralysed the whole industry.

While Cheddi Jagan has surrendered political control in Guyana to the more ruthless Forbes Burnham, he remains the undisputed leader of the Indian sugar workers. From the pathetic huts of these workers there still flutter the little Jagan flags, signalling their continuing allegiance, in every Indian village in the land. In 1977 Jagan tried to reassert his power, and that of the Indian community, by bringing GAWU out on strike. All production was halted and the national economy shuddered to a halt. The Burnham government refused, however, to negotiate with GAWU and totally rejected its demands. Black strike-breakers were brought in to harvest and process the cane. Gradually, as the strikers and their families drifted into want, Indian fieldworkers began to check in: the sons, brothers, and cousins of the men on strike, for only thus could some money be brought home. The strike lasted six months, and at last GAWU gave in to Burnham. Not a single demand was conceded: not even the demand that strike-breakers be dismissed from employment. The Indo-Guyanese had to eat the bitter taste of defeat. They who were the main supporters of the Guyanian economy had to accept that they would remain totally excluded from any access to control and decision.

Probably the key to Burnham's success was the manner in which management identified totally with the determination to break the strike. The grandsons of the indentured Indian coolies saw themselves in the position of the white bosses of yesterday, ignoring all those legends of oppression they had learnt at their mother's knee. Class, not community, provided their identification when the crunch came. The master-slave technique, which provided a buffering mechanism, out of the aspirations of the coloured children of the slaves to escape from servility, still paid off handsomely as late as the 1970s.

How long?

The Moyne Commission predicted that the former impulse to protest against *worsening* conditions had given way to a new determination to claim 'a better, less restricted life'. Perhaps Moyne's conclusion was premature, but are there signs in the late 1970s of a delayed demand for a better life? The answer is to be sought, perhaps, not only on the plantation but also at the ballot box. Elections held in 1976 indicated a massive discontent with the buffering, pariah-capitalist formula which had been the basis of independence.

In Trinidad Eric Williams and his People's National Movement had to resist a powerful electoral attack by the United Labour Front, led by Basdeo Panday and Raffique Shah, supported by the great mass of the sugar workers. The PNN managed to retain 26 seats while the ULF secured 10, but subsequently Shah and Panday fell out, leaving the Williams regime apparently firmly in the saddle. The electors of Mauritius expressed their dissatisfaction with the party in power since independence, the Labour Party, even more trenchantly. Labour could only retain 25 of the total of 62 seats, with the planters' party, the Social Democrats (PMSD), holding on to 7, while the radical *Mouvement Militant Mauricien* captured 30, many being sugar constituencies with an overwhelmingly Indian population. Labour stitched together a hasty coalition with the PMSD and clung to office. It was only a matter of time before this coalition of convenience collapsed, but when the MMM won the long-delayed election they discovered that dependence on world sugar prices inhibited anything like real change in the conditions of their supporters — the exploited sugar workers.

5

THE IMPORTATION OF BRITISH INDIANS INTO SURINAM (DUTCH GUIANA), 1873-1916

PIETER EMMER

'Jobo tanbasi' (The white man is still the master), the ex-slaves of Paramaribo are said to have remarked, when the first ship with indentured labourers arrived in the colony.[1] The following pages are written in order to show how right these creole labourers in Surinam were. At the very moment the period of apprenticeship ended, the first indentured labourers arrived. The planters had succeeded in escaping from a labour-market of demand and supply, as they had done before, by obtaining a period of apprenticeship after slavery had ended.

Slavery and the plantation society

Geographically, Surinam (or Dutch Guiana) belongs to the South American mainland; its socio-economic characteristics, however, call for a comparison with the plantation islands in the Caribbean. Like Jamaica, Barbados, Guadeloupe, Martinique, and Saint-Domingue, Surinam could be labelled as an early West Indian cash-crop colony where the whole economy was geared to the export of sugar, coffee, and cotton, produced on plantations which had been developed during the period 1650 to 1780. After 1800 the plantation economy spread to new areas such as British Guiana, Trinidad, Cuba, and Puerto Rico.

The growth of these plantations in number and size had far-reaching consequences for the development of the colonial societies in which they were situated. In principle the plantation was a closed unit, a socio-economic entity with very few local ties, but with a strong and direct link with the North American and European metropoles. On these Caribbean plantations African slaves provided most of the labour, while the managerial positions were mainly reserved for whites. The colonial state in the West Indies had one important task: to provide the plantation managers with a defence force against slave revolts as well as against attacks from foreign invaders.

TABLE 5.1:   DEMOGRAPHY

	British Indian immigrants			Creole and other unindentured labourers death-rate
	birth-rate	death-rate	male:female ratio	
	per 1,000	per 1,000		per 1,000
1874	10.3	185.4	100:40.7	57.5
1875	23.8	63.5	100:39.6	47.3
1876	27.8	36.3	100:39.8	55.5
1877	22.9	38.3	100:39.6	49.6
1878	33.5	27.1	100:37.6	40.7
1879	38.9	20.8	100:36.3	33.2
1880	39.4	18.1	100:35.2	35.9
1881	27.9	32.6	100:35.9	42.5
1882	31.8	26.0	100:37.3	27.0
1897	39.5	24.3	100:34.9	26.1
1898	35.0	19.7	100:35.0	20.8
1899	46.2	13.6	100:34.6	24.5
1900	42.3	15.5	100:34.4	23.0
1901	42.1	13.4	100:32.0	16.7
1902	18.9	25.0	100:26.3	23.0

Sources for all tables: Yearly Abstracts of the Immigration Department in: *BPP,* 1877, xxviii, 1861, *Slave Trade, No 3 (1877) Reports respecting the conditions of coolies in Surinam,* pp. 41-4, 73-8, 91-4; India Office Records, Emigration Proceedings, vols. 1332, 1348, 1502, 2058, 2278, 5442 and 6830, Files J + P/6/555, 582 and 625; and Public Record Office, London, FO 37-884.

The Caribbean plantation colonies usually possessed one capital city: there was hardly any need to set up additional villages and towns because most colonial subjects had to remain forever within the boundaries of 'their' plantations. Only in cases of severe criminal acts were slaves sent to the colonial law courts, while in most instances the slaves were judged and punished by their managers. In principle a plantation colony in the West Indies could be described as a collection of small, inward-looking island societies separated from the outside world by a common defence. The plantations in Dutch Guiana were in fact small islands as they were separated from one another by rivers and canals.

The ending of slavery

In the British and French Caribbean some features of the old plantation societies disappeared after the abolition of slavery in 1833 and 1848, respectively. In all these post-emancipation colonies the administrative, judicial, and military apparatus was enlarged in order to enable the colonial state to cope with the greatly enlarged direct responsibility for all its inhabitants, including the ex-slaves.

The planters, however, tried to retain the plantation as much as possible as a total institution, dominating the colonial economy. The ex-slaves were unable to resist the plantocracy in those areas where there was no unoccupied land available. On Barbados the planters were able to retain most of the ex-slaves as plantation labourers. In more sparsely populated areas the planters were faced with a growing movement among the ex-slaves to leave the plantations in order to become free subsistence farmers. In British Guiana the movement among the ex-slaves to leave the plantations was particularly strong: 53 per cent of the slaves left and production went down by 40 per cent.[2]

In the Dutch West Indies the planters were well aware of the results of emancipation in the neighbouring British and French colonies. In the Dutch Antilles (Curacao, Aruba, Bonaire, St Eustatius, St Maarten, and Saba), the plantations were of no importance for the production of cash crops for export; they mainly provided foodstuffs for local consumption. In addition, there were hardly any free plots of land allowing the ex-slaves to leave the estates and to settle as independent farmers. Barbados provided the planters in the Dutch Antilles with the example that ex-slaves without land turned into an agricultural proletariat. As a consequence the Antillean planters did not press the Dutch government for the institution of a period of apprenticeship.

In Surinam the land-population ratio was completely different and very similar to that of neighbouring British Guiana, where the majority of the ex-slaves had left the plantations. In order to prevent this, the Dutch government allowed the Surinam planters a period of ten years' apprenticeship, commencing on the date of the actual emancipation: 1 July 1863. In addition, the Dutch government tried to provide the planters with additional labour from outside the colony.

The quest for indentured labour

The long parliamentary debate in the Netherlands regarding the precise conditions of the West Indian slave emancipation enabled the Dutch government to remedy several of the shortcomings in the process of abolition which had occurred in the British and French Caribbean. The relatively long period of apprenticeship in Surinam has already been mentioned. In addition, the Dutch government tried to introduce indentured labour into the colony even before slavery itself had been abolished. Between the years 1853 and 1873 China, Barbados, Madeira, and the Dutch East Indies provided around 5,000 contract-labourers. On the other hand, the plantation managers had been faced with a slowly diminishing creole slave population ever since the abolition of the Atlantic slave trade in 1807. In 1800 Surinam still counted 50,000 slaves; in 1863 only 30,000. During the period of apprenticeship, between 1863 and 1873, the Surinam plantations were confronted with a further reduction in the supply of creole labour — by 20 per cent — since household and artisan slaves were not forced to remain on the estates.[3] This tendency continued right until the beginning of World War I.

The plantation management in Surinam (and this holds true for most of the Caribbean) tried to counter the decreasing supply of labour by concentration of acreage and crops. Small plantations disappeared and sugar became by far the most important export crop. In 1833 Surinam counted around 344 plantations, in 1863 (emancipation) 230, and around 1900 only 4. The volume of sugar production, however, remained more or less the same between 1800 and 1900.[4]

The ownership of the diminishing number of plantations became increasingly more local. This development started long before emancipation and it continued during the period of apprenticeship, when many foreign (i.e. Dutch, English, Scottish) owners received compensation for the freeing of their slaves and then sold their plantations to local (Surinam) planters. It should be kept in mind, however, that some of the largest sugar estates remained in the hands of overseas consortia.[5]

Whatever the nationality of the owner or the manager of the Surinam plantations, most of them were in dire need of labour in order to make up for the increasing number of creole ex-slaves who were leaving the plantations during the period of apprenticeship. No wonder the Surinam planters petitioned the Dutch government to conclude a treaty with the British government allowing the recruitment of indentured labourers in India. The importation of such indentured workers into neighbouring Guiana had been very successful. The Surinam planters hoped to do even better than their neighbours and to escape an interim period between the ending of apprenticeship and the arrival of indentured labour, which had been so detrimental to the plantations in British Guiana. In that period the

Guianese planters had been dependent on the remaining creole plantation labour, which had demanded very high wages.[6]

In fact the Dutch government did manage to avoid the development of a free labour market in Surinam. On 1 July 1873 apprenticeship ended in Surinam and on 5 June of the same year the first ship with British Indian indentured labourers arrived in the colony. In order to achieve this smooth transition from apprenticeship to indentured labour, the Dutch government had to grant special concessions to the British government, which made the institution of indentured labour in Surinam somewhat different from that in the neighbouring British colonies, notably British Guiana.

The main differences were: (i) after a five-year period of indenture the 'time-expired coolies' would immediately be entitled to a free return passage to India, while in British Guiana such a return immigrant would have to wait for an additional five years; and (ii) the Surinam colonial authorities had to accept the presence of a full-time British consul, who was to report to London on the well-being of 'Her Majesty's British Indian subjects.' These consular activities were an extra safeguard for the protection of the immigrants, in addition to those of the Agent-General for Immigration who, as a colonial civil servant, was to supervise the allotment of the indentured labourers to the plantations as well as the labour and housing conditions and the payment of wages on the plantations. In this respect the situation was drastically different from that in British Guiana, where there was only an Agent-General. The British consul in Surinam was completely independent of the local colonial government and its civil service, both of which were heavily influenced by the powerful plantocracy. Several of the British consuls took their duties very seriously and their reports on the alarmingly high death-rate among the first groups of indentured labourers from India prompted the British government to suspend the importation of Indian immigrants completely between 1875 and 1877. The flow of Indian emigrants to Surinam was reopened only after the British consul in that colony had sent a favourable report to London indicating that the death-rate had gone down and that several Surinam planters had been prosecuted in defence of the rights of the immigrants. Owing to these international pressures the Surinam colonial government reluctantly had to extend its influence beyond the boundaries of the plantations and to take seriously its responsibility for all its subjects.

In practice, however, the plantation system was difficult to change, whatever labour system prevailed and whoever were appointed as colonial officials or consuls. The plantations remained a set of isolated units of production and consumption, social entities in themselves. Outside the plantation the words 'slavery' and 'indentured labour' indicated a world of difference; for the workers on the plantation they meant continuity in recruitment, in work-load, daily life, health care, and, in resistance, crime and punishment.

Recruitment in India

Like the other colonies importing Indian indentured labourers, Surinam maintained a 'coolie-depot' in Calcutta. During most of the period the Dutch consul in that town acted as Emigration-Agent for Surinam. The actual process of recruitment was the same for all countries importing indentured labour. The Emigration-Agent appointed a number of agents, who in turn hired a number of sub-agents. These sub-agents used recruiters, who actually approached the intending emigrant and brought him to the sub-depot.

In theory, the process of recruiting was regulated in such a way that it was distinctly different from enslavement. Both at the sub-depot and at the main depot in Calcutta, the intending emigrants were brought before a magistrate and asked whether they were leaving the country voluntarily. In practice, however, there were several aspects which bear resemblance to the enslavement of Africans during the previous period.[7]

First, few of the Indians had any idea where they were going. African slaves were known to have committed suicide before reaching the Americas, out of fear of being eaten alive at their final destination. Some of the intending indentured labourers feared:

that they will be converted into Christians both Hindoos and Mohammedans and the Hindoos will be fed with beef and the Mohammedans with pork; the thread of the Brahmins and the heads of the Hindoos will be taken off and they will not be able to keep their caste.[8]

In theory, all indentured labourers were recruited to go to one specific country. The Emigration-Agents at the main depots in Calcutta all helped one another, however, when a shipment of contracted labourers had to be made up in a hurry, in particular when a waiting ship could not sail because the numbers of women among the emigrants did not meet the minimum requirement. No doubt in such cases the intending emigrants were told that their new destination was as good as the old one. As in the slave trade, the British Indian migrants, like the Africans, had no idea where they were being taken.[9]

A second factor, common to both the slave trade and the indentured transports, was the selection of the migrants with regard to their future employment on a plantation. Slaves were selected only according to their physical strength. They did not have to qualify as experienced agricultural labourers. Both slave traders and planters assumed that all Africans had some basic knowledge of agriculture. Gang-labour on the plantation had such specific demands that it could only be taught 'on the job' during a period of seasoning.[10]

As had been the case with the Africans, the planters complained heavily about the agricultural skills of their indentured labourers:

the reason ascribed by the planters is that in general the immigrants are not capable of great exertion and require to become acquainted with the handling of the cutlass and shovel, while at the same time, it is said, they are very indolent. Many are to be found weeding and thrashing in a sitting posture, having shortened the handles of their cutlasses for convenience; and in the distant field erect a small awning and there quietly pass the day. It is the general opinion that the class of agricultural labourers is badly represented in the selection made by the Dutch Agent in Calcutta; the majority having formerly been house servants, soldiers, policemen, barbers, shopkeepers, hawkers, etc.[11]

After the first three ships with indentured labourers had arrived in Paramaribo, the Dutch government complained to the British government that only one-eighth of the immigrants had been accustomed to agriculture, the others belonged to a 'ramas de classes de toutes les professions et peu propres aux traveaux de champs'.[12] '. . . . A great many were beggars, old sepoys, brahmins and people from great cities.'[13]

In spite of these protests nothing changed. As with the slave trade, the planters were dependent on a supply system in which there was no place for 'quality control'. The Dutch government dismissed its first agent in Calcutta, but it was virtually impossible for his successors to do any better. All the Emigration-Agents were completely dependent on the supplying recruiters, who were paid one flat fee for each intending emigrant. These recruiters as well as the sub-agents are known to have carefully orchestrated the interviews before a magistrate; the future emigrant was told to stress his agricultural background and, if necessary, to dirty his hands and change his clothes beforehand.[14] In fact similar devices had been used by the slave-brokers to increase the value of their merchandise.

In conclusion, it seems that the recruitment of Indian indentured labourers — at least in the beginning — and that of African slaves had two important features in common: both groups of migrants were highly suspicious of their future and were not particularly prepared for work on a plantation.

The arrival in Surinam

There is little doubt as to the motives behind the keen interest of the Surinam planters in the importation of British Indian immigrants. Slavery in Surinam had been abolished as late as 1863 and had been followed by a period of apprenticeship, which was ended in 1873. During the last years of slavery as well as during the period of apprenticeship all sorts of attempts had been made to lure contract-labourers to Surinam: between 1863 and 1873, 4,919 labourers were imported to Surinam from Madeira, Barbados, China, the Dutch East Indies, and even a few from the Netherlands. None of these attempts were successful: except for the Chinese, the contracts with the other labourers were all made for one or two years only and very few were willing to reindenture.[15] In addition, free wage labour became increasingly expensive; right after the period of apprenticeship creole labourers were asking between Dfl 0.90 (7½p) and Dfl 1.20 (10p) per day.[16] For the first time in the history of Surinam the planters came close to a confrontation with an unrestricted labour market based on supply and demand.

At this moment, however, the first ship with indentured labourers arrived. According to the governor of Surinam, this occasion had a 'wholesome effect' on the labouring classes.[17] In addition, the smooth transition from apprenticeship to indentured labour had a social effect: the plantocracy was not made aware of a basic change in the rights of the labourers:

The consequence of allowing coolies to emigrate from India to this colony in the same year that apprenticeship of the former slaves expired, was that the Surinam planters not yet having become accustomed to work with free labourers, found in the meek Hindu a ready substitute for the negro slave he had lost.[18]

In fact, many of the procedures around the actual arrival of the immigrants resembled those of the days of slavery. The ships with indentured labourers were first inspected by a doctor before the immigrants were allowed to disembark. From the ship they were taken to the 'coolie-depot', where they stayed for a couple of weeks. In that depot the new arrivals had time to acclimatise while the Agent-General of the Immigrant Department decided on their allotment to those planters who had asked for them.

Slaves had been sold to the highest bidder, and it seems natural that the planters tried to influence the Agent-General's decision regarding the allotment: there are two indications that bribes were used.[19] In addition some well-to-do labourers, who had already settled in the colony, came to look for a wife among the new arrivals. If such a labourer was able to pay the planter's share of the cost of transport, he could 'buy' her freedom.[20] In conclusion, it seems that most indentured labourers entered their employment as the newly arrived slaves had done during the eighteenth century: neither were allowed to choose their new masters.

On the plantation: the cost of labour

Indentured labour cost the employer less than labour rented on the free market. As mentioned above, immediately after the ending of the apprenticeship period wages seem to have jumped to between Dfl 0.90 and Dfl 1.20 (7½p to 10p) per day for an adult male labourer. The indentured labourers had only been promised a minimum wage of 1s (5p) per day, and only the adult males seemed to have been able to earn a little more (table 5.2). In addition to the wage paid to the indentured labourer, the employer had to pay a lump sum of Dfl 156.00 (£13.00) per indentured labourer towards the cost of immigration, which covered about three-fifths of the actual costs of introducing an adult immigrant into the colony. The colonial government paid the rest.[21]

Because of this subsidy the indentured labourer cost the planter a minimum of Dfl 0.10 per day above the daily wage. In 1879 the total amounted to an average cost of Dfl 0.75 per day for an adult male labourer. These figures on the relative labour costs show the normal patterns of the Caribbean labour market: imported labour was cheaper than labour available locally. As in the days of slavery, the planters resorted to local labour only in specific cases, if at all. After the arrival of indentured labour in Surinam, free labourers were hired only to do the cane cutting during harvest time. Gradually the immigrants took over these jobs, just as the slaves had replaced the whites on the plantations during the course of the seventeenth century.[22]

The planters were faced with a high capital outlay for acquiring indentured labourers, as had been the case in buying slaves. In order to minimise additional expenses the planters had several alternatives: (i) At the Parimaribo 'coolie-depot' all immigrants were divided into three classes. Only the best among the adult males were promised the minimum wage of Dfl 0.60 per day. Women and second-class males were supposed to earn a daily minimum wage of Dfl 0.40. The employer was supposed to provide work for five days per week.[23] (ii) When the first indentured labourers arrived in 1874 a task system existed in the colony. The planters as well as the colonial government were

TABLE 5.2: WORKING DAYS/SICKNESS/WAGES OF BRITISH INDIAN IMMIGRANTS

	I	II			III	IV	V		
		M	F	Children			M	F	Children
1875	2,959	165.25	124.81	—	52.5	25.4	0.65	0.56	0.25
1876	2,940	168.73	119.36	65.33	47.3	25.2	0.69	0.64	0.49
1877	3,215	177.42	124.08	69.47	32.8	12.3	0.67	0.59	0.46
1878	3,160	172.97	132.68	83.41	26.8	7.8	0.70	0.63	0.53
1879	2,873	191.04	135.70	48.87	25.2	10.5	0.74	0.63	0.69
1880	3,728	202.63	138.30	50.52	25.3	20.3	0.60	0.59	0.55
1881	4,156	197.12	150.04	28.05	30.4	7.7	0.72	0.58	0.46
1882	4,428	196.08	151.66	29.93	21.0	9.9	0.72	0.64	0.54
1896	7,066	187.13	137.39	92.97	16.5	2.7	0.69	0.58	0.39
1897	5,919	188.79	129.85	90.65	17.6	2.7	0.70	0.59	0.25
1898	5,919	189.90	129.69	104.57	16.6	2.7	0.66	0.58	0.33
1899	5,058	194.16	132.56	111.57	16.5	2.4	0.68	0.57	0.28
1900	3,727	199.53	134.77	70.88	15.6	3.0	0.67	0.56	0.29
1901	2,845	202.68	121.44	62.33	16.8	2.8	0.66	0.56	0.40

I   Total number of immigrants
II   Average number of working days per year
III   Average number of sick days per year
IV   Average number of days of 'wilful absence'
V   Average daily wages (Dfl)

in favour of the task system. The British government was opposed to the task system and thought it a factor in the exceedingly high death-rate among the first shiploads of British Indians, which caused London to suspend the migration of British Indians in 1875. Only after the resumption of immigration in 1877 were the intending immigrants told that they had the option of either working according to the task system or providing a day's work of seven hours for the minimum wage.[24] In practice, however, it was difficult for the immigrant to get his minimum wage. In both systems he was usually given such a heavy task that he had to labour more than seven hours in order to finish it.[25] On the sixth day he had to make good the unfinished portions of his five previous tasks. The working week was officially extended to six days in contracts concluded after 1877.[26]

(iii) Special rules had to be made for those indentured labourers who were unable to earn even half the minimum wage. During the first six months they had no problem: their employers had to provide them with rations. After this period, however, the immigrant's debt for rations would have run up to Dfl 15.60 (£1.35), to be deducted from his earnings at half the minimum wage of Dfl 0.30 per day. When a labourer was unable to earn half the daily minimum wage, he was in danger of receiving no money at all during his second half-year on the plantation. After lengthy discussions between the governor and the British consul in Paramaribo, it was decided that in such cases the labourers would not receive any wages in cash but would continue to receive rations 'free of charge'.[27] In such a case the planter would make a profit of about Dfl 0.18 a day, since the rations cost him only about Dfl 0.12 a day. No wonder the immigrants were opposed to any prolongation of the initial period of six months in which all indentured labourers had to be provided with food at their own expense.[28]

(iv) As can be seen from Table 5.2, the planters imported 25 per cent too many indentured labourers. If we take into account that in 1877 the six-day week was introduced, the planters only provided their labourers with an average of 188 working days, while they should have asked the indentured workers to work around 250 days, allowing for Sundays, the 'coolie-holidays' (Hindu or Mohammedan festivals), and sick-days. As in the days of slavery, the planter must have calculated his labour needs in order to meet the maximum requirements in the harvest season. The payment of wages, however, had caused the planters to reduce work for part of the work-force during the slack season, while most of the indentured labourers were kept on their toes all year round. During the period of slavery the whole work-force of a plantation would have been able to profit from a reduction in the work-load during the off-season.

As far as the figures for women are concerned, their average number of working days was affected by maturity and childbirth. Here, a female indentured labourer might have been worse off than her enslaved counterpart. The managers had no business interest in the birth of a child of indentured parents, whereas, at least in the period between the ending of slave imports and emancipation, the birth of a slave child could be advantageous to the slave-owners. In addition, the aged among the plantation slaves usually looked after the new-born babies to enable the mothers to return to the fields. During the last decades before emancipation pregnant women were actually treated with unusual care. The husbands of pregnant female indentured labourers, however, usually had to pay for their rations and mothers were not necessarily promised the services of a nurse.[29]

More in line with the custom of the previous slavery period was the work done by boys and girls. The figures in Table 5.2 show an increase in the average number of working days during the year, but a decrease in the average daily wage. The reason for this might be found in the increasing supply of youths from India, who came over with their indentured parents. Subsequently the employers could ask for more working days from and give lower wages to each child. Children born of indentured parents in Surinam could hardly have been of any use to the plantation work force; only after a possible second indenture of their parents did they approach the minimum working age of ten years. Education was unpopular with the parents; in spite of a colonial law providing for compulsory education and heavy fines, only 20 per cent of the immigrant children went to school.[30]

On the plantation: daily routine, provision-grounds, and housing

Even today, the regimentation of every-day plantation life seems to have retained some of the features of the original seventeenth-century institution.[31] When the indentured immigrants arrived little had changed since the slaves and 'apprentices' had left. Every morning a roll-call was held and the indentured labourers were divided into groups. Work started early, around 7 a.m. and was usually finished around 4.00 p.m., when the immigrants retired to their houses. Saturday afternoon and most of Sunday were free. Each gang had a driver, usually an East Indian, since the immigrants disliked taking orders from a creole or a mulatto. Higher positions on the plantation seemed to have remained closed to East Indians, and overseers and managers were mulattoes or whites.[32]

Like the slaves, the British Indian immigrants were allowed to cultivate small plots of land on the plantation for their own use during their time off. Like the slaves, the indentured labourers cultivated mainly foodstuffs. This might explain why the immigrants were keen on receiving wages rather than provisions, and why the period was reduced during which these rations had to be provided. There are indications that this situation was different for the first groups of indentured labourers who arrived in the colony. Immediately after immigration started, the British consul suggested to the colonial government that not only should rations provided be cooked but also that the period of six months should be extended to twelve![33] Later on the immigrants became more versed in cultivating their own plots and in raising cattle, fowl, and pigs. The new arrivals could usually buy livestock from those who were leaving, while the provision-grounds were already there.

In 1878 the British consul noted a further development: the Indians not only used their provision grounds to cultivate food for themselves; they specialised and sold their produce (plantains, cassava, and other vegetables) to other immigrants as well as to creoles.[34] Four years later it was reported that the *sirdars* (drivers) saved money by trading the surplus produce of the indentured labourers in their gang at the town market. In this way the *sirdars* could undercut the high prices usually asked by the plantation shops, which were mainly in Chinese hands.[35] The slaves had used their profits from peddling to buy their freedom; the Indians wanted their savings remitted to India.[36]

Another parallel with the slave era was the housing arrangement. Sometimes the immigrants had to move into the old slave huts, sometimes they had newly constructed dwellings:[37]

The dwellings of the British Indian immigrants are built apart from buildings occupied by other labourers. They are arranged in rows of four to six at equal distances, some containing a set of two and three rooms in double row, back to back, while others of three apartments are in single file, each having a roofed gallery and separate entrances. No space is allowed under those having planked floorings. No more than three single male immigrants are assigned to one room or one family, husband, wife and children.[38]

In principle the managers were responsible for the housing conditions of their indentured labourers; in practice they were hardly interested in what happened in the 'coolie-ranges', as had been the case with regard to the slave quarters. Time and again the Agent-General instructed the managers that the indentured labourers should not be allowed to cook in their rooms and that separate kitchens and privies should be provided.[39] However, the managers and overseers had nothing to gain by changing the life-style of their work-force; they were probably as reluctant to go to the 'coolie-houses' as their predecessors had been to intrude into the houses of the slaves.

Like the slave population, indentured labourers on a plantation became members of a village community. During the last decades before emancipation many plantations had been closed down and the slaves moved elsewhere. These moves were usually violently opposed by the slaves, who refused to mix with the alien workforce of another plantation.[40] Taking into account that the planters and, in exceptional cases, the immigrant workers themselves could ask for a transfer, in 1890 only 1,427 indentured labourers had been moved to another estate out of the 13,962 who had been allotted up to that year.[41]

In conclusion, it should be noted that the plantation remained a closed unit and that the indentured workforce became a social entity, like the slave community in the period before abolition. Of course, the indenture period of five years meant more changes in the workers' quarters than during the time of slavery after the abolition of the slave trade. The plantation management had, however, to be very bad before an indentured labourer who had decided to stay on would want to move to another plantation in order to re-indenture.[42]

On the plantation: medical care

Health care on the Surinam plantations was far from perfect during the days of slavery. Every plantation with more than a few slaves was supposed to have a hospital. The sick-quarters were usually housed in the same building as the prison-room. Most managers had made contracts with private doctors, who would visit the plantations regularly for a flat fee per slave per year.[43]

Very little changed during the time of apprenticeship, and the immigrants were also expected to use the existing medical system. The level of medical care in the colony became a bone of contention between the Dutch and British governments, and was the main reason for the suspension of the indentured migration from India in 1875.[44] In his reports the British consul in Paramaribo pointed out that many estate hospitals were not sufficiently equipped to cope with the maximum number of patients, set by law at 10 per cent of the indentured work force on a plantation.[45] The high mortality among the first arrivals in 1874 was devastating, as shown in Table 5.1, being more than triple the mortality among creole labourers in Surinam. The Surinam authorities blamed the bad selection made of intending emigrants in India. They set up a committee to look into the matter which concluded that there seemed to be no relationship between the conditions on the estate hospitals in Surinam and the rate of mortality:

In conclusion, it may be remarked that the sickness and mortality among the Immigrants from British India, which have caused immense losses and disappointment to the planters — far too heavy to be overcome — is ascribed by all members of the medical staff to the diseases with which the immigrants were affected before their arrival in this country, amongst which syphilis and poverty of blood appeared the most general cause.[46]

As can be seen from Table 5.3 this statement is untrue: the most lethal diseases were those caused by a new bacteriological environment: syphilis was a minor killer, and anaemia is not even listed as an important fatal illness among the immigrants. The mortality aboard the first eight ships amounted to an average of 4.44 per cent, which was certainly not an omen for an abnormal death-rate after disembarkation.[47]

It seems difficult to establish the exact cause of the high death-rate among the first groups of indentured labourers during their first year of residence in Surinam. During the second year of immigration the death-rate had dropped by almost two-thirds and it declined even more in the third year, where it stayed well below that of non-indentured creole labourers. It should be noted, however, that the indentured labourers as a group had a specific demographic feature: people older than 30 years of age were usually not indentured.[48] The high rate of mortality among the newly imported immigrants corresponds with the high death-rate of newly arrived slaves from Africa.[49]

In 1879 the medical system in Surinam was placed on a new footing, which might explain the decline in the death-rate among the new arrivals after the resumption of the imports. New regulations created the position of a Medical Inspector, and the doctors practising in the districts were no longer allowed to take fees from the planters. In 1882 a 'medical school' was opened in order to provide the colony with more and better trained medical men. The estate hospitals were regularly visited by the Agent-General and the British consul.[50]

It should be stressed that this innovation in the health care of the colony

TABLE 5.3: CAUSES OF DEATH AMONG BRITISH INDIAN IMMIGRANTS (%)

	1876	1877	1878	1879	1880	1881	1882	1896	1897	1898	1899	1900	1901
malaria	—	—	—	—	—	—	—	24	—	—	12	11	17
febris pernicosa	23	19	9	12	17	18	8	—	14	—	4	3	—
dysentery	3	8	7	4	2	15	4	—	—	20	—	3	4
marasmus	—	1	12	5	7	12	12	6	7	—	10	7	7
convulsions	14	13	11	21	10	8	5	1	10	—	13	27	7
debilitas	—	7	11	11	14	—	10	23	12	—	—	12	15
hydropsy	6	4	3	2	4	1	2	—	—	—	—	—	—
syphilis	—	1	—	—	—	1	—	—	—	—	—	1	—
apoplexia cerebri	3	2	7	4	—	2	—	10	—	—	—	—	4
gangrene	5	—	2	2	—	3	—	—	—	—	6	—	—
phthisis	2	4	7	9	7	5	9	—	8	10	—	—	—
diarrhoea	4	5	5	2	2	4	12	—	1	—	—	—	—
drowning	1	3	1	4	3	5	3	2	2	3	3	5	2
suicide	—	—	—	4	—	2	2	2	2	2	—	1	2
manslaughter	2	1	1	—	3	1	4	1	—	—	—	—	—
opium	1	1	—	—	—	1	—	—	—	1	—	—	—
nostalgia	—	1	1	—	—	1	—	—	—	—	—	—	—

(Terms used in original documents.)

did not come from the planters themselves. Without pressure from abroad they would have changed little. In 1876 the British consul reported that one of the estate hospitals was still used as a prison.[51] Most of the nurses were native creoles, 'totally illiterate', obviously the old 'dress negroes' who had also supervised the slave hospitals.[52] The average number of sick days during the first period of immigration, as shown in Table 5.2, was above even that of the slaves on the plantation Catharina Sophia during the decade before emancipation.[53] The planters seemed to take little interest in reducing the number of working days lost owing to illness.

The same continuity existed between the behaviour of indentured servants and that of the slaves. They would, allegedly, rather go to hospital than to work. Apparently the immigrants liked to be admitted after the visiting doctor had left, and they went back to work before the doctor returned. In this way their time of indenture diminished without their having to do any work: a not unfamiliar form of informal resistance to exploitation. Again, the labour incentives offered to the immigrants seemed too small to bring about a change in attitude which would have made an indentured labourer differ in this respect from a field slave.

On the plantation: crime, punishment, and resistance

The number of immigrants who came into contact with the Surinam legal system was considerable. Most of the cases, as Table 5.4 shows, resulted from offences against the Labour Law allowing a 'penal sanction' in disputes between employers and indentured labourers. This law made it possible for employers to have their indentured labourers imprisoned for 'refusing to begin to work, threatening or insulting employers, leaving the estate during work hours, idleness, drunkenness during work time, destroying machinery, tools, for striking and enticing others to strike.'[54] In contrast, employers could be fined for imposing tasks which were too heavy, for not providing work at all, for turning their indentured workers out of their houses, for insufficient food in hospital, or for refusing a pass.[55]

A comparison with the punishment of similar offences committed by slaves is impossible. In those cases the manager of the plantation would have acted simultaneously as prosecutor, judge, and prison-warder. After abolition the manager of a plantation lost all his legal functions, and in theory both planters and immigrants had to comply with the judicial system of public prosecutor, judge, and state-supervised prisons, as it had always existed in the world outside the plantation.

In practice, the legal rights of indentured labourers were, to use an understatement, less equal than those of the planters. The figures speak for

TABLE 5.4:   BRITISH INDIAN IMMIGRANTS CHARGED
WITH OFFENCES (%)

	Labour law	Petty offences	Correctional cases	Criminal cases	Total
1874	5.5	2.8	0.5	0.3	9.1
1875	10.8	7.3	0.7	0.6	19.4
1876	5.9	6.4	1.7	0.8	14.8
1877	4.6	9.4	1.6	0.5	16.1
1878	5.7	14.5	0.6	0.0	20.8
1879	8.8	12.1	1.1	0.2	22.2
1880	7.7	12.2	0.4	0.2	20.5
1881	15.0	9.1	0.7	0.3	25.1
1882	13.6	11.2	1.2	0.5	26.5
1896	9.6	4.0	0.2	(0.05)	13.8
1897	11.2	3.4	0.1	(0.03)	14.7
1898	14.8	4.4	0.8	0.1	20.1
1899	13.4	3.8	0.7	0.1	18.0
1900	12.9	3.3	0.6	0.0	16.8
1901	12.7	4.3	0.6	0.1	17.7
1902	16.4	3.6	0.4	0.1	20.5

themselves: 71.4 per cent of indentured workers charged with offences against the Labour Law were convicted, and only 10 per cent of managers (Table 5.5).

If the immigrants tried to lodge a complaint against their employer, they first had to ask for a pass from their employer. In this respect the situation resembled exactly that of the slaves, who, in Surinam, had obtained the right to complain in 1851.[56] Assuming a pass had been given, the slaves had to file their complaint at the nearest police station, which could mean more than a full day's travelling. The indentured labourers, however, were allowed to complain to the visiting district commissioners. These commissioners regularly visited those estates employing indentured labourers in order to check the pay-sheets, the estate hospitals, and the housing of the indentured immigrants. They also acted as referees when managers or overseers disagreed with a contract labourer about his work-load. Most of them were native mulattoes who could not speak a word of Hindi. The immigrants had little trust in them; they were regarded as mere puppets of the managers.[57]

In order to complain, many immigrants wanted to see the Agent-General in Paramaribo in person or the British consul. Passes to go to town

TABLE 5.5: COMPLAINTS MADE BY BRITISH INDIAN IMMIGRANTS
AGAINST THEIR EMPLOYERS

	% LODGING A COMPLAINT	ILL-FOUNDED OR WITHDRAWN COMPLAINTS	NUMBER OF EMPLOYERS: ACQUITTED	CONVICTED
1875	0.81	13	6	5
1876	1.36	31	3	6
1877	2.11	51	7	10
1878	1.17	24	6	9
1879	3.06	71	6	11
1880	2.62	71	16	11
1881	2.07	76	—	10
1882	2.08	78	10	4
1896	0.42	21	2	7
1897	0.41	24	—	—
1898	0.87	32	15	2
1899	0.40	20	—	—
1900	0.35	10	1	2
1901	0.60	16	1	—
1902	1.05	41	—	—

were rarely given. Some employers only gave them on Sunday when the immigrants were free to go anyway and all Paramaribo offices were closed. One British consul had to distribute his own 'passes' in order to ensure that the indentured labourers could at least show some kind of document when they were picked up by the police. When the consul made his tour of inspection on the estates, all indentured workers were usually out of sight, working in the fields. 'Later on I found that the immigrants did not even know that I existed.'[58]

Not only the penal sanction made the indentured labourer a special target; severe punishments were also applied in regular criminal cases. The British consul reported: ' . . . and I am reluctantly compelled to observe that there is a determination manifested by the judges to inflict on Indian immigrants the highest penalty of the law, which would appear to be modified in cases of local subjects.'[59] It seems that the old division in legal practice between blacks and whites had been replaced by a new division between indentured labourers, the native blacks, and the whites. For arson, immigrants were sentenced to fifteen years' imprisonment; burglary was punished by eight years' hard labour in chains.[60] As in the days of slavery, both the colonial government and the planters tried to keep the workers confined to the plantations. Many managers and overseers were reluctant to have their indentured labourers officially prosecuted: time spent in prison could be no reason for extending the period of indenture.[61] Frequently immigrants must have been punished by being forced to do dirty or heavy work on the plantation. In addition, the colonial government planned to have all indentured labourers charged with Labour Law offences sentenced to hard labour. This punishment would kill all hope the immigrants might have entertained of passing their time of indenture in prison without doing any work. In addition, the colonial government planned to have vagrancy laws ready in order to cope with immigrants who were unwilling to re-indenture. They would also be made to labour at public works.[62] It should also be noted that justice in Surinam was not disinterested: most judges were part-time planters or had a financial interest in a plantation.[63] The alarming reports from the British consul to London and the subsequent questions from London to the Dutch government at The Hague were able to stop some of the repressive plans regarding the position of the 'time-expired coolies' remaining in Surinam.

How did the indentured labourers react to all these regulations and laws so heavily biassed against them? In fact, their reaction very much resembled that of the slaves during the first half of the nineteenth century. There were relatively few important uprisings among indentured labourers: only five small revolts during the whole period of immigration between 1873 and 1916. These riots were all confined to one or two plantations. The odds were heavily against the insurgents: in total, 38 immigrants were killed and only 3 Europeans. The official reports stressed that small issues were usually the cause of these riots: too much work or too low wages.[64]

Few indentured labourers ran away: in 1890, after eighteen years of immigration, 161 immigrants had taken to the bush, mostly in order to abscond British Guiana.[65] In order to express protest, the immigrants mainly resorted to day-to-day resistance, as the slaves had done previously. The consular reports mention strikes and the destruction of buildings and crops.[66] The frequent conflicts over the work-load have already been mentioned. Frustrations among the immigrants also found an outlet in manslaughter, mainly among themselves, suicide, and 'wife chopping' (Tables 5.3 and 5.4). During the period 1880-83, 31 immigrants died an unnatural death: 10 because of manslaughter, 3 accidental manslaughter, 7 drowned, 9 suicides, and 2 cases of either suicidal or accidental drowning.[67] Jealousy among the men because of their common-law wives seems to have been a consequence of the unbalanced proportions of the two sexes (Table 5.1). In 1890, 588 men and women were married, only 6 per cent of the total number of immigrants at that time. Official marriages were very rare: 2-3 per year during the first ten years.[68]

Special mention should be made of the 'escapism' the immigrants resorted to by using alcohol, opium and ganga (hashish): ' . . . Saturday night, after the wages are paid, drinking, quarrelling and fighting commence, and Monday, instead of going to work, many of them enter hospital or jail.'[69] Table 5.3 shows the opium victims. The high number of deaths caused by debility was attributed to the widespread use of ganga by a medical inspector from India who visited Surinam in 1890.[70] Like the slaves, all celebrated the 'New Year Games', aided by the extra rum rations from the planter; the immigrants all participated in the Tadja festival in August, with plenty of alcoholic stimulants.[71]

As a last resort, some indentured labourers wrote to the Protector of Emigrants in Calcutta to complain about the conditions in Surinam:

If any coolie fails to work for a single day of the week, he is sent to jail for two or four days, where he is forced to work while day and night kept under chains. We are tortured very much. For this reason two to three persons died by swallowing opium and drowning themselves. If any of us says anything to a sahib, he lodges a complaint and sends him to jail for two or three weeks.[72]

The comparisons relating to crime, punishment, and resistance between slaves and indentured workers are numerous. In spite of the increased responsibility of the colonial state during the course of the nineteenth century, the plantation survived to a large extent as an entity both in punishment and in resistance.

Conclusion

In many respects both slaves and indentured workers had had the same experience when they entered the plantation to which they had been sold or allotted. This applies to the process of enslavement and recruitment, to the arrival in the colony as well as to the labour conditions, medical care, housing, and the use of leisure time. Furthermore, the patterns of resistance and criminality as well as those of punishment and oppression show multiple comparative elements between the time of slavery and that of indentured labour. The continuity between these two systems of labour supply must also have been obvious from the planter's point of view. In both systems the planter was offered labour specially imported for work on the plantations and cheaper than the labour available locally.

The continuity of management and labour conditions on the Surinam plantations was greater than elsewhere in the Caribbean, for several reasons. First, the Surinam planters were never faced with new attitudes by their workers (demands for wage increases, better housing and medical care, greater personal freedom) arising from the conditions of a free labour market, as was the case in the British Caribbean.

Secondly, in Surinam the change-over from one labour regime to another did not coincide with a drastic change in ownership of the plantations or in the kinds of cash crops produced. The direction of the changes in ownership and of cash crops had been the same since the beginning of the nineteenth century, long before the abolition of slavery: (i) the number of Surinam-owned plantations increased, while the number of Dutch and foreign-owned plantations decreased; (ii) more and more Surinam plantations produced only sugar, reducing the output of coffee and cotton; and (iii) the number of plantations declined, while the acreage and output of the remaining estates increased considerably.

Thirdly, the system of indentured labour had already been introduced into Surinam during the period of slavery. Indentured labourers (mainly from China) and slaves had worked on the same plantations. The simultaneous rise of the system of contract-labour and demise of slavery did not make the plantocracy aware that a fundamentally different kind of labour had been introduced.

All these factors helped to make the introduction of indentured labour into Surinam seem continuous with the importation of African slaves. In other areas of the Caribbean the change-over from slavery to different forms of unfree labour may have been an adaptation to the changes in the ownership of the plantations or to the change in the production of export crops. In Surinam this was not so; the importation of contract labourers in fact obstructed new development in agriculture and industry in that it helped to lower the costs of labour and consequently slowed down the modernisation of sugar cultivation, the 'Sweet malefactor'.

6

THE NATURE AND ORIGINS OF PACIFIC ISLANDS LABOUR MIGRATION TO QUEENSLAND, 1863-1906

ADRIAN GRAVES

Introduction

Between 1840 and 1915 the south-west Pacific was a vast labour reserve.[1] Approximately 280,000 Melanesians and Micronesians were recruited to indentured labour in Queensland, Fiji, Samoa, Hawaii, New Caledonia, French Polynesia, Nauru, and Peru. About half that number again were involved in contract work within the region either in New Guinea or in inter-island labour migration.[2] The recruitment of nearly 64,000 Pacific Islanders to work in Queensland between 1863 and 1906 was probably the most significant of the Western Pacific migrations. Certainly, it has attracted the most attention in the literature, a central concern of which is to explain this vast movement of communal agriculturists to work in capitalist agro-industry. The discussion ranges from descriptions of the methods of labour recruiters to lists of the immigrants' motives.

Popular treatments of the subject give the impression that most Pacific Islanders were either kidnapped or tricked into their contracts,[3] and it is a view expressed in scholarly works too. This conclusion seems merely to reflect the sorts of data on which much of the literature is based, namely British Official Papers. The labour trade attracted an enormous critical attention, especially in its early years, from the powerful anti-slavery lobby in Britain. Consequently, Parliamentary Papers and Colonial and Foreign Office material dealing with the system primarily catalogues recruiting abuses and Whitehall's attempts to regulate the trade. The literature based on this material, which is preoccupied with the administrative and juridical background to the labour trade, treats its sources very insularly and uncritically.[4] And the rather one-dimensional conclusions drawn in some popular and scholarly literature has reproduced itself in other historical works.[5] Thus the image of the Pacific islands immigrant as hapless victim of an unscrupulous and coercive recruiting industry is surprisingly persistent.

Nevertheless, a revisionist view has recently emerged. The revisionists argue that the labour trade passed 'from an early and brief period of coercion through several decades of systematic recruiting well understood and willingly entered into by the islanders'.[6] 'The belief that the labour trade was nothing but blackbirding', writes another critic, 'defies logic and logistics.'[7] The aim of the new Pacific history is to demonstrate that the immigrants 'had a shrewd understanding of the rules, rewards and costs of the game' and to undermine the literature which treats the migrating Islanders merely as 'natives'.[8] Consequently, the revisionists seek the explanation for migration in the individual motives of the immigrants.

The desire to travel, it emerges, was a major dynamic in Pacific islands labour migration. O.W. Parnaby, for example, writes: 'Missionaries on almost every island from which the Natives were recruited spoke of the eagerness of the Islanders "to see the world". This passion for travel combined with a childlike curiosity about anything new and strange made relatively easy the task of the labor recruiter. . . .'.[9] Peter Corris rates the 'novelty of travel' particularly high in his list of the 'stimuli' to migration.[10] According to Richard Bedford, one of the 'most common explanations' for New Hebridean labour migration is the anxiety to experience 'some of the excitement of living outside the social domain of the village'. 'Young men', he says, 'frequently went walkabout.'[11]

In addition to having the travel bug, the Islanders were very materialistic and acquisitive. The labour trade continued with the workers' consent, it is argued, because the migrants appreciated that in the long term colonial labour worked to their advantage. Not only could they taste the 'excitement' of civilisation, more importantly the immigrants could purchase 'alien novelties'.[12] It is not altogether clear what lay behind the clansmens' want of commodities but at least two writers maintain that the sight of return labourers' overflowing trade boxes 'infected' Melanesians with the desire to migrate.[13] However they are expressed, voluntarist or psychologistic explanations predominate in the more recent studies. And they appear in the most surprising quarters. In his admirable little book, *The Trumpet Shall Sound,* Peter Worsley wrote: 'The native was. . . torn by his dislike of leaving home to work for the Whites, . . . yet he was attracted by the hope of obtaining a portion of their riches, and by the fascination of many aspects of town, plantation and mine life.'[14]

Usually, however, revisionist analyses of individual motives take place within the conceptual framework of neo-classical economics. Thus it is assumed that the decision to migrate was rational and progressive, the operation of free choice in the context of a competitive labour market. J. A. Bennet writes, for example, that 'labour recruiting was a business conducted on orderly lines with the principles of the market place determining whether or not the Solomon Islander signed on'.[15] The most subtle and sophisticated expression of neo-classical economic analysis of Pacific migrations has appeared recently in the scholarship of Colin Newbury.[16] In its treatment of coercion, its psychological explanations, or its neo-classical assumptions, however, the 'new' Pacific historiography has serious shortcomings.

The new view does not satisfactorily explain the periodic emergence of kidnapping. Certainly, coercion was not confined merely to an 'early and brief' period of the labour trade. The best documented cases of kidnapping, involving more recruits and recruiters than previously, occurred in the 1880s, twenty years into the system, and there were isolated instances reported in the 1890s. Thus coercion is not an insignificant aspect of the trade, nor can it be attributed simply to a 'lapse' in the standards of the recruiters or to the behaviour of one or two 'irrascible' ship's captains.[17] We shall briefly discuss kidnapping later in the essay. Suffice it to say here that the methods employed by labour recruiters in the south-west Pacific must be seen in the context of the changing capital structure, organisation, and difficulties of the recruiting industry. The articulation of these aspects with fluctuations in the demand for labour or its supply is equally important. The treatment of coercive recruiting in the literature is confused and contradictory because it does not address these issues.

The emphasis on voluntarist explanations in the new historiography is not illuminating either. Ideas examined in isolation from their economic or social mainsprings are ahistorical. Thus, the reification of an idea, its expression as a fact or a cause, effectively divorces the individuals whose behaviour it ostensibly explains from their own history. Rather than fulfilling the admirable aim of rescuing 'natives' from the old history, the revisionists have by their own historical method reduced the Pacific island immigrant to a caricature, a Pacific Sambo, mindlessly lusting for the bright lights of civilisation. This is also the weakness of locating the causes of migration in the conceptual framework of neo-classical economic theory. Reducing the dynamic of migration to the exercise of 'free choice' in a competitive labour market obviates any serious consideration of changes in the immigrants' own society and economy, which may have forced them into wage labour.[18]

Not that the revisionists entirely ignore the 'traditional' society. When the literature cites 'pressures from within' the Islanders' own societies as a cause of migration, however, it invariably means 'unsatisfied needs and aspirations' or the odd cases of criminals and eloping couples who escaped their societies' sanction by engaging for colonial labour service.[19] The most serious connections made between labour migration and Melanesian society is in the work of Peter Corris, especially his study of *compradors* or 'passage masters' in the Solomon Islands. But even here the treatment is largely descriptive, with a stress on the essentially harmonious nature of the passage masters' activities.[20] This conclusion overlooks the coercive mechanisms of clientage and control or outright force employed by the passage masters to mobilise recruits for colonial capitalist development and the subversion of the communal economy which this entailed. In this lies the ultimate failure of the revisionists: their inability to recognise the interactive and disruptive effects of expansive, intrusive capitalism on the agricultural subsistence economy and its role in the migration of clansmen to colonial labour service.

This essay considers Pacific islands labour migration to Queensland as an historical process with concrete, material origins. At the heart of the analysis is the transformation of the Melanesian economy during the nineteenth century, its increasing dependence on the sale of labour power to secure the subsistence of its members. There is no question that this process, which is termed proletarianisation by some writers,[21] is extremely complex. Only its broad contours can be outlined here and further avenues of research suggested. We shall proceed by examining the relationship between the mobilisation of the colony's Pacific islands labour force and the growth of commercial activity and missionary endeavour in the south-west Pacific; the impact of labour migration on the Melanesian gift economy; the collaboration of passage masters with the recruiters and the effects of natural or social disasters on migration. The discussion will be made more cogent, however, if we first turn to a brief outline of the involvement of Pacific Islanders in the Queensland sugar industry and the nature of the labour trade.

I

At its foundation in 1859 Queensland became a self-governing British colony. In 1901 it was incorporated into the Federation of Australian states. As the colonial period progressed cane sugar production vied with mining and pastoralism as the major industry in the economy.[22] For the greater part of the period the sugar industry was based on plantation production. After 1885 rising factor costs, low sugar prices, and other marketing difficulties forced the reconstruction of the industry on the basis of the central milling system. Under this system the two principal aspects of sugar production, cane cultivation and milling, were separated. Cane was cultivated on small family farms, employing seasonal labour at harvest time and it was crushed in very large, centrally located mills. The effect of the new technology was markedly to reduce labour inputs and to bring considerable savings of scale to the industry.

The growth and development of the Queensland sugar industry, especially in the era of plantation production, turned on sufficient supplies of cheap unskilled labour. Until the turn of the century, however, Queensland was a labour-starved economy. Aborigines were unsuitable for the tasks involved in sugar production and the industry found it difficult to obtain workers from outside the colony. The best source of labour proved to be the islands adjacent to Queensland in the south-west Pacific. The immigrants engaged in the industry on three-year contracts of indenture. Under this contract they were paid a minimum wage of £6 per annum and provided with accommodation, clothing, food, and medical care. When they finished their initial contract the workers could return to their homes or re-engage in the industry. Because of the endemic shortage of labour in the colony, 'time expired's' contracts were usually more favourable than those of 'new introductions' and the duration of the contracts were usually shorter. It is notable that as the industry was reconstructed on the higher technology of central milling, the labour cycle of the immigrants significantly increased. Now, the industry needed experienced workers and, as plantations withered, the demand for first contract labour fell off. In any case by 1900 sugar production had become labour sufficient and the large-scale importation of Pacific Islanders had become unnecessary. Accordingly, the Queensland labour trade was abolished by the Commonwealth Parliament in 1901, a move which was encouraged by the Australian labour movement which bitterly opposed the system.

The recruiting of Pacific Islanders was undertaken by individuals who were, by and large, indirectly associated with the sugar industry.[23] It was small investors, freelance ship's captains, or merchants who set up as labour agents and small companies of local businessmen in the sugar belt who engaged in the trade. Planters and investors in the sugar industry tended to recruit labour on their own behalf in periods of intense competition for the limited supplies of labour in the region, or later in the period when merchants and ship's captains fell out of the trade because of falling demand for indentured labour or because the investment risks associated with labour recruiting had become too high.

By any standards the labour trade was a very hazardous business. Periodic cyclones, monsoons, the strong prevailing winds of the region, and the formidable dangers posed by the Great Barrier Reef subjected vessels, crew, and passengers to great risks. These risks were greatly enhanced by the fierce resistance some Islanders put up to the recruiters as well as by the difficulties associated with approaching landing or pick-up places on the islands. Imperial and colonial legislative and administrative controls on the labour trade imposed further constraints on the industry's profitability.

While demand for Pacific island labour in Queensland remained high, the labour traders invoked a broad range of measures to reduce the investment risk in the industry. They used small, relatively old, even superannuated, sailing vessels which were cheap both to acquire and to run. Crews of highly paid European sailors were kept to the minimum and an elaborate collaborative structure of Islander interpreters, guides, sailors, and guards was employed.

The means by which labour traders reduced their outlays in the industry were reinforced by the methods they utilised which were directed at optimising their vessels' recruiting quotas. Trade goods were offered to clansmen in exchange for the labour of their junior kin. As we shall discuss later in this essay, recruiters struck bargains with senior clansmen who became effective middlemen in the trade. There is much evidence that men were tricked into recruitment on the basis of lies about their proposed length of service, where they were to work, and the level of pay. And a comparatively small number of people were kidnapped to Queensland.

It should be stressed, however, that kidnapping was confined to specific phases and circumstances in the history of the trade. Periods of rapid development of plantation production, namely 1868-74 and 1879-84 and the early 1890s, saw the demand for labour in Queensland far outstripping its supply. These conditions attracted into the labour trade speculative recruiters whose object was to cash in on the inflated returns the recruiting industry was able to command at these times. To achieve their aims, it was necessary for the speculators to optimise both the number of voyages their vessels made and their recruiting quotas.

Direct coercion or kidnapping proved a very successful means by which the speculators reduced the length of recruiting voyages and at the same time optimised their complement of indentured workers. It is important to note further that periods of rapidly increasing demand for labour stimulated the labour traders to make deeper forays into the labour reserve, into the hitherto unrecruited parts of the region. Here the local economies were little disrupted by the impact of colonialism. In the absence of other processes by which the Islanders were incorporated into existing labour markets, force proved to be the most reliable means of mobilising recruits in the so-called 'low contact' areas. That is not to say that kidnapping was never resorted to at other times in the long-frequented parts of the labour reserve. Here it was sporadic, less systematic, and usually involved a few victims at a time.

The necessity for outright coercion in parts of the south-west Pacific labour reserve reinforces the view that an 'available' labour force is not a feature of pre-capitalist societies.[24] Communal agriculturalists, such as those in the south-west Pacific, are tied to the land because it forms the foundation of their subsistence, and by way of a complex web of social obligations and institutional controls which secure the reproduction of such societies. Normally, this matrix of structure, controls, and obligations renders communal societies internally resistant to change. Consequently, when they are tapped to service the cheap labour requirements of capitalist economic development, the flow of labour out of the pre-capitalist community has to be effected either by force or by the radical transformation of the communal economy and society. Most Pacific Islanders were incorporated into labour markets by this latter process of which the encroachment of commercial and missionary activity in the region was a major aspect.

II

During the nineteenth century, the south-west Pacific was increasingly drawn into the web of British, French, German, American, and Australian imperialism. The penetration of traders, settlers, missionaries, and foreign navies in this period generated the disintegration of the communal economy and society, as production and the region's resources were directed towards the imperial and colonial centres. Eventually the region was turned into a vast labour reserve serving the needs of capitalist development among the islands and in the colonies on its fringes.

Before 1860 the major commercial activities in the region were whaling and sealing, sandalwood trading, *beche-de-mer* or sea-slug fishing, and copra and coconut-oil processing. The whale fishery area extended from New Caledonia to the southern Solomon Islands. Besides European and American whalers, at least forty Australian ships were engaged in the industry by 1830.[25] The sandalwood trade was concentrated on New Caledonia, the Loyalty Islands, and the New Hebrides. Although the trade dates from the 1820s, the peak of its activities was reached in the 1840s when a speculative scramble sent British, American, European, and Australian traders into the islands in search of even the most isolated stands of the highly profitable scented wood.[26] *Beche-de-mer,* or sea-slug, a delicacy valued by the Chinese, was actively exploited in the region before 1860.[27] By that date these three industries had all but collapsed because of unfavourable markets or the exhaustion of the resources in the islands.

But the post-1860 period saw a more intense penetration of the region by western economic interests, for in this period, land alienation on a large scale, accompanied by European settlement, characterised developments in the islands. At first, relatively small cotton, sugar, or coffee plantations were established in the New Hebrides but, after 1870, large tracts of land were purchased in the group by individuals and companies set up for the purpose. The pace of land alienation was stepped up even further in the 1880s when companies such as the Compagnie Caledonienne des Nouvelles-Hebrides (CCNH) purchased enormous quantities of land in the New Hebrides.[28] Subsequently, large estates producing a variety of crops ranging from cotton to arrowroot were founded by large Anglo-Australian, French, and German companies. Land alienation occurred later in the Solomon Islands and was confined mainly to the purchase of coastal strips for copra stations. The changes which this growing commercial development wrought in the south-west Pacific were dramatic and far-reaching, the most important of which was the radical transformation of the local economies and the initiation of capitalist relations of production in the region.

Whaling, sandalwood gathering, and *beche-de-mer* fishing involved not only the exploitation of raw materials but the processing of the product in the islands. In this sense, the early commercial activity was both industrial and labour intensive necessitating the establishment of factories and processing plants and resulting in the emergence of a local stratified labour force. Islanders induced or coerced into working for the traders became boat-crews, divers, firewood gatherers, boiler attendants, sea-slug curers, lumberjacks, storemen and packers, or even interpreters and labour recruiters.

The labour supply for the early industries was obtained from within the region by a combination of local and migrant labour. By 1860, New Caledonia, the Loyalty Islands, most of the southern and central New Hebrides, and some of the northern New Hebrides and southern Solomon

Islands had been brought firmly into the nexus of western economic activities in the region, including a migratory labour network which extended at different times as far as the Hawaiian Islands in the north, Peru in the east, and Australia and Fiji, in addition to the region's own internal network.

The incorporation of the local economies into incipient capitalist activities through the supply of labour was associated with the transformation of subsistence agriculture in the Pacific. The establishment of even temporary European settlements and trading stations which employed considerable numbers of workers require reliable supplies of food. Village production was thus assimilated into a 'refreshment trade' in which surplus products, including pigs, fish, vegetables, or poultry, were traded for weapons, ironmongery, tobacco, trinkets, alcohol, or money. The production of surpluses for the refreshment trade was later extended to include the development of peasant agriculture, or cash-cropping. The variety of local subsistence crops was thereby increased to include tapioca, sugar, coffee, maize, tomatoes, rice, pineapples, and melons alongside the traditional yams, taro, sweet potatoes, arrowroot, nuts, breadfruit, and citrus fruits.[29] After a period of coconut-oil production in the Gilbert Islands, copra gathering and drying, either industrially or naturally, also emerged in the region.[30]

The transformation of the local economy and society was achieved not only through a web of economic pushes and pulls but included more direct physical disruption. Because fertile land was relatively scarce in the islands, land use and occupation were highly defined in the south-west Pacific. Specific areas of land were attributed to individuals or clans and land ownership, including its resources, was integrated into and protected by traditional custom and law.[31] Normally, land utilisation was extended far enough to meet the immediate needs of the local community. The advent of traders and settlers in the region dislocated the established patterns of land use and disrupted the traditional system of land tenure. The establishment of trading stations and settlements with the infrastructure necessary for industrial or large-scale agricultural activities — storage facilities, wharves, housing, factory sites, plantations, and the inevitable store or alcohol canteen — resulted in the physical dislocation of Islander communities. Moreover, the pre-1860s exploitation of raw materials, especially enormous, indiscriminate consumption of timber, permanently changed the physical features of some islands, seriously disrupting local agriculture.[32] Villagers were thereby forced on to less fertile land, into conflict with adjacent communities, or into colonial labour migration.[33]

Eventually the onset of colonialism in the region also eroded the belief system and social formations which derived from and buttressed the communally-based economic life of the villagers. Less land, greater cash demands, less labour time, and the encroachment of a new belief system founded on the individual forced tension and conflict within the ancient system of communal living. For example, women, children, the infirm, and old people were relatively secure in their subsistence within the milieu of the cycle of domestic and communal economic life and its process of redistribution. However, the reduced labour power of the communities subject to out-migration, mounting obligations, changed values, and falling living standards placed the least productive members of the community at risk. For many such people labour migration provided a means to secure their livelihood and indeed, in the Queensland case, a relatively high number of children and infirm individuals were engaged for colonial labour during intense recruiting phases.

In more general terms, the pattern of Queensland recruiting articulated with commercial developments in the south-west Pacific. The first Queensland ships worked the already well-established recruiting grounds of the Loyalty Islands and the southern and central New Hebrides.[34] The trade moved northwards through Melanesia as labour supplies in the southerly islands diminished and in their northwards movement the Queensland recruiters were able, in part, to capitalise further on the preceding disintegration of the communal economy and society initiated by commercial activity in the region.[35]

But the patterns of labour migration associated with the commercial development of the south-west Pacific were extended by the emergence of capitalist agriculture and mining in the colonies on the periphery of the region, which utilised the islands as a source of cheap labour. Apart from the sugar industry in Queensland, German colonialists in Samoa pursued copra production and tropical agriculture after 1860, while cotton and sugar plantations were in the ascendancy in Fiji. Nickel mining was pursued on New Caledonia, along with a burgeoning dairy and meat industry. Later, planters and miners in New Guinea also recruited labour from the south-west Pacific, as did flax growers in New Zealand and planters in the Society Islands. A survey of recruits in latter stages of the Queensland labour trade reveals that up to 10 per cent of those recruited had worked in other colonies before engaging for the Queensland sugar industry, and up to 30 per cent of recruits were so called 'old hands'.[36] In this sense, the emergence of colonial industries which utilised Pacific island labour extended and consolidated the transformation of the traditional sector in the region and, in particular, contributed directly to the process whereby clansmen became workers.

Christian missions played an important and distinctive role in the process of proletarianisation in the south-west Pacific.[37] Anglican and Presbyterian missionaries were the most numerous in the region. The London Missionary Society arrived in the Pacific as early as 1795, but its major penetration of the region occurred after 1849, when a base was established at Norfolk Island and subsequent stations opened in the northern New Hebrides and the southern Solomon Islands. The Presbyterians entered the islands in 1842, and consolidated their position with particular zeal in the New Hebrides, where, by 1890, there were at least twenty-four established Presbyterian missions.[38]

Both Anglicans and Presbyterians considerably extended their influence in the region through a collaborative structure of trained indigenous personnel, who were used in the vanguard of missionary expansion in the region.[39] In 1883 the Presbyterians alone claimed 150 native teachers, outnumbering the sect's European missionaries in the region by over ten to one.[40]

To attain their goals missionaries required large, stable communities. For this reason they acquired land and established gardens or plantations employing local labour.[41] Missionaries thereby contributed to the transformation of traditional economies in much the same way as secular commercial activity. But missions also had special features. As they were often the first Europeans to settle on an island, the disruptive presence of missionaries set in motion the process of proletarianisation, thus preparing the ground for the traders, settlers, and labour recruiters who followed in their wake. In another sense they extended even further the cycle of debt which tied the Islanders to their occupations in the secular plantations and industries. Since the mission regimen usually demanded the wearing of clothes, daily shaving, contributions to the church for buildings and running costs, bibles and hymn books, they substantially increased the obligations of the mission flock.[42] Colonial recruitment presented the opportunity to escape both the debt and the social ties peculiar to the missions, and it also offered relatively liberal returns to the migrant, compared with incomes on mission stations.[43] This was especially true of mission-educated Islanders who were able to secure positions as interpreters and recruiters in the labour trade.

Mission ideology, 'christianising and civilising', was also important in the mobilising of colonial work forces. Missionaries asserted that it was their duty to replace the barbarous societies of the Pacific with what they perceived as civilised forms of government, society, and values. Concomitant with this belief was a highly defined commitment to the values of steady, productive labour and a disdain for communal values and practices. This dogma was particularly strong among the missionaries of the Pacific who were 'born again' evangelical Christians and puritanical Scots to boot, or dissenting Anglican clergy closely associated with the world of small business.[44]

This particular world view meant that missions, as distinct from the secular institutions, *systematically* set about dismantling traditional structures and belief systems, including the established pattern of communal production. Missionaries were also important pioneers of imperialism. Not only did they encourage economic activity which connected the islands to the colonies but also the permanent settlement of Europeans on 'converted islands'.[45] The Presbyterians, for example, urged the formation of the Australian New Hebrides Company, which was founded in 1889, and included such companies as Burns, Philp and Company, who were prominently involved in the Queensland labour trade.[46] When the Western Pacific High Commissioner (anxious to preserve the rights of Australian labour recruiters) refused the new company a labour licence in 1890, the Presbyterian mission urged: 'That the Imperial Government be moved to provide that British subjects may be enabled to obtain legal title to their land and also. . . . lawfully to engage the natives of one island. . . . to labour on another.'[47] Although some missionaries opposed the labour trade, many applauded it, cooperating with the recruiters and endorsing contracts as voluntary agreements as was required under the laws regulating the trade.[48] One missionary even proclaimed, as early as 1869, that 'the employment of Polynesians in Queensland had done more to promote their social advancement than all the missionary efforts heretofore',[49] sentiments endorsed by later missionary writers.[50] Certainly, traders and labour recruiters appreciated the 'civilising' function of the missionaries in the Pacific. One contemporary observer went so far as to credit missionary endeavour as the major reason that 'trade and commerce' were possible in the region.[51] In any case, the extensive and unique role that missionaries played as agents of proletarianisation in the Pacific is indicated by the predominance of mission-trained labour among the early recruits to Queensland.[52] Later, in 1876, evidence suggests that as many as half of the Islanders in the Maryborough district were so-called 'mission boys'.[53]

The implantation and extension of capitalism in the south-west Pacific was thus a primary agent of proletarianisation in the region and a major stimulus to labour migration. But it should not be assumed that the transformation of the regional economy in the period under examination was complete. On the contrary, even as the Queensland labour trade was abandoned, clan-based production co-existed in Melanesia with capitalism and articulated with it. Perhaps one of the most remarkable aspects of this articulation was the link between commodity consumption in Queensland and exchange in Melanesia. This process was so important in the migration of young men to Queensland that it warrants closer examination.

III

The exchange of gifts or prestation, is the pivot upon which the communal economy of Melanesia turns. As the region became incorporated into the international economy, clan production increasingly articulated with the consumption of colonial goods which in turn promoted labour migration. To understand this process we have first to study the basis of exchange in Melanesia.

In this classic study, *Essai sur le Don*, Marcel Mauss demonstrated that exchange in Melanesia conformed to a type he named 'agonistic total prestation' or the 'potlach'.[54] Now this mode of circulation of goods is extremely difficult to re-express in conventional economic terms and in anthropology and sociology the forms and functions of exchange in the so-called 'archaic' societies are subject to much debate.[55] For our purposes it is sufficient to take note of certain important characteristics of the system. First, the essence of potlach is the obligation to repay gifts received and it implies two other equally important factors; the obligation to give presents and the obligation to receive them. As Mauss explained, the circulation of goods by means of a

. . . . pattern of symmetrical and reciprocal rights is not difficult to understand if we realise that it is first and foremost a pattern of spiritual bonds between things which are to some extent parts of persons, and persons and groups that behave in some measure as if they were things. . . . Food, women, children, possessions, charms, land, labour, services, religious offices, rank — everything is stuff to be given away and repaid. . . . [Thus] Clans, age groups and sexes, in view of the many relationships ensuing from contracts between them are in a perpetual state of economic effervescence. . . .[56]

Secondly, the transaction of gift exchange in Melanesia is a total institution. For all kinds of forms find simultaneous expression in the potlach: moral, economic, juridical, aesthetic, magical, religious, mythological, and social phenomena. This aspect has been re-emphasised by Claude Levi-Strauss as follows: 'Everything in a society — even the most special things — everything is above all a function and is functioning. Nothing can be comprehended except in relation to everything else, to the complete collectivity and not simply to particular parts. There is no special phenomena which is not an integral part of the social whole.'[57]

Mauss identified a third important characteristic of the potlach, the connection between the material transfer of objects and the social hierarchy. 'To give is to show one's superiority', he wrote, 'To accept without returning or repaying more is to face subordination.'[58] The notion of the hierarchical nature of prestation was later expanded by Karl Polanyi and his associates. They stressed the need to view the circulation of goods in communal economies in terms of its mechanisms; the identity of its participants, the sequential order of gifts, and the frequency of prestation.[59] But it was left to scholars in the school of French Marxist anthropology to extend the original work of Mauss by explaining the links in the potlach between rank, production, and distribution and the reproduction of the lineage group. For our purposes the work of Claude Meillassoux is especially relevant.[60]

The basic unit in Meillassoux's analysis of production is the kinship group or community. Goods circulate in the community between senior members who exercise authority over the clan and juniors who work for a senior and hand over the product of their labour to him. Thus, while goods are essentially produced by junior clansmen, they are entirely controlled by seniors. What then is the basis of this relationship, this form of dependence?

Whereas in other economies kinship ties, the transmission of technical knowledge, the ownership of the means of production, and direct coercion are mechanisms for the social control of production, this is not so in agricultural subsistence communities. The key to the seniors' dominance over the productive output of junior clansmen is their hegemony over the mechanisms of social and economic advancement in the clan. Social knowledge, for example, clan lore, history, genealogies, marriage rules, and even special skills such as magic, religious rituals, prophecy, and medicine is retained for the seniors' sole access. They control its transmission through institutional barriers such as initiation and esoteric barriers which determine that only chosen individuals are endowed with magical or ritual information. Juniors are thus dependent upon seniors to acquire social knowledge and for advancement in rank, status, and authority in the clan that this acquisition encompasses. Upward mobility is sought by the juniors through acts of prestation they make to their patrons. Thus the seniors' authority is based in part at least on the possession of knowledge which justifies their control over the output of their junior kinsmen's labour. Far more crucial to advancement in the clan, however, is marriage, since it is only through having people dependent on him, a wife and children, that the junior clansman himself can achieve authority in the community.

Again, the seniors play the decisive role in the arranging of marriages, for they control access to women through their possession of 'elite goods'. Elite goods are usually non-perishable items such as shell necklaces, copper, iron goods, cloth, and so on, which seniors accumulate through prestations but which are not redistributed back through the clan. The composition and bulk of these goods testifies to the status and authority of the owner. Since elite goods form the basis of bride-wealth exchanges, marriage contracts can only be made between seniors of opposite status in the clans involved in the negotiation. Thus the possession of elite goods, and the control over access to women which it entails, operates as a collective form of control among the seniors of different groups over the output of their junior clansmen. On this point Meillassoux writes:

. . . . a more inclusive alliance is necessary between the seniors of these neighbouring communities in order mutually to preserve their respective authority. . . . any senior who would accept such a transaction with an individual without the required status would be weakening his counterpart's authority and consequently his own. It is in the joint interests of all seniors to respect established order.[61]

This control over matrimonial exchange serves two important functions. On the one hand it is vital to the maintenance of an extended kinship group and its biological perpetuation, but it also guarantees reproduction of the dependence relationship of juniors towards seniors. Thus, by extending a precept originally suggested by Marx, Meillassoux shows that a junior of the clan must follow a continuous progression in the social hierarchy to become a senior in order to reproduce himself as an 'objectively individual man'.[62] The rate of this progression is in the hands of clan seniors, both within the junior's own clan and outside it, who regulate the junior's admission to rank and authority ultimately through gift exchange.[63] Now, what is the relevance of all this to the migration of Pacific Islanders to Queensland?

First, it is well established, through historical and anthropological enquiry, that commodities produced externally were readily accommodated into the Melanesian gift economy. They not only became a medium of exchange between clan members, but, in the form of 'elite goods', they were transferred in inter-clan prestations. In his important study of the Siane of the interior New Guinea Highlands, R.F. Salisbury found that a considerable influx of goods had preceded even the limited involvement of this group in the capitalist economy.[64] For Salisbury, the most dramatic expression of this was that steel axes had completely replaced stone axes. Thus, communities involved more intensely with capitalism became sources of supply of durable commodities through acts of prestation with more isolated clans. Prestations in these cases were invariably connected with ceremonial exchange, the establishment of alliances, and, most importantly, with bride-wealth exchanges. Salisbury and others have noted that the accommodation of commodities into the gift economy was associated with an increasing inflation in the volume of the goods exchanged in prestations.[65]

Young men thus became dependent on wage labour to acquire goods in sufficient volume to fulfil their obligations, to reduce indebtedness, and to establish a basis for advancement in the clan. This inevitably involved clan juniors in indentured labour migration. Since labour migration is inevitably the experience of young men at a particular stage in their advancement in the clan, it is considered a *rite de passage* in the communities. But this process was not confined to Salisbury's Siane, for it is a feature peculiar to the whole of Melanesia and it was of great importance to the Queensland labour trade.

Pacific Islanders' migration to Queensland was made up overwhelmingly of males under the age of thirty,[66] most of whom returned to their villages after a period of colonial work.[67] As with the Siane, the clansmen returning from Queensland distributed commodities acquired in the colony to kin, and some of these goods were incorporated into inter-clan prestations. Increasingly, colonial commodities displaced traditional goods in Melanesian exchange during the time of the labour trade. So effectively were colonial commodities incorporated into Melanesian prestations that on at least two islands, San Cristobel and Guadalcanal, the local shell money industries declined and became defunct during the period of the labour trade and the region at large experienced an inflation in the composition of matrimonial prestations.[68] It should not, however, be assumed that colonial commodities were always involved directly in ceremonial exchange, for practices varied from region to region and from clan to clan. In the Solomon Islands Corris records that 'migrants exchanged trade goods for porpoise, dog or shark teeth and shell money, which were then used in the potlach'.[69]

Whether directly or indirectly, the consumption of colonial commodities became locked into the forms and functions of Melanesian exchange through the labour trade. On the other hand, colonial labour service was a decisive experience for young men, because it provided the most effective means for them to acquire the goods necessary to reduce indebtedness and to secure their promotion in the clan. On the other, the transformation of goods into gifts became a powerful instrument of social control which served the interests of colonial economic development. It contributed to the flow of migrants to Queensland. And in the colony itself the process of commodity consumption by the immigrants helped to stabilise the Pacific labour force and stimulate its productivity.[70] Not that exchange was the only mechanism of the Melanesian economy coopted to the service of capitalism. The history of *compradors* in the recruiting industry, known in the trade as 'passage masters', suggests that the political structures of the community, the authority and power of clan seniors, was also incorporated into Queensland's drive for labour supplies.

IV

One of the most remarkable features of the pattern of labour recruiting in Melanesia was the exceptional number of Queensland recruits from Malaita in the southern Solomon Islands. Between 1871 and 1904, 9,186 Malaitans went to Queensland, constituting about 14.7 per cent of the Pacific island labour force in the colony or over double that of any single island.[71]

The prominence of Malaitans in Queensland can be partly explained by elements of the previous discussion. As early as 1828 Malaita was an established source of labour for the whaling industry.[72] The early traders were able to exploit a number of economic, social, and ecological characteristics which subjected Malaitans to a precarious daily life, predisposing the people to recruiting for contract labour. Illustrative of this factor were the Lau lagoon and other coastal areas of Malaita, which were the major sources of colonial labour in the early phases of recruiting in the Solomon Islands. Apart from the fact that they were simply the most accessible to the recruiters, coastal people depended on the narrow and unstable economy of fishing for their subsistence. To obtain trade goods or vegetables, the fishermen were utterly dependent on the willingness of the landed villagers to engage in trade, an activity which hostile relations sometimes precluded.[73] This economic insecurity was reinforced by the vagaries of the weather. The Lau lagoon is on the weather side of Malaita and because of its position is liable to great damage in the hurricane season. Also, both mainland and coastal Malaitans suffered from a variety of endemic diseases and population pressures resulted in frequent inter-communal warfare throughout the island. The abundant population of Malaita, reputed at the time to be the largest in Melanesia, itself presented attractive possibilities to the labour recruiter.[74]

But these factors alone do not explain the exceptionally large recruitment of Malaitans to the Queensland cane fields. For this, an examination of the enduring institutional structure of recruiting in Malaita is necessary. This system was based on the collaboration of local headmen who acted as labour agents for the Queensland recruiters and who became known in the trade as 'passage masters'. The most powerful of these collaborators were Kwaisulia of Ada Gege, an artificial island in the Lau lagoon, Foulanger of Walande, a small island off the south-east coast of Malaita, Mahooalla of Mgai Fou in the Langalanga lagoon, and Goreally of Kwai, an island off the east coast of Malaita.[75] All these men had several important characteristics in common. First, they were Malaitans; second, they were so-called 'salt water chiefs'; third, they were former labourers in the colonies; fourth, they derived and extended their political power and personal wealth from their collaboration in the labour trade. To illustrate how the conjunction of these factors contributed to Malaita's importance as a source of cheap labour for the Queensland sugar industry, we can turn to the personal history of the most prominent of the passage masters, Kwaisulia of Ada Gege.[76]

Ada Gege is one of a chain of about thirty artificial islands which stretch for about thirty miles down the north-east coast of Malaita. These highly populated tiny islands are inhabited by Lau speakers whose main productive activity is fishing, hence their designation as 'salt water people'. As has already been suggested, inhabitants of islands such as those in the Lau lagoon were easily accommodated into the regional labour market of the south west Pacific. It is not surprising, therefore, that the first Queensland labour ship to call at the Lau lagoon in about November 1875 recruited no less than thirty-one migrants for labour in the sugar industry.[77] It is almost certain that Kwaisulia was among these recruits.[78] Working for at least part of the time in the Rockhampton district, Kwaisulia stayed in Queensland for at least six years, serving out his time as an indentured labourer for the first three years and then as a time-expired or 'free' labourer. On his return to Ada Gege in 1880, Kwaisulia began his thirty-year collaboration with the Queensland and Fiji labour trade. Several factors facilitated this association.

While he was in Queensland, Kwaisulia learnt English, an accomplishment which specially helped him to act as a go-between in the labour trade. Being sited at Ada Gege was another advantage in his favour, since this island was in the centre of the Lau group and was adjacent to a stretch of beach known as the Urassi Cove. The central position of Ada Gege gave easy access to the rest of the Lau islands and the beach provided an excellent pick-up point and protection for the labour ships. Rendezvous points such as this became known in the trade as 'passages', hence the term 'passage masters', ascribed to local chiefs like Kwaisulia who dominated the recruiting of labour at these places. For an explanation of how the passage masters achieved positions of such power and the direct relation this bore to the mobilisation of labour for Queensland, it is necessary to survey the sources of political authority in Melanesia.

Power and prestige in Melanesia are seldom inherited. In the vast majority of communities, positions of eminence and leadership depend on how wealthy a man is. As has already been discussed in this essay,[79] it is the process of the accumulation of wealth itself which sets in motion the chain of causation which leads to the consolidation or extension of status within the clan. A scenario for this process might be as follows. An individual, by good fortune, hard work, or skilful manipulation of personal wealth, may accumulate enough goods to meet the exchange obligations of his immediate family. This makes him more attractive to older and remoter kin as a patron of their dependants' affair. Thus, in the course of time, he acquires control over a widening circle of junior clansmen. At the same time he has enough wealth at his disposal to put others in debt. In turn, an expanding circle of clients and dependants gives a burgeoning senior access to a labour pool with which he can raise pigs and produce large quantities of food and commodities. With a substantial surplus at his disposal, he can further consolidate his seniority in the clan by distributing the produce as gifts at community feasts and widen further the numbers obligated to him under the mechanisms of the potlach. Still greater authority is obtained in the sponsoring of village club houses or in the underwriting of elaborate festivals. At this point the ambitious man achieves the status of a clan head man, arbitrating in disputes, negotiating with other communities, and playing host to visitors. Moreover, his wealth provides him with the means to hire sorcerers to punish dissidents and to enforce his authority by way of hired killers and henchmen.

Now with authority based directly on the acquisition of an economically productive following of dependants and clients, large and stable political units under the power of a paramount chief were rare.

There were several reasons for this. First, in the New Hebrides secret societies based on clan limited the extension of power and influence. Here the accumulation of wealth meant entry into and promotion up the scale of the societies' grades. The highest grades extended beyond the particular clan only in so far as the spirits of men who achieved ultimate rank before they died may have become local deities. In the Solomons, where the constraints of secret societies were not present, furious rivalry for power and prestige often led to the formation of new and independent villages by dissident factions which limited the development of large political units. The unity of political formations in the Solomon Islands could, however, be enforced when the leader had extraordinary wealth and a powerful army to enforce or extend his authority. This rare circumstance emerged at Malaita in the case of the passage masters.

Through their association with the labour trade, the passage masters were able to manipulate the political structures of the community. The wealth they obtained as labour agents enabled them to become powerful 'big men'. They used their political authority to mobilise more labour for the colonies, which further increased their wealth and entrenched their power. Again, this process is illustrated in the case of Kwaisulia.

In the earliest years of his activity as a labour middle-man, Kwaisulia obtained recruits who were forced into the regional labour market for social or economic reasons. In October 1883, for example, he offered to the Queensland schooner, *Alfred Vittery*, two recruits who were fugitives from island justice.[80] It is likely, too, that Kwaisulia obtained recruits by fraud or trickery.[81] Using the wealth thus obtained,[82] he was able to establish a following of dependants and clients to the point where he mobilised recruits by the use of debt extraction or sheer force.[83] He required obligated individuals to sign indentures for Queensland, levying taxes from the debtors either before they left for the colonies or on their return. With his increased wealth and influence and the trade goods, arms, and dynamite with which his services to the Queensland sugar industry were repaid, Kwaisulia was able to extend his territory beyond Ada Gege in frequent and highly successful war campaigns against adjacent communities, installing close kinsmen as head-men over the defeated peoples.

Kwaisulia's military dominance was strengthened by his alliance with the British Navy. The regime of terror which ruled the mobilisation of labour at Malaita evoked a violent resistance of the locals which was directed against the recruiting ships. In addition, Malaita was a particular target of the Royal Navy because of its reputation for being constantly embroiled in inter-communal warfare, a state of affairs the Navy wanted to change as part of its policy of 'pacification' in the region. Kwaisulia collaborated directly with the Navy in the capture of fugitives and punishment raids.[84] Enabled thus to maintain control over an extensive and secure sphere of influence, Kwaisulia supplied labour to Queensland continuously for the rest of the period of the Queensland labour trade, despite the resistance of the local communities and the rise of other competing 'big men'. Although he was undoubtedly the most important of the passage masters in the Solomon Islands, Kwaisulia's manipulation of Melanesian political structures through the wealth obtained in collaboration with the labour traders was repeated in the experience of other Malaitan salt water chiefs who became, effectively, *compradors* to the recruiting industry.

In so far as the passage masters were all coastal chiefs, the system illustrates a more general feature of recruiting in the south-west Pacific. The labour frontier of each island advanced differentially.[85] At first it was the coastal people who were tapped for colonial labour and then, successively, the tribes and clans of the interior of each island, called in the trade 'bush-men'. Following this development, the coastal clans became involved in cash cropping, especially in the copra trade, and they became intermediaries in the recruiting industry.[86] 'Bushmen do not recruit', wrote John Brenan in 1896, 'without the aid of the salt water people'.[87] It was this feature that the passage masters exploited to provide labour to the recruiters and to establish their own position.

The system of passage masters which was used to mobilise labour for the Queensland sugar industry is significant for several reasons. The system was clearly an important contributory factor in the exceptionally high number of recruits to Queensland emanating from Malaita. The bulk of these workers were engaged in the period 1888 to 1904. The recruiting industry had become by this period a costly and dangerous enterprise. By providing a ready supply of recruits and ensuring the labour vessels of security at the recruiting passages, the operations of the passage masters were vital to the survival of the recruiting industry at a crucial moment in its history. Labour voyages were safer, quicker, and more fruitful when they utilised the middlemen of Malaita.[88]

But the passage masters were created by the labour trade. They were invariably returned labourers who were able to put their personal skills to use as labour agents. It was their association with the recruiting industry which enabled them to entrench themselves in the communal society and polity which, in turn, made them more effective agents of labour supply.

This collaborative system is yet another illustration of how the mechanisms and institutions of the pre-capitalist economy were accommodated into and harnessed to serve the needs of colonial industry. But Islanders were not always connected to wage labour by such systematic means, as we shall now observe.

V

Disaster, natural and social, was an important element in the mobilisation of a work force in the south-west Pacific. To appreciate the importance of this process we should examine first the nature of crisis in pre-capitalist communities and its impact on production and reproduction.

In pre-capitalist societies natural or social catastrophe results in the material destruction of the elements of reproduction.[89] In other words, hurricanes, drought, disease, war, or depopulation all destroy societies' productive forces, the producers or the means of production. Following this, there is a decline in both human and productive consumption, which leads to a reduction in the amount of labour available for production in the next cycle. In this way, crises in pre-capitalist societies reproduce themselves, the break in the normal productive process causing a shrinkage in the starting basis of the process. Now it is important to stress that there are features of crisis in the pre-capitalist society which make it both relatively and absolutely more important than, say, the business fluctuation in the capitalist economy. Crisis in the pre-capitalist economy has a reproductive, spiral effect. This manifests itself in an overall reduction in both current production and social reserves. When agriculture is the basis of all expanded production (as it was in the south-west Pacific) it is, above all, a reduction in agricultural production which lies at the root of persistent crises. Whereas capitalist crises occur as a result of an over-production of exchange values, pre-capitalist crises are due to an under-production of use values. In direct contrast to the capitalist economy, hunger in people's homes in pre-capitalist society is the cause of a decline in the output of labour which leads to more hunger and the subsequent reproduction of the crises. Again, unlike crises in the capitalist economy, pre-capitalist crises is by definition local and limited in space.

Because of its nature, crisis in the pre-capitalist society may have important effects on the process of labour migration. The spiral, reproductive effect of persistent crises forced communal producers, caught in the midst of local catastrophe, to adopt any of the available means to secure their subsistence, and this often meant a resort to colonial labour recruitment.

Other writers have described that part of the south-west Pacific which stretches from the Solomons to New Caledonia as one of the world's most inhospitable habitats.[90] This is not only because of the region's uncomfortable climate, or the unproductiveness of some islands, but because it is often harassed by hurricanes or drought. Frequent and violent hurricanes sweep through the south-west Pacific between January and April of each year. These catastrophic gales coincide with that time in the agricultural cycle when the tuber crops are maturing and the stored surpluses from the last season are low. Hurricanes, therefore, not only destroyed maturing crops in the islands, but they afflicted the cultivators at the most precarious period of the production cycle.

The climate of the region is controlled by trade winds, and this factor presents drought as a persistent threat to the livelihood of the inhabitants. Whereas the trade winds bring heavy rains to the windward side of the high mountainous islands, the opposite side can be so dry that yam and taro crops are seriously threatened. The low coral islands of the Pacific basin normally derive little precipitation from the trade winds, and rainfall is consequently very low in these habitats. In the Gilbert and Ellice Islands or the Banks and Torres group, drought occurs frequently and even drinking water is scarce.

Many writers have described the notorious morbidity of the south-west Pacific.[91] This can in part be attributed to the ecological instability of the region. Some prevalent diseases such as scurvy, yaws, and filiariasis, were related directly to food scarcity and dietary deficiencies. Malaria was rife in both the Solomon Islands and the New Hebrides. In addition to these illnesses, the advent of colonialism brought smallpox, measles, typhus, hookworm, leprosy, and syphilis to the islands. New diseases associated with unsanitary conditions on plantations and mines, such as tuberculosis, phthisis, and dysentery, also emerged. As we have already discussed, the prevalence of disease in a pre-capitalist community is tantamount to a natural disaster because it erodes the group's productive forces and thereby the community's ability to secure its reproduction.

There is much evidence that Islanders accepted recruitment for labour in Queensland to escape the effects of crises of the habitat. In 1869, for example, J. Campbell, a Queensland sugar grower, told of overcrowding on the recruiting vessel *Black Dog* as a result of the failed yam crop in the New Hebrides. '. . . . it was complete starvation in the islands at the time', he explained, 'periodical starvation takes place on these islands and the people are glad to get away.'[92] Similarly a significant number of Islanders engaged with Queensland recruiters, suffering from the diseases common to the region and the general morbidity of first contract workers, contributed to the high death rates in the colony's migrant population.[93] Clearly then, colonial service was resorted to by communities seeking relief from natural disasters in the south-west Pacific. But some catastrophes in the region were man-made.

Human conflict was a major form of crisis in the south-west Pacific. Warfare took place between the Islander communities, with the state in the form of the Royal Navy, and with traders, settlers, and labour recruiters. The huge trade in arms which was associated with the labour trade had an important impact on the nature of conflict in the region.

Snider rifles made at Liege and Birmingham for general commerce formed the greater number of weapons that were distributed throughout the Pacific after 1860.[94] The first Snider rifle was a British Enfield muzzle-loader converted into a breech-loader by fitting a hinged breech block with a firing-pin passing through it, the invention of Jacob Snider of Philadelphia. By all accounts the weapon was powerful and effective.[95] These rifles were supplemented by 'Tower' mark Sniders which flooded on to colonial markets after they had been withdrawn form the British Army between 1867 and 1875 to be replaced by the Martini Henry rifle. Australian traders bought the surplus obsolete weapons and redistributed them through the labour trade where there was an enormous demand for them.[96]

The Islanders wanted rifles for defence and because they had become a mark of status and prestige in the traditional society. Weapons were handed to the kin of migrants who engaged in the labour trade and they were a major item of consumption in Queensland to be taken home by time-expired workers in their trade box. One trader wrote that on Tana in 1870 he saw 'every man with a musket over his shoulder'.[97] In the period between 1871 and 1880 the quantity of rifles and ammunition exported to the south-west Pacific from New South Wales alone amounted to 1,304 cases of small arms, 336,773 pounds of gun or blasting powder, 16,752 pounds of dynamite, plus appropriate supplementary supplies.[98] In 1878 the sale of arms to the Islanders was forbidden for reasons of internal security in Queensland, and because the number of rifles in the islands put the labour trade at risk. Planters believed, however, that unless the trade in weapons was maintained the Islanders would stop engaging for Queensland.[99] Consequently the regulations were flouted by shopkeepers, planters, recruiters and immigrants, alike. When inspections of labour vessels were stepped up to control the trade, elaborate tricks were devised to smuggle rifles on board repatriating vessels. Trade boxes:

. . . . were fitted with false bottoms and carbines were stowed in them, the barrel being cut short or the stock being taken off. Innocent boxes of Queensland plants were found to have earth on top and a layer of cartridges underneath. During the Government inspection, rifles were sunk in the water butts or stowed away in the sheep pens, or even lowered over the side into the sea. The native crews would always stow away rifles for a fee, concealing them on the ship or up aloft or even under the ballast . . . . It was a common practice for returns to bring back charges of dynamite with fuse and cap all fixed for firing. . . . such charges of dynamite have been found stowed away under the ballast next to the vessel's skin. . . . What wonder vessels like *Sybil* were lost at sea.[100]

In 1882 it was estimated that one hundred rifles and one thousand five hundred muskets plus ammunition went to the New Hebrides alone from Queensland while the ban on rifle trading was in force.[101]

Ironically, the trade in arms helped to deepen the crisis of colonialism in the south-west Pacific. On the other hand, the island communities were impoverished by the trade in arms. Their resources were wasted on a commodity which did nothing to improve local production. Their subsistence was thus made even more dependent on colonial labour. But the advent of colonialism also exacerbated the intercommunal tensions which were a feature of the region. Fertile land was scarce on most islands and the allocation of plots in traditional society was highly defined. The establishment of plantations and trading stations had the effect of dislocating the villagers from their land. In an attempt to secure land to maintain the community's subsistence, the Islanders were thus forced into war with neighbouring people.[102] With the advent of powerful weaponry, inter-communal wars were a much more deadly affair.[103]

But the Islanders also responded to their expropriation by attacking the Europeans in the region. As the activity of traders and settlers increased after 1860, there was a concomitant increase in conflict between Europeans and the Islanders. On some islands there was an almost continuous state of war between the two groups.[104] The Islanders also made many attacks on the labour recruiters and their vessels. Indeed, settler and trader insecurity was reinforced by the reputation of the Islanders as savages, predisposed to indiscriminate murder, and led to demands for the protection of the Royal Navy.

Counter to the prevailing imperial policy against the expenditure of funds on the defence of colonies, The Pacific Islanders Protection Act of 1872 facilitated the construction of five warships to patrol the south-west Pacific.[105] Almost exclusively serving the interests of the settlers and traders, the navy ships carried out punitive expeditions against the

Islanders. Prompted usually by the spontaneous or organised resistance of the locals to western exploitation or expropriation, and sometimes by acts of brigandage or plunder, the naval expeditions involved the bombardment of villages, followed by landing parties or marines who systematically destroyed huts, canoes, fishing nets, gardening tools, coconut plantations, pigs, yam gardens, or other items of economic or cultural significance. If the alleged offences of Islanders could be tied down to specific individuals, these expeditions were highlighted by the public execution of the alleged culprits. Less spectacular sanctions included fining communities in quantities of local produce or by punishing guilty Islanders with gaol terms or labour service in the colonies. The threat of terror, or of cumulative fines, was placed on villages which protected or hid people accused of murder or theft.[106] So enthusiastically did the Australian Naval Squadron prosecute its duties between 1872 and 1900 that several minutes and letters passed between the Admiralty and the Australian Station, urging more temperate dealings with the Islanders of the region.[107] To a lesser extent the German, French, and American navies emulated the activities of the British Navy in the Pacific in the same period.[108]

Warfare, in whatever form, connected Islanders to colonial labour in a number of ways. The most obvious of these is that warfare involved the destruction of the means of production, simple and expanded production, and sometimes the producers themselves. This, as has been stressed, constituted a major crisis for pre-capitalist communities, aside from the immediate effects of disruption and terror associated with violent human conflict. But there is evidence that the activities of the navies in particular contributed directly to labour migration. The frequency and intensity of punitive raids bore a direct relation to the intensity of Islander resistance. The periods of active Islander resistance coincided with aggressive colonial recruiting drives which were characterised by the arbitrary use of coercion, the penetration of hitherto unrecruited areas, and the culling of islands already under-populated. Naval 'pacification', therefore, was aimed at making the labour recruiters' task both safe and fruitful, especially during the periods of high labour demand. This connection between naval activity and labour recruitment was observed by at least one island resident during the period, who wrote: 'the gunboats built at great expense to the nation. . . . have actually encouraged and promoted directly and indirectly the traffic in savages',[109] and 'the gunboats of the "Kidnapping Act, 1972" are perceived (by the natives) to favour this traffic'.[110]

Warfare, combined with the ravages of natural or social disasters and the disintegration of the communal economy and society through the growth of commercial activity in the south-west Pacific, contributed to a serious crisis of depopulation in the region. By the latter part of the nineteenth century missionaries and administrators were expressing serious concern at the magnitude of the problem.[111] There is little doubt that depopulation itself contributed directly to labour migration. The loss of irreplacable labour power through disaster or migration placed island communities at risk. That village survival was often threatened by labour migration is clear, for it was this that was at the core of Islander resistance to the labour trade, whether by force of arms or more peaceful forms of protest.[112] At the same time, a motive commonly ascribed to the recruitment of time-expired labourers was the poverty and disarray that the workers found in their villages on their return from Queensland.[113]

In its widest sense, catastrophe was an important determinant of Pacific island labour migration. Natural or social disasters were purely local affairs, however, confined in both time and space. Consequently, crises merely supplemented the process of proletarianisation which was initiated and promoted in the first place by the advent of imperialism in the western Pacific.

Conclusion

The migration of Pacific Islanders to Queensland in the nineteenth century, was not merely the product of a coercive recruiting industry nor can it adequately be attributed to 'wanderlust', 'acquisitiveness', or the exercise of free choice in the context of a competitive labour market. The purpose of this essay has been to suggest that the movement of clansmen to work in capitalist agro-industry had concrete, material origins. At its core lay a long-standing historical process, the transformation of the subsistence agricultural economy through the impact of capitalism. The penetration of the region by traders, settlers, recruiters, missionaries, and foreign military forces generated the disintegration of the pre-capitalist economy. Increasingly, the inhabitants of the South-west Pacific became dependent on wage labour to secure their reproduction. Aspects of this process were subtle and pervasive, such as, for example, the incorporation of the mechanisms of Melanesian exchange through the transformation of colonial commodities into gifts or the cooption of the political structures of the community to the service of the labour trade, as in the case of the passage masters. But Islanders were also forced into labour migration by less benign, more dramatic, processes, including disasters, both natural and man-made.

The historical foundations of labour migration are multi-faceted and complex, and there is very much that we have yet to learn and understand about the process in the south-west Pacific. In this essay we have just touched on aspects of conflict and change within the region itself which forced villagers into wage labour. There is much that future research should uncover about the effects of capitalism on clan-based production for example, or the emergence of peasant production in the islands and its articulation with the ebb and flow of men in search of work. Generalised studies can be useful in plotting the broad contours of history. They cannot, however, adequately cope with the analysis of such issues, whose forms and functions can differ markedly in both time and location, especially in an area as vast as the western Pacific. The detailed micro-histories which will help solve these puzzles, of individual islands, of villages, even of clans, remain to be written.

7

CAPITALISM AND MIGRANT LABOUR
IN SOUTHERN AFRICA:
THE ORIGINS AND NATURE
OF THE SYSTEM

MARTIN LEGASSICK & FRANCINE DE CLERCQ

In South Africa industries generally are based upon the employment of low-paid native labourers. This has inevitably involved the
question of bringing natives to places where the industries were
being established . . . . While the natives had ample land from
which to supply their needs they could not, at the rates which were
then offered, be induced to come out from their reserves to work at
strange occupations. Thus there arose a demand for low-paid non-
European labour from abroad . . . . The importation of natives
from outside the Union increases the supply of native labourers and
therefore reduces the wage which even the reserve native can secure
and ties down the detribalized native to a wage on which he cannot
maintain himself and his family. The effect, therefore, of importation, is to keep down the standard of living of the native workers of
the Union. This, in turn, keeps down the standard of wages for
unskilled white workers . . . . The coloured people are depressed
in the same way.[1]

From a historical point of view, mining and agriculture were the
predominant employers of extra-Union Natives until the thirties.
Since then, the greatest part of the increase of their numbers has
been absorbed by the service industries and secondary industries
. . . . This elastic source of labour helps to increase the flexibility of
the South African economic system. In periods of prosperity and
'boom' conditions it serves as a medium to obviate relative
scarcities of unskilled labour or to limit their intensity, while
during depressions the labour supply shrinks automatically. For the
industrialist and the businessman, the additional labour signifies
that the elasticity of the labour supply is maintained, or at all events,
is not greatly decreased, so that wages need not be raised at all, or
not much, to attract labour. For the indigenous or settled Native,
on the other hand, this means that he must compete with the immi-

grants, to whom, rightly or wrongly, preference is frequently given. As a consequence of this, in all probability, his wage has risen less during the past few years than would have been the case in the absence of immigration.[2]

THE accumulation of capital in Southern Africa has, from its inception, been associated with the employment of migrant workers. The conditions which create and perpetuate this migrant labour system have altered dramatically over time, as have the forms taken by the system.[3] Nevertheless, it has retained certain characteristics which mean that it is described more accurately as a penal contract or indentured labour system. 'The system which has grown up, as far as unskilled labour is concerned', wrote the head of the Witwatersrand Native Labour Association in 1906, 'is obviously a branch of the indentured labour system . . . . The natives on the mines are, in all essential respects, indentured labourers. They are brought from long distances and mostly from other countries. They engage in the first place for fixed periods. They do not have their homes at or near their place of employment . . . . They are even subject to a special code of law.'[4] For significant sections, although not the whole, of the work force in South Africa, the centre of southern African capital accumulation, all these conditions still apply. It is the purpose of this paper to examine why such a system originated, why it has continued, and the nature and causes of the changes it has undergone. To examine such questions is an essential part of establishing the conditions under which this system, with all the misery, degradation, and suffering that it has produced, can be abolished.

Subjection to a migrant or indentured labour system has been the condition, not of all workers in South Africa but of black African workers alone. Immigrant workers from Europe ('whites') have (with insignificant exceptions) never been subjected to any constraints over movements, once admitted to the country. Coloured workers (the descendants of imported slaves and indigenous Khoi) and Indian workers (descendants for the most part of nineteenth-century indentured labourers) are subject to various forms of racial oppression, but not to the migrant labour system.[5] Indeed, not all African workers have been, or are, migrants in this sense. Through the early period of capitalist development, African workers came to settle with their families near their jobs in the town and legal inhibitions on this process of urbanisation were comparatively ineffective. Only after World War II, in terms of Section 10 of the Natives (Urban Areas) Consolidation Act of 1945, and in its subsequent amendments, did there begin effective procedures for limiting and controlling this process of urbanisation and only after this period was the state in a position effectively to enforce these procedures. At present, therefore, there exists a substantial African work force *not* subjected to the full migrant contract labour system because of permanent residence (whether legally or illegally) in urban areas near work-places. Nevertheless, one of the intentions of the Bantustan policy, particularly the granting of so-called 'independence' to the Bantustans, is to transform the majority or the whole of the African work force into 'foreign' contract workers.

Among those workers subjected to the migrant labour system there exist, and have existed, differences of condition and legal status. These differences exist at a given point in time, and they have also varied over time. One such difference, which is a principal concern of this paper, is between that part of the African work force in South Africa which is regarded as 'South African' and that which is regarded as 'foreign'. Even this distinction, however, has taken different forms at different times. Leaving aside the question of the use and significance of the term 'foreign' in the nineteenth century in southern Africa, we can see changes even since 1910. The Admission of Persons to the Union Regulation Act (22 of 1913) formalised different statuses of 'foreignness' in South Africa, and classified migrant African workers from Mozambique (PEA), Malawi (Nyasaland), etc., as essentially 'prohibited immigrants', those who 'on economic grounds or on account of standards or habits of life' were regarded as unsuitable for permanent settlement in South Africa. Such persons could enter South Africa only in terms of a treaty with a neighbouring state, or in accordance with a labour recruitment scheme approved by the South African government. Although labour recruitment from north of latitude 22° was prohibited in the same year, when it was resumed in the 1930s and after, a similar status of 'foreign prohibited immigrant' was accorded to persons from Nyasaland, Northern and Southern Rhodesia, Tanganyika, etc. On the other hand, persons from the High Commission Territories, although under the 'foreign' rule of Britain, were not subjected to the conditions of the 1913 Act. Workers from such areas were seen as part of 'British South Africa', and the High Commission Territories were regarded as 'native reserves' whose inhabitants were subject to the forms of regulation of the 'internal' rather than the 'foreign' part of the migrant labour system. Only in the 1950s, and then finally in measures promulgated in 1963, did migrant labour from the High Commission Territories become transformed in status to the condition of 'foreign' workers. At the same time the South African state was beginning the implementation of the Bantustan policy, which has now brought the Transkei and Bophutatswana to so-called 'independence'. The consequence, as we have already pointed out, is the gradual transformation of the majority of black South Africans into legal foreigners in their own country.

These changing definitions of who are to be regarded as 'foreign' workers, no less than the changing character of the social and status implications of 'foreignness', are in themselves an indication that the role of 'foreign' labour in South Africa cannot be considered in isolation. We cannot simply add an examination of the role of foreign labour to an examination of the 'internal' labour situation. Nor can we deal with the problem by regarding it simply as one of the 'stratification' of a work force, with 'foreign African migrant', 'internal African migrant', 'internal African non-migrant', 'Coloured/Asian', and 'White' layers. This stratification is indeed one of the aspects of the situation: in South Africa, white workers are heavily concentrated in skilled supervisory, or mental jobs, while African workers are heavily concentrated in unskilled or manual jobs. The 'foreign' African labour force is in these respects more particularly concentrated than the African work force in general. According to the 1970 census, 97.3 per cent of 'foreign' Africans were employed in work classified as unskilled (and very much concentrated in the mining sector), and only 1.63 per cent were categorised as in 'skilled' work. 'Foreign' workers made up 8.4 per cent of the total unskilled African work force, and only 2.5 per cent of the skilled work force.[6] Nevertheless, such concentration on stratification alone does not explain the role of the migrant labour system, or of the status of 'foreignness' within it. It does not take account of the fact that there is an interrelationship between the conditions and status of the different 'strata' of the work force as a whole; that the condition of one part is the corollary of the condition of another part. It is by understanding the relationship of the migrant labour system and of the status of 'foreignness' to the dynamic of capital accumulation in southern Africa as a whole that this will become clear.

The accumulation of capital:
formation of a proletariat and industrial reserve army

Capitalism is characterised by the system of wage-labour through which workers, deprived of the means of production and subsistence, are compelled to seek employment from the capitalist, those who possess those means. Engaging in wage-labour, the workers produce a greater value of products than the value represented by their wages: They perform unpaid labour for the capitalist, which is appropriated as surplus value. The accumulation of capital occurs through the reconversion of part of that surplus value into capital, for the purpose of appropriating more surplus value. One of the factors which jeopardise this process of accumulation is a shortage of wage-labour, that is, the separation of an insufficient number of workers from direct access to the means of production and subsistence. Such conditions, that is an excess of capital and shortage of wage-labour, tend to lead to increased wages. Hence, as Marx argued, a necessary condition for the continuation of capital accumulation is not simply the formation of a proletariat, i.e. a population separated from direct access to the means of production and subsistence, but of a surplus population, 'A population of greater extent than suffices for the average needs of the self-expansion of capital'.[7] This surplus population acts as an industrial reserve army, which

during the periods of stagnation and average prosperity, weighs down the active-labour-army; during the periods of over-production and paroxysm, it holds its pretensions in check. Relative surplus-population is therefore the pivot upon which the law of demand and supply of labour works. It confines the field of action of this law within the limits absolutely convenient to the activity of exploitation and to the domination of capital . . . . the course characteristic of modern industry, viz. a decennial cycle (interrupted by smaller oscillations), of periods of average activity, production at high pressure, crisis and stagnation, depends on the constant formation, the greater or lesser absorption, and the reformation of the industrial reserve-army or surplus-population.[8]

In developed capitalism it is the increasing productivity of social labour which comes to constitute the main lever of accumulation. This increasing productivity of social labour means, essentially, a growing mass of the means of production in relation to the mass of labour in motion, or a progressive increase in constant capital in comparison with variable capital. This means that the tendency to increased productivity of social labour is the same as the tendency for the creation of a surplus population, both absolutely and relatively. Developed capitalism, therefore, through its process of self-expansion, itself generates an industrial reserve army or, if for various reasons it does not, crisis is likely to ensue which will throw workers out of production and create such an industrial reserve army. The capital relation in developed capitalism thus reproduces itself, although it does so as a contradictory relation and through crisis. In the historical process of the seizure of the social relations of production by capitalism, their transformation into the relations of capitalism, these conditions may not, however, obtain. Direct and forcible intervention, the 'artificial' expansion of the proletariat or of an industrial reserve army, becomes necessary to sustain the conditions for the accumulation of capital. this is not to imply that in developed capitalism force is absent: on the contrary. But its uses and its forms change in relation to the special circumstances and contradictions of particular moments.

Within southern African the accumulation of capital and the formation of a proletariat may be said to have begun in the nineteenth century. The concrete circumstances in which that process occurred explain the origins of the migrant labour system, as a means of 'artificially' expanding the proletariat and the industrial reserve army. Thereafter, certain moments in the process of capital accumulation, with their particular contradictions, have produced certain transformations in that system, necessitating an increasing, and changing, role for the state in its relation to the migrant labour system. To be more specific, capital accumulation in South Africa has occurred under continuous conditions of a relatively large surplus population which, even under boom conditions, has not been wholly re-absorbed into production. Initially, this was because of its 'artificiality'. But, as the dynamic of capital accumulation has created a work force fully separated from direct access to the means of production and subsistence, the conditions of accumulation have reproduced the same situation. In this context state policy has moved through a series of stages. At the start it was directed towards attracting labour into production. Over time this role was supplemented by state intervention to redistribute labour in production. In the more recent period the role of the state has been increasingly to repel labour from production. The particularly punitive penal forms which have characterised state policy are a condition of the size of the industrial reserve army, combined with the rapid pace of accumulation. These statements are clearly generalisations. We now turn to examine more concretely the successive moments of accumulation and state policy, to refine and qualify these generalisations.

Capital accumulation, the state, and the creation of the migrant labour system in southern Africa

During the nineteenth century the accumulation of capital in southern Africa gave birth to a rural proletariat formed predominantly from the indigenous (black) people, although supplemented by indentured labour from India. Much of this proletariat existed, whether as wage-labourers or labour-tenants, immobilised on the farms where it worked, although it was supplemented seasonally by labour migrating from areas still in the communal possession of African communities, coming to earn money to buy guns, pay taxes, etc. As a subordinate tendency, both in areas of communal possession and in areas under rentier landlords, a peasantry was also emerging. The rural proletariat as a whole was subjected to a penal contract system, enforced either by the direct force of the commando or by the legal system of the state. It was in this period, moreover, that various forms of state intervention in the attraction-redistribution-repulsion of labour emerged (pass laws, the Durban *togt* labour system, etc.).[9]

Towards the end of the century the discovery in South Africa of precious minerals, particularly gold (the money-commodity) which was in short international supply, quickened the pace of accumulation. Mining production expanded rapidly and along with it agriculture, transport, commerce, services, etc. The expanded opportunities for accumulation meant a dramatic increase in the demand for labour. In all the territories of what was to become South Africa pressures were exerted on the state for increased intervention to promote the supply of labour. The state sought to attain these ends by various means, including (i) increased taxation (in money) of Africans, and (ii) a legal assault on the position of peasants and immobilised farm labour, restricting conditions of land tenure and the amount of land which could be occupied on state-owned land, seeking to 'unlock' labour tied up on private land. In the short term, however, neither the economic nor the political forces which were expanding the proletariat in such areas were sufficiently powerful. The general level of wages was driven up, although the benefits often accrued not directly to the workers but to middlemen (traders, chiefs, labour recruiters), who were able to create the linkages between the areas of supply and of demand.

To reduce the general level of wages or restore the rate of exploitation it was therefore necessary either to increase the productivity of social labour or to expand the geographical area from which the work force was being generated. The second of these alternatives was the predominant response, and the lead in this respect was taken by the gold-mining industry, organised in the Chamber of Mines. The gold-mining companies represented the largest concentrations of capital in South Africa; they had absorbed large amounts of finance capital from the centres of imperialism; as producers of the money-commodity they were (and remained) crucial in the general accumulation process in South Africa, and critical in the whole system of world accumulation. In the interests of the world economy and of the South African economy overall, both British imperialism and the dominant local political forces were compelled to look to the interests of the gold-mining industry. And the conditions of accumulation were such that raising the social productivity of labour was a less attractive or immediate possibility than the recruitment of a work force from new geographical areas or, in other words, the artificial creation of an industrial reserve army.[10]

In the 1890s, through independent recruiters, the mining industry tapped new supplies of labour in the Northern Transvaal and Portuguese East Africa (in the latter case this represented a diversion of some labour from Natal sugar). Just before the Anglo-Boer War over 70 per cent of the work force of 97,000 was from PEA. After the war the Chamber, on the terms regulated by the Transvaal (and later the South African) state, moved to centralise and rationalise this recruitment with the establishment of the Witwatersrand Native Labour Association (WNLA). As an immediate expedient in the context of disruption of labour supply lines, the WNLA introduced indentured labour from China between 1903 and 1908, but was soon forced to abandon this policy. In its place there was a return to PEA (and, until 1913, 'tropical') labour, whose contribution to the mine labour force remained around 50 per cent or more until the onset of the depression in 1929. It was the ability to create this 'artificial' reserve army which allowed the Chamber to institute a system of 'maximum average wages', which from 1900 exerted a downwards pressure on real wages. In 1910 average wages per shift were 18c, in 1911 20c, and here they remained (1931 22c; 1943 23c) until World War II.

Thus conscious large-scale recruitment efforts organised by private capital formed the major means of 'attracting' labour to the mines. At the same time the state played a critical role in reinforcing and regulating this system of private recruitment. All black mine labour was subject to criminal liability for breach of contract. And the status of 'foreignness' was initially established because recruiting in Mozambique became the subject of inter-state agreements. The first of these of importance was the *modus vivendi* of 1901, which led to the Mozambique Convention of 1909 (amended in 1928, 1934, 1936, 1940, 1964, and 1970). As already noted, 'foreign' labour secured through these means had a special status in terms of the 1913 Aliens Act (and its later amendments). Moreover, the Mozambique Convention provided the precedent on which the South African state and the WNLA established later agreements with the colonial governments of Northern and Southern Rhodesia, Nyasaland, Tanganyika, Botswana, etc.

There were certain specific corollaries to this creation of an 'artificial' reserve army. Its artificiality consisted in the incomplete separation from the means of production and subsistence of the labour force from which it was drawn. Thus within the span of a working life these workers divided their time between direct domestic subsistence production and wage-labour, with minimal economic compulsions on the latter activity. Workers therefore attempted to organise the term and frequency of wage-labour to cause the minimum disruption to the seasonal and sexual organisation of production and reproduction.

The employers, on the other hand, were interested in a term and frequency of work which would (i) make the costs of long-distance recruiting acceptable, and (ii) recoup such costs as were involved in on-the-job training. Here was a conflict of interest which, particularly in the period of independent recruiting, produced the predominant worker response of desertion (whether to another mine offering more favourable terms or back home). It was gradually resolved in two ways. For the 'internal' labour force, the norm for a single period of service stabilised around three to six months until after World War I. For the 'foreign' labour force, on the other hand, the norm stabilised around a contract of twelve months. The role of the state was (i) to enforce these contracts; (ii) to enforce pass laws which would prevent desertions (the chamber of Mines first formulated the necesssary legislation for the Transvaal government in 1885-96); and (iii) to agree these contract lengths with the relevant foreign governments[11]

The early gold-mining period was therefore associated with the institutionalisation, through the Chamber, the WNLA, and the state, of divisions already present in the relation to production of different workers: whites, 'internal' migrants, and 'foreign' migrants. These divisions tended to be reproduced within the labour process, in types of housing, and in forms of organisation. In particular, conditions existed for white workers to organise politically and economically. For blacks, on the other hand, subject to the penal contract system, housed as single males in socially insulated compounds, subjected to periodic return to their homes, the conditions of organisations were different. And the system provided the basis on which further division — ethnic, foreign/internal, etc. — could be created within the black work force. The constitution of the South African state, establishing democratic representation for the white minority (and for some blacks only in the Cape), and autocratic administration over the black majority, built on these processes. This dual system of rule was territorially and politically consolidated in such measures as the Native Land Act of 1913, the Native Affairs Act of 1920, and the Native Administration Act of 1927 which (along with other laws and practice) served to ensure that the 'internal' labour system would also develop on the basis of migrancy. It is to the reasons for this that we now turn.

Martin Legassick and Francine de Clercq

Capital, the state, and the redistribution of labour in production: 1910-1933

The forms in which the division of the working class became institutionalised in the early mining period gave a particular character to the manifestation of capital-labour conflict. The comparative 'immunisation' of the black labour force through the creation of an industrial reserve army and the associated institutions meant that the pressure on wages was reduced to the organised pressure of white workers. It was this pressure that compelled capital in South Africa, and particularly mining capital, to increase the productivity of social labour, particularly through reorganisation of the labour process. It was on the mines that this had the most dramatic effects, for white miners could not organise on the basis of craft skills to oppose alteration in the labour process. Instead, in their economic and political organisation, their leadership accepted the existing modes of working-class division and called on the state to intervene in two ways: (i) to redistribute labour in production by protecting jobs on a racial basis as the labour process was reorganised; and (ii) to ensure that the undercutting effect on wage levels of the penal contract system did not extend to them. (In its extreme forms, this was the demand for a white labour policy, abolition of indentured labour, and the institution of total segregation.)

As a result of the economic and political struggles of white workers from the early 1900s to the 1920s, the state did intervene in these chauvinistic, racist ways: the job colour bar regulations under the 1911 Mines and Works Act, and the renewed Mines and Works Act in 1926, are examples. The ending of 'tropical' recruitment in 1913, although the result of a complex variety of pressures, was also supported by the leaders of the white workers' organisations. Simultaneously, the state and employers began to institutionalise an 'internal' recruitment network which, to the extent that it could secure a sufficient supply, would provide the basis for a nationalistic phasing out of 'foreign' labour. In 1912 the Native Recruiting Organization was established by the Chamber, in terms of the Natives Labour Regulation Act of 1911, to serve these ends. Slowly, this organisation began to push towards minimum contract lengths approximating to those of 'foreign' labour. In 1919 a seven-month minimum was established, and bonuses were being provided for those returning within four months; in 1924 the minimum was extended to nine months. By 1931 the average length of contract for 'British South Africans' was 10.8 months (with an average rest of 8.1 months), and by 1934 it was over twelve months.[12] These extensions of contract length were not achieved simply through the instrument of the law; they simultaneously reflected the fact that 'British South Africans' were being separated from the means of production and subsistence under conditions which were creating surplus population (although a surplus population very often remained in a 'latent' state in the 'native reserves' and on the 'white farms').

Through reorganisation of the labour process (in particular the introduction of the jackhammer drill), especially on the new mines of the Far East Rand, the mining companies were able to overcome the profitability crisis which had threatened after the First World War.[13] Working costs, which were 25/10d per ton in 1921, fell to 19/3d by 1932; in the same period working profits rose from £11.2 million to £15.3 million. This was achieved within the limits imposed by the state's racist and nationalist forms of redistribution of labour in production. The possibility of achieving this in the mining industry, moreover, resulted from the overall slowing of accumulation in comparison with the pre-war period, a slow-down which reached its culmination in the depression at the end of the 1920s. Nevertheless, the necessity for a 'foreign' section of the industrial reserve army persisted. All that was altered and limited (another aspect of the redistribution of labour) was the functions of this industrial reserve army. Thus the Low Grade Mines Commission of 1920, while opposing any displacement of 'British South African' migrants by 'foreign' Africans, recommended that the latter should be employed particularly on low-grade mines.[14] In coal mines and the newly developing base minerals mines it also appears that there was extensive use of 'foreign' labour. In the 1930s a standard text argued:

The supply [of labour] from Portuguese East Africa can be adjusted to counteract both seasonal and cyclical fluctuations in the numbers of Natives from the Union and British Protectorates. The Natives from Portuguese territory are, moreover, to a marked degree miners of experience, and they can be drafted by the central authority to one mine or another with greater freedom than those from other South African sources.[15]

Over the period from Union to the depression, moreover, it is likely that agriculture, particularly in areas adjacent to 'foreign' countries, drew on seasonal labour as an industrial reserve army. Thus a commission in 1935 reported that in Natal sugar plantation workers from Mozambique were preferred to local labour because they worked for longer periods and did not take weekends and Mondays off. The bulk of such migrants (as well as those who found their way into the towns from the mine compounds) would have been illegal but the initial inter-state agreements provided for the regularisation of the position of illegal 'foreign' migrants provided that they had six months' service contracts with employers. These provisions began to be tightened in the 1920s to strengthen the state's control over redistribution and (as the depression intensified) repulsion. The 1928 Mozambique Convention prohibited Mozambiquans from work outside mining, imposing a ceiling on mining recruitment of 100,000 in 1929, falling to 80,000 by 1933, and prohibited re-recruitment in less than six months. Act 46 of 1937 extended the prohibition on urban employment outside mining to all 'foreign' labour (for this was the period during which 'tropical' recruitment commenced again). In the same period there were more stringent inter-state measures agreed concerning the repatriation of 'foreign' workers at the termination of their contracts, and the deferred pay system, hitherto voluntary, was made a compulsory part of the contract (which also served to strengthen the 'repulsion' aspects of state policy).

1933-1946

At the height of the depression, therefore, the labour trends of the second phase of capital accumulation in South Africa reached their culmination. White labour was in the most protected position (although even here the depression exacerbated tendencies to unemployment and 'poor whiteism'). The 'internal' recruiting system was able to generate a substantial part of the labour force for the mines (a peak of 74.8 per cent in 1932), reflecting the extent to which proletarianisation had proceeded and a surplus population been created. Indeed, this was sufficiently the case for the Chamber to be able to cut recruitment costs without forgoing the advantages of re-recruitment by instituting the Assisted Voluntary System on the mines. By 1932 32 per cent of the mine labour force was on AVS, and in 1942 49.2 per cent. Comparisons made by a wartime commission on the length of time between contracts in 1931 and in 1943 indicate a substantially increased level of proletarianisation. The 'foreign' work force, however, was substantially reduced as a percentage of the mine labour force, and was to some extent reduced even in absolute numbers, while (despite the reintroduction of 'tropical' recruiting) it was being subjected to an increasingly limited role in the economy, and even to the pressures of 'repulsion'.

The abandonment of the gold standard (and consequent devaluation), as a result of South Africa's particular relation to the world capitalist economy as supplier of the money-commodity, produced comparatively rapid economic recovery, at first in gold-mining, but spreading into other sectors (particularly those that had been artificially stimulated in the 1920s). The increased pace of accumulation, in mining, in manufacturing, in agriculture, once again created an accelerated demand for labour. This was occurring, in a context where the pressures of rural proletarianisation were beginning to erode the effectiveness of the institutions reinforcing the migrant labour system. Workers, 'internal' as well as foreign, in short, were moving from the farms, the 'reserves', their home territories, to settle in the towns, often with their families. Given that wages had been 'stabilised' by the industrial reserve army at levels which took for granted migrant labour and rural domestic production, these conditions meant that wages for urban black families had fallen increasingly below the value of labour-power. In response to the class pressures created by this situation, the state did not move, in the first instance, to implement a minimum wage policy (though this was advocated by some organised workers in manufacturing and by liberals). Instead, in the 1930s the state legislated a restructuring of the 'reserve' economies which had been under discussion for some ten years. This aimed to increase 'reserve' domestic production, but on the basis of further limitations on the extent of cultivable land, i.e. to stabilise the reproduction of a surplus population confined to the rural areas, except when 'attracted' to labour. It was complemented by urban areas legislation which provided for 'quotas' of a permanent urban black population. A new division in the 'internal' black labour force was to be institutionalised: between the 'urbanised' (largely in manufacturing) and the migrant, available for mines and farms.[16]

The particular form of this state intervention in the 1930s was vitiated by the pace of accumulation during and immediately after World War II. The demand for labour produced considerable re-absorption of surplus population, and in conditions where Africans organised effectively for the first time in 'African only' and multi-racial industrial trade unions, created upward pressures on wages. The drift of surplus population from the rural areas to the towns intensified, moreover. The crisis point for accumulation, however, was reached when trade union organisation among Africans spread into the mining sector. Since 1920 the operation of the migrant labour system had tended to insulate mine-workers from the dynamics of urban class struggle. Now the conditions of continued declining rural production, rising urban prices, and stagnant real wages brought African miners to the forefront of the struggle. In August 1946 African miners brought twelve mines to a halt in a strike lasting some three days. It was brutally repressed, but thereafter there was some upward movement in wages: 23c a shift in 1941, 29c in 1946, 36c in 1951. What the strike highlighted, however, was the substantial gap that had developed between the levels of African wages in manufacturing and in mining (and, for that matter, on the farms). Mining and export farming production remained crucial to accumulation in South Africa (as did the relative reduction of domestic food prices, i.e. the restructuring of locally oriented agriculture, in order to restore rates of exploitation). And mining and farming could not afford to bring their wage rates into levels competitive with other sectors of the economy. These problems were those addressed in the post-war period, through a substantial intensification in the role of the state *vis-à-vis* 'labour policy', and an alteration in the forms of such intervention.

1946-1960

In the conditions of the immediate post-war period, accumulation would have slowed down in general unless rates of exploitation were restored. The initial role of the state was to ensure that the strategic sectors in terms of South Africa's relation to the world capitalist economy were insulated from this process.[17] Whatever happened in manufacturing, the mining and farming sectors had to be protected and encouraged to restructure. In both cases, this occurred through a combination of processes: on the one hand, raising the productivity of social labour, and on the other hand, by tapping, through recruitment networks, new sources of surplus population. Thus from 1945 to 1951 the percentage of 'foreign' labour within a relatively static mine-labour force increased substantially: from 34.3 to 48.4 per cent. The increase came almost entirely from 'tropical' re-cruitment with the Mozambiquan contribution constant. Hence the decision probably came from the Chamber, seeking by this means (i) to decrease its reliance on potentially more militant black South African labour and (ii) to rely more on a less completely proletarianised work force which could still supplement its wages from domestic production. An equivalent process occurred on the farms. Although research on this is limited, one suspects that farmers (especially in border areas) began to call increasingly on 'foreign' and High Commission Territory labour to make good the deficiencies which were being produced by the drift of 'South African' farm labour to the towns. The state encouraged this process, in the first instance by the conscious redirection of 'foreign' workers in the towns into agriculture, on pain of deportation. Under these conditions manufacturing, in the immediate post-war period, was relatively 'deprived' of access to surplus population: wages tended to rise, stimulating capital-labour substitution. By the early 1950s this process in manufacturing (involving imports of capital goods) was running up against balance of payments constraints, and the consequence was a period of stagnation in manufacturing, leading to the re-enlargement of a South African surplus population.

During this period the state also set about constructing an institutional apparatus through which an 'internal' system of migrant labour, which had begun to disintegrate before and during the war, could be re-created. It must be pointed out that this involved by no means all African workers in the first instance. Under the Native (Urban Areas) Consolidation Act of 1945 certain conditions were laid down under which Africans could acquire rights of permanent urban residence. These provisions were coercive in that they required such persons to fulfil positive criteria for the first time: criteria, moreover, which place a premium on steady employment. Thus workers dismissed by employers for militancy in the factories were also automatically punished by the state by being denied the right of permanent urban residence. These provisions were consistent with the recommendations of the Fagan Commission (1948) for the continued presence of some urban surplus population:

In estimating labour requirements one has to remember that where there is great industrial activity, it is also necessary that there should be a substantial reserve of labour people who are ready to step in when others fall out or when there is increased activity in some industry; and there are many industries that are constantly contracting and expanding for seasonal and other reasons.[18]

Correspondingly, the state was compelled to intervene in the area of urban African housing (previously under municipal control) in order to make increased provision for such urban residents. Whereas in the inter-war period the characteristic urban housing for African workers had been compounds for single men under employer ownership (or municipal barracks), there now developed the arid mass-constructed housing of the segregated urban township, with provision for families.

State policy was simultaneously to limit and to regulate this urbanisation. The pass laws were tightened up, and extended for the first time to women (since the establishment of urban families was regarded as the crucial factor to control). A network of labour bureaus began to be established, at first in the urban areas and subsequently in the rural areas, to provide mechanisms through which migrant labour could be channelled. In contrast to the privately operated recruiting network of the Chamber, this system was under the control of the state. This reflected the fact that

154

the new migrant labour system was being created in conditions of much more complete separation from the means of subsistence of the African population. In other words, the role of the labour bureaus was not one of attraction of labour but of redistribution and repulsion of labour. During the 1950s (and even thereafter) state officials believed that such 'repulsion' could be encouraged by continuing the process of 'agricultural rehabilitation' in the 'native reserves', i.e. increasing the carrying capacity of the land.[19] At the same time (from at least the time of the Lansdowne Commission in 1943) it has been recognised that landlessness existed in these 'reserves', which should be catered for by the establishment of 'rural villages'.

During the 1950s the implementation of a policy of 'repulsion' was relatively limited, especially for South African workers. There were 'endorsements out' of the urban areas, but the main effectiveness of the new state policy may have been to bring new entrants to the labour market in the 'reserves' under the control of the labour bureau system. In fact the resources of the state were largely occupied with combating the mass movement of resistance, urban and rural, which developed in the period against the increased intervention of the state in the control of labour. The most significant effects of this period, in fact, were in terms of the transformation of the status of High Commission Africans to that of 'foreign' workers and the actual weeding-out of 'foreign' Africans who had acquired permanent residence qualifications. New legislation and regulations meant that 'foreign' Africans (now including those from the High Commission Territories) could no longer qualify for permanent residence, could not bring their families with them to the country, and were required to spend at least six months at their homes prior to re-employment 'so that they do not lose their ties with their own country'. Special provision, however, was made for 'foreign' workers seeking employment on the farms. The extent to which the implementation of these measures involved actual 'repulsion' and disruption of social ties appears from the census figures. In 1936, 333,777 foreign Africans were enumerated, in 1946 556,807, and in 1951 606,992. The Tomlinson Commission, in the early 1950s, estimated that some 35 per cent of foreign Africans qualified for permanent residence. In 1960 the census enumerated 585,429 foreign Africans, a decline from 1951. Since all sources are agreed that this figure is a substantial underestimate, it is clear that large numbers of persons were being compelled to disguise their origins to avoid being thrust into the surplus population being generated in the surrounding territories, able to enter South Africa legally only for employment on the mines or the farms.[20]

1960-1978

By the late 1950s the accumulation process had begun to re-create a surplus population which may well have been declining throughout the 1940s. In the gold-mining industry a peak in absolute employment levels was reached in 1962. At the same time the post-war mechanisation of agriculture was generating an increasing (though partly latent) surplus population on white farms. The relative stagnation of manufacturing was adding to surplus population.[21] This is indicated, *inter alia,* by the decline in overall real wage levels during the 1950s, and a corresponding increase in industrial strikes throughout the period. Conditions existed, in fact, for a new thrust in the pace of accumulation led by manufacturing, a policy whose encouragement by the state was advocated by the Viljoen Commission (1958). This acceleration of the pace of accumulation was what occurred in the 1960s, accompanied by massive inflows of foreign capital securing high profit rates. The overall conditions for this accelerated accumulation were, however, 'political' as well as 'economic'. It involved the smashing of the movement of mass African resistance in the 1950s, as well as the existence of a re-expanded surplus population.

There are aspects of the process of accumulation in the 1960s which raise certain problems. In the first place, it is fairly clear that it occurred in the context of a relatively high level of surplus population. Recent retrospective analyses of African unemployment levels suggest figures of the order of one million around 1960, which must be supplemented by the accessible surplus population of the High Commission Territories, Mozambique, and Malawi. (On the other hand, Tanzania cut off its supply of workers to South Africa in 1961, and Zambia in 1966, while the contribution of Rhodesian labour to South African accumulation may or may not have diminished after UDI.) At the same time, both in manufacturing and in mining, this accumulation appears to have occurred on the basis of substantially increased mechanisation, i.e. increase in the productivity of social labour. Aspects of state policy, intentionally or not, served to stimulate this mechanisation. For example, a series of Wage Board determinations in the early 1960s may have served to increase minimum wage levels (for the first time since the 1940s); and certainly there was a rising trend in wages in manufacturing during the 1960s. All else remaining the same, the payment of higher minimum wages would have reduced the rate of exploitation. Employers would have sought to compensate for this by various means, among which the substitution of machinery for living labour would have been an important one. In addition, the implementation of measures creating a new migrant labour system may have caused temporary 'bottle-necks' between the areas of supply (the 'reserves') and the urban industrial centres. The Physical Planning Act of 1967, attempting to enforce white-black labour ratios in the cities, may also have contributed to mechanisation. Alternatively, the levels of mechanisation may be explicable in terms of the kind of 'technology' necessary for manufacturing to become internationally competitive, or in terms of the 'technology' accessible to foreign companies engaging in investment.

TABLE 7.1:   MINIMUM AND AVERAGE EARINGS (PER SHIFT)

	Minimum (underground)	Average
1910	—	18c
1911	—	20c
1913	—	20c
1916	—	20c
1921	—	22c
1926	—	22c
1931	17c	22c
1936	—	23c
1938	n/a	23c
1941	n/a	n/a
1943	18c	23c
1946	22c	29c
1948	24c	n/a
1949	27c	n/a
1951	30c	36c
1956	n/a	43c
1961	n/a	48c
1964	34c	n/a
1965	n/a	n/a
1966	n/a	59c
1969	40c	65c
1971	42c	n/a
1972	50c	81c
1973	72c	R1.10c
1974	R1.60c	R1.78c
1975	R2.20c	R3.00c
1976	R2.50c	n/a
1977	R2.50c	n/a

Source: 'Capital Restructuring and the South African State'.

Whatever the causes, the effects of the increased pace of accumulation at particular levels of the productivity of social labour were to lead to the increased generation of a relative surplus population, extruded from mining and manufacturing, in addition to an absolute surplus population which had come into being in agriculture in the 1950s and 1960s. Indeed, the mechanisms of labour 'redistribution' which had been established in the post-war period persisted. The mining industry, for example, continued to draw on its 'separated' labour force and industrial reserve army constituted by 'foreign' workers. If High Commission Territory workers are considered to be transferred to this category in the 1960s, then the 'foreign' work force comprised a consistent 60 per cent of the total through the 1960s, rising to 70 per cent in the early 1970s and a peak of nearly 80 per cent in 1973. This was labour employed on a penal contract basis, serving lengthy contract periods, and was correspondingly accompanied by a decline in the numbers of AVS workers. Evidence of the average length of service at one stretch from Anglo-American mines in 1960 indicates (i) the generally increased level of proletarianisation of mine-labour and (ii) the continued differentiation between 'foreign' and

TABLE 7.2: UNEMPLOYMENT IN SOUTH AFRICA

	Number	Percentage of labour force
1960	1,236,000	18.3
1961	1,311,000	19.0
1962	1,375,000	19.5
1963	1,401,000	19.4
1964	1,378,000	18.6
1965	1,448,000	19.1
1966	1,389,000	17.8
1967	1,394,000	17.5
1968	1,645,000	20.1
1969	1,589,000	18.9
1970	1,758,000	20.4
1971	1,747,000	19.8
1972	1,891,000	20.0
1973	1,898,000	20.3
1974	1,990,000	20.8
1975	2,014,000	20.6
1976	2,139,000	21.4
1977	2,306,000	22.4

Source: C. Simkins, 'Measuring and Predicting Unemployment in South Africa,' in Simkins and Clarke, *Structural Unemployment in South Africa,* p.87.

South African labour: Mozambiquans 412 shifts, 'tropicals' 393 shifts, 'British South Africans' 245-8 shifts. By this time the number of AVS recruits had fallen to some 23 per cent of the total labour force; and by 1969 AVS recruits were only 9 per cent. The situation with regard to farming is not so clear. If 'foreign' labour was being 'redistributed' into farming in the late 1940s and the 1950s, then the evidence of censuses is that the numbers of 'foreign' Africans on white farms have declined considerably since 1960. It is not at all clear, however, whether these figures are accurate, and whether they conceal 'illegal' or even legal 'seasonal' foreign labour on such farms, particularly in 'border' areas.[22]

Instead the state during the 1960s was involved in somewhat different forms of 'redistribution', accompanied by positive 'repulsion'. The latter involved the massive removals of surplus population from white farms and so-called 'black spots' and its re-siting in the 'reserves'. This was accompanied by the transformation of the 'reserves' into 'Bantustans', involving politically a change in the structures of government, devolving more authority on to Bantustan governments for the administration of this surplus population and labour force and involving economically different strategies (including encouragement of full-time farming, some encouragement of minor industry, etc.). At the same time there was more active pursuit of 'endorsement out' of any excessive surplus population from the towns. This provided a basis on which (i) the reserve army of labour for agriculture could be drawn from the Bantustans rather than from 'foreign' sources; (ii) through the labour bureaus, increasingly established in the Bantustans, workers could be channelled on yearly contracts into the towns as necessary, and channelled to the particular sectors that required them.

Conclusion: present situation and future trends

The contradictions generated by the acceleration of accumulation in the 1960s began to become manifest in the 1970s. In the first place inflation began to assume alarming proportions and was probably the single most important factor leading to the mass Durban strikes of 1973, the continued militancy of the black urban working class, and the wave of mine strikes from 1972. The result of this upsurge of struggle was substantial immediate wage gains, particularly marked in the mines. These, however, were soon undermined by continued inflation, nor did they eat more than marginally into the huge increase in mining profits which resulted from the gold price increase. Secondly, the boom in manufacturing production ran

into balance of payments constraints which, in the context of the current
world capitalist recession, have forced the South African economy into
recession during the 1970s. Although the temporary world upturn, and

TABLE 7.3:   AFRICAN 'RESIDUAL LABOUR' IN SOUTH AFRICA

	Minimum Number	Maximum Number	Minimum %	Maximum %
1946	265,000	1,258,000	9	35
1951	272,000	1,330,000	9	34
1960	850,000	1,769,000	21	38
1970	1,092,000	1,988,000	20	34

Source: J. Knight, *Labour Supply in the South African Economy*, SALDRU
Working Paper No. 7 (Cape Town, 1977), p.27.

further gold price rises, led to a recovery of the economy during 1978-80, it
is now once again turning downwards. A pattern of small upturns
followed by deeper downturns is likely to continue, indicating that South
African capitalism will not be able to overcome its contradictions,
particularly now that the post-war boom period for world capitalism has
decisively ended. Thus the surplus population generated during the
preceding period, estimated at some 1½ to 2 million in 1976, is being
enlarged. This has occurred simultaneously with the victory of
FRELIMO and the MPLA in Mozambique and Angola, the achievement
of independence in Zimbabwe, the sharpening of the independence
struggle in Namibia, and the temporary withdrawal of Malawian labour
from South Africa.

For the overall migrant labour system there have been two significant
changes associated with these developments. In the first place, the mining
industry after 1974 pursued a deliberate policy of reduction in the 'foreign'
labour force (and, more specifically, that from Mozambique and Malawi)
to less than 25 per cent by 1977. Correspondingly, both the 'High Commission Territories' and the South African (especially Transkeian)
contributions have increased. This has been associated with a return to
short-term contracts of six months, and to an average period of service (on
recent estimates) of some twelve months.

In the second place the so-called 'independence' of the Transkei and
Bophutatswana alters the status of those Africans who have been compelled to become 'citizens' of such territories. For those already subjected
to the migrant/contract system of such areas (in its 1950s and 1960s
forms), this represents a transition from *de facto* to *de jure* 'foreignness'

while working in South Africa. At the same time it makes the first major inroad into the status of those who could formerly qualify for permanent residence in South African cities, for it appears that all those whose ancestry can be traced to a particular 'Bantustan' are being reclassified as 'foreign'. Moreover, in the case of the Transkei an inter-state agreement governing labour has been signed, thus according to the Transkei government an integral role in administering the migrant labour system on the basis of the precedent originally established by the Mozambique Convention.

What are the implications, actual and potential, of these changes, in particular for strategies aimed at abolishing the migrant labour system? It has been argued here that the migrant labour system in its various forms must be understood in the context of capital accumulation in the region. This capital accumulation has been characterised by the generation of a surplus population with has continually been relatively large. Even in the periods of most rapid accumulation it has not been totally absorbed/re-absorbed into production. On the other hand, in the periods of recession, South African capitalism has continued to call on internal and foreign migrant labour. These characteristics of the surplus population (which are equivalent to the fact that the black proletariat has always been a relatively 'new' and 'undisciplined'/militant proletariat in terms of the restructuring of the forces of production) have had contradictory effects. On the one hand, it has been associated with the existence of a cheap labour system,

TABLE 7.5: ECONOMICALLY ACTIVE FOREIGN AFRICANS PER SECTOR OF EMPLOYMENT, 1970

	men	%	women	%
Agriculture	39,580	8.9	5,140	10.9
Mining	352,480	79.6	40	0.1
Manufacturing	11,020	2.5	660	1.4
Electrical	900	0.2	0	0
Construction	6,080	1.4	20	0.1
Commerce	5,120	1.2	340	0.7
Transport	3,420	0.8	0	0
Finance	660	0.1	40	0.1
Services	11,660	2.6	9,620	20.4
Not economically active/ unemployed	12,020	2.7	31,200	66.3

Source: D. Clarke, *Foreign African Labour Supply in South Africa, 1960-77,* Development Studies Research Group, University of Natal, (1977), p.42.

TABLE 7.4: NUMBER OF FOREIGN-BORN AFRICANS IN SOUTH AFRICA BY COUNTRY OF ORIGIN (AND BY EMPLOYMENT IN MINING AND NON-MINING SECTORS)

	Total foreign African population in South Africa					
	1911	1921	1936	1946	1951	1960
Lesotho		111,773	163,838	199,327	219,065	196,996
Botswana		11,959	4,048	38,559	51,017	59,286
Swaziland		29,177	31,092	33,738	42,914	38,892
HCTS		152,909	198,978	271,624	312,996	295,174
SW Africa		2,926	1,879	4,990	4,129	2,499
N Rhodesia		6,511	13,871	45,549	46,241	33,696
S Rhodesia		—	—	—	—	—
Malawi		2,122	17,657	61,005	63,655	62,623
Mozambique		110,245	98,031	141,417	161,240	160,945
Angola		942	28	6,716	6,322	10,748
Tanzania		—	118	2,937	7,127	1,117
Others		4,164	3,215	22,569	2,816	5,323
Total	229,000	279,819	333,777	556,807	604,526	542,125
Foreign Africans employed on mines:						
Lesotho		6,646	45,982	38,200	35,700	51,400
Botswana		853	7,155	7,000	9,100	16,000
Swaziland		3,602	7,027	5,500	5,600	5,600
HCTS		11,101	60,164	50,700	50,400	73,000
Mozambique		89,767	88,499	96,300	106,500	95,500
Tropical		2,888	3,402	32,400	41,200	82,800
Total	106,326	103,756	152,065	179,400	198,100	251,300
Foreign Africans not on mines:						
Lesotho		105,127	117,856	161,127	183,365	145,595
Botswana		11,103	—	31,559	41,917	43,285
Swaziland		25,575	24,065	28,238	37,314	33,292
SW Africa		2,926	1,879	4,990	4,129	2,499
N Rhodesia		6,511	13,871	45,549	46,241	33,696
S Rhodesia		—	—	—	—	—
Mozambique		20,478	9,532	45,117	54,740	65,445
Tropical		176	14,941	39,837	37,370	4,992
Others		4,164	2,675	20,990	2,816	5,323
Totals	122,674	176,060	184,819	377,407	407,892	334,127

Source: 'Capital Restructuring and the South African state'

Total foreign African working population in South Africa						
1969	1970	1971	1972	1973	1976	1977
169,682	147,400	118,856	131,748	148,850	152,188	—
35,642	47,160	31,891	31,960	36,500	37,016	—
11,346	24,260	11,251	10,109	10,000	16,390	—
—	—	—	—	—	—	—
—	1,420	—	—	—	—	—
—	—	—	—	—	—	—
5,751	11,640	5,245	6,200	3,250	8,895	—
69,417	106,640	109,185	131,291	139,700	39,308	—
133,021	144,900	124,866	121,709	127,200	150,738	—
270	3,440	29	154	42	623	—
—	180	—	—	—	—	—
8,229	1,980	8,952	7,978	10,000	914	—
433,358	589,020	410,005	441,149	475,542	406,072	290,000 (estimate)
65,000	71,100	68,700	78,500	87,200	85,000	—
14,800	16,300	16,000	17,500	16,800	26,000	—
25,000	5,400	4,800	4,300	4,500	13,000	—
—	—	—	—	—	—	—
99,800	113,300	102,400	97,700	99,400	79,000	
69,900	98,200	107,800	129,200	128,000	20,800	
274,500	304,300	299,700	327,200	335,900	223,800	200,000 (estimate)
104,682	76,300	49,886	53,279	62,000	67,188	—
20,842	30,860	15,891	14,460	19,000	11,016	—
6,346	18,860	6,451	5,809	5,000	3,390	—
—	—	—	—	—	—	—
—	—	—	—	—	—	—
33,221	31,600	22,466	24,009	28,000	71,737	—
13,767	8,440	15,531	16,423	25,000	18,508	—
—	—	—	—	—	—	—
—	—	—	—	—	—	—

and with penal forms of state policy (Masters and Servants Acts, pass laws, compounds, segregated townships, repatriation provisions, resettlements, etc.) which have inhibited worker organisation, and also inhibited political and economic 'reformism'. On the other hand, the South African proletariat has been subjected to the ongoing daily experience of widespread, intimate, and open connection between economic exploitation and political coercion and regulation. Through its history of struggle, therefore — from the post-World War I period, through the upsurges of the 1940s and 1950s, to the new and unprecedentedly large workers' movement of the present period — it has tended to reject any rigid separation between 'trade union' and political struggle. Because of the particular conditions of the 1890s, capital accumulation accelerated on the basis of the migrant labour system. The tendency since that point has been towards a periodic restructuring of this system, which at each point has brought a greater state involvement, although in changing forms. Apart from the penal aspects of this, it has meant the constant creation and re-creation of new divisions in the working class. Not only have white workers become incorporated as allies of the ruling class, but the remainder of the working class has been fragmented: Coloured-Indian-African; permanent-contract; 'South African'-'foreign'; as well as the 'ethnic' tribal divisions which are created. This is not an 'ideological' phenomenon, but is reflected in political and industrial rights under law, positions in the labour process, conditions of housing, education, welfare benefits, etc. Where the migrant labour system. The tendency since that time has been towards a and out of the social movement of workers between domestic production and wage-labour under limited compulsions, it has become increasingly a system regulated by the state and by inter-state agreements limited by the pace and forms of accumulation.

The future of the migrant labour system is therefore bound up with the future course of capital accumulation as a process of class struggle. The very nature of the system has, however, meant that this class struggle has become to some extent mediated in terms of negotiation-diplomacy between supplier states and the 'demanding-repelling' South African state. A strategy in the interests of the workers must thus be one which combats the consequences of the migrant labour system: division among workers, penal and other inhibitions on worker action. What this will mean for the government or worker organisations of different supplier countries cannot be answered abstractly, but only in terms of the particular orientation and role of workers from such countries within the South African accumulation process, and their ability to detach themselves from it. Does the actual or potential level of capital-intensification in the South African economy mean that accumulation can continue on the basis of a more confined geographical hinterland, excluding, for example, Mozambique or Malawi? Or, on the other side, is in possible for such governments to withdraw their workers and re-absorb them through economic development programmes? Does the elaboration of the 'Bantustan' workers as 'foreigners' strategy imply any changing orientation of South African capital to the role and status of 'High Commission Territories' workers? What, on the other side, can supplier countries do to combat the attempt to divide the working class of South Africa? Here it would seem that unilateral attempts to institute development-re-absorption strategies, i.e. on a national basis, can only encourage the South African state in its activities of fostering 'national' divisions among workers.[23]

Finally, the historical evidence on the nature of the migrant labour system seems to suggest not only that it rose with the rise of capitalism in South Africa, but that it has a fate intertwined with that of capitalism. From the period when the tendency was 'attraction' to the present tendency towards 'repulsion', the fate and lives of the African working people of South Africa have been subjected to a movement between home and work dependent on the dynamic of accumulation, rather than the satisfaction of their needs. The abolition of the migrant labour system in southern Africa as a whole would have to involve co-ordinated economic planning in the region, planning conducted on an inter-state basis, guided not by the search for profit but by the satisfaction of needs: planning able to provide work where workers wanted to live, and homes where workers wanted to work. This is what the black workers of southern Africa are struggling for, and what they must ultimately achieve.

TABLE 7.6: RECRUITMENT TO THE SOUTH AFRICAN MINE LABOUR FORCE BY COUNTRY OF ORIGIN

	South Africa %	High Commission Territories (Lesotho, Botswana, Swaziland) %	Foreign (PEA & Tropicals) %
1904	23.6	4.1	72.3
1905	14.6	3.4	82.0
1908	39.2	4.9	55.9
1909	39.0	4.0	57.0
1912	42.8	7.3	49.9
1913	37.8	8.7	53.5
1915	47.2	10.2	42.6
1918	37.7	10.3	52.0
1920	34.3	9.8	55.9
1922	43.2	12.4	44.4
1927	39.3	10.4	50.3
1929	39.0	13.6	47.4
1931	49.8	17.3	32.9
1932	56.5	18.3	25.2
1936	52.2	19.0	28.8
1939	48.0	20.0	32.0
1942	69.0	Recruiting stopped in	31.0
1943	65.8	the protectorate at	34.2
1944	63.7	the request of the	36.3
1945	65.7	British High Commissioner	34.3
1946	41.3	16.6	42.1
1951	35.3	16.3	48.4
1956	34.7	16.7	48.6
1961	36.5	17.5	44.0
1963	39.1	19.5	40.4
1964	37.9	20.7	41.4
1966	34.1	22.7	43.2
1969	31.2	22.4	46.4
1970	24.2	23.0	52.8
1971	22.4	22.9	54.7
1972	21.1	24.1	54.8
1973	20.5	25.5	54.0
1974	24.8	27.0	48.2
1975	23.4	29.8	36.8
1976	43.2	31.6	25.2

Source: 'Capital Restructuring and the South African State: the case of foreign labour', unpublished mimeo, Sociology Department, University of Warwick, August 1977. Similar tables may be found in van der Horst *Native Labour in South Africa*, pp. 216-7 for 1904-39, and Wilson, *International Migration in South Africa*, for 1946-75.

8

COOLIES, PEASANTS, AND PROLETARIANS: THE ORIGINS OF CHINESE INDENTURED LABOUR IN SOUTH AFRICA, 1904-1907

PETER RICHARDSON

IN the aftermath of the South African war of 1899-1902 an acute labour shortage in the gold mining industry led directly to the importation of indentured Chinese labourers for unskilled work on the Transvaal gold fields.[1] This importation began in June 1904 and continued until January 1907, during which time approximately 63,000 Chinese were brought over to the Transvaal on three-year contracts.[2] The use of indentured labour to supplement and replace African long and medium-term contract labour in the gold mines has attracted considerable and varying attention from historians.[3] Nevertheless, emphasis has to a very large extent been centred on the origin of the labour shortage in the Transvaal, the effect of Chinese importation on black and white labour in the Witwatersrand mines, and the political consequences of importation for Milner's policy of anglicanisation in the new colony.[4] Little or nothing is known of the background to this migration, or the methods by which recruits were secured. This is a surprising omission for it has an obviously limiting effect on our appreciation of the importance of this short-lived but notorious experiment. The paper which follows is an attempt to redress this balance by an examination of the context and background of Chinese migration to South Africa between 1904 and 1907, and to illustrate a broader significance for it than has been revealed by a concentration on its purely South African aspects. In short, this paper attempts to show that factors making possible a widespread mobilisation of Chinese labour in these years were in marked contrast to those by which many Africans were forced on to the mining labour market of Southern and Central Africa.[5]

II

Chinese indentured migration to the South African mines was, as the discussion below reveals, largely northern in character. In its predominance of northern migrants, Chinese movement to the Witwatersrand was very different from that of earlier migrations of Chinese across the Indian ocean to South Africa. The small number of southern Chinese settlers who came, mainly between 1870 and 1900, to the Cape, Natal, and the Transvaal, were emigrants from Kuangtung, Fukhien, and Hainan Island. Alternatively they were migrants from Chinese communities in Malaysia, particularly the Straits Settlements.[6] Furthermore, the migration of 1904-7 was temporary, the maximum period of settlement permitted being five years, with an initial contract of three years. By contrast, Chinese migration in the last thirty years of the nineteenth century was more often than not permanent. Nevertheless, the northern migration was substantially larger than its southern counterpart. As late as 1920-1, there were only 5,000 Chinese — all southerners — in the Union of South Africa.[7] In 1904, immediately before the arrival of the mine workers, there were a mere 981 Chinese in the Transvaal colony, virtually all of them in Johannesburg.[8] Between 1904 and 1907 this number was eclipsed by the influx of indentured workers. In the six years between 1904 and 1910 in which the Chinese formed a significant proportion of the mine labour force, 63,695 were imported into the country, of whom 62,006 came from northern embarkation ports. Only 1,689 came from south-east China, the traditional emigrant recruiting grounds.[9]

In its northern character, Chinese migration to the South African mines foreshadowed trends in the population pattern of twentieth-century China, rather than continuing those of the nineteenth century. Thus, the French and British armies in the First World War were able to make use of much of the recruiting machinery established by the Transvaal Chamber of Mines in north China, and the British even contemplated bringing the South Africans' general manager in China, J.R. Brazier, out of retirement to conduct the operation.[10] Moreover, Chinese migration to South Africa took place in the context of one of the most significant interregional migrations of the Chinese people in the twentieth century, the colonisation of Manchuria. Although Manchuria was not divided into provincial boundaries until 1907, from 1860 there had been a partial lifting of the ban on Chinese colonisation in certain areas. This was largely the result of the Russian occupation of the Trans-Amur and the Trans-Ussuri regions after 1860. The colonisation of Manchuria was even more energetically pursued after the Sino-Japanese war of 1894-5 and the Russo-Japanese War of 1904-5, and before 1907 all legal bans to Chinese colonisation in the area had been lifted.[11] The link between Chinese migration to South Africa and the colonisation of Manchuria was more than a purely temporal one. The emigrants to both these areas came chiefly from Shantung, Chihli (Hopei), and Honan, and the Peking-Mukden railway and the ports of Chefoo, Weihaiwei, Tsingtao, Tientsin, and Chinwangtao were common transport approaches to these new areas. (See Maps 1 and 2). Interestingly, in this earlier phase both movements were also temporary, that to Manchuria being mainly seasonal, that to South Africa determined by the politico-economic requirements of the gold mining industry of the Transvaal.

III

Discussion of the context and background of Chinese indentured migration to South Africa has been, in the past, bedevilled by lack of basic information on the geographic and socio-economic origins of the migrants. Any meaningful discussion of this topic has to establish whence these men came, and seek to explain the significance of the pattern which is produced. The problem is essentially one of source material. Most accounts of Chinese migration to South Africa, whether in English or Chinese are noticeably brief and are more concerned to describe the phenomenon of migration than to explain it. Nor is this unique to South Africa. In many instances of Chinese overseas indentured migration this is the case: contemporary observers and historians concentrate on the more sensational aspects of the so-called 'coolie trade' rather than seeking to explain its operation or its success from the employers' point of view.[12] Although contemporary observers of the South African case vary little from this established pattern, historians are more fortunate in having a considerable volume of archival evidence which can offer some broad answers to these important questions. In essence this material consists of a very large number of manuscript copies of the contracts which the labourers signed prior to embarkation.[13] Much of the information in this paper is based, in the first instance, on an analysis of these contracts and is an attempt to relate these findings to an analysis of why it was possible for the Transvaal gold mining industry to tap such an extensive labour market. However, the paucity of readily available local information makes these conclusions necessarily tentative and speculative.

The contracts in the archives owe their existence to stipulations in the

Anglo-Chinese Labour Convention of May 1904, and instructions issued under the Transvaal Labour Importation Ordinance of February 1904, that all emigrants had to sign a contract of service in the presence of a British Consul or his appointed delegate, in this case the Transvaal Emigration Agent, and a Chinese Government Inspector.[14] They are a record of the financial and legal obligations undertaken by the Chinese during their stay in South Africa, and a list of the recompense which could be expected for incurring such obligations. The contract lists for every man engaged his name in English and Chinese, his contract number, age, and province, prefecture (*fu*), district (*hsien*), and village of origin.[15] It also records his degree of indebtedness to the mining companies either in the form of advances on wages or monthly allotments against wages payable in China. Finally it contains the labourer's signature or mark. Of the thirty-four shipments made to South Africa from China, contracts for twenty-one remain, dated October 1904 to November 1906. For the early shipments documentation is far less complete, but some information can be pieced together from other sources.[16] The licenced passenger capacity of these emigrant steamers was between 1,500 and 2,500.[17]

Analysis of these contracts and related information reveals much about the geographical origins of Chinese labourers on the Witwatersrand. A provincial breakdown of shipments nine to thirty-four, for example, reveals that the overwhelming majority of men came from Chihli and Shantung provinces, the former being predominant. The case of the SS *Sikh* may be cited as an example. The ship left Chinwangtao in Chihli on 8 January 1905. 2,038 men were originally contracted for employment on four different mines. Of these 1,798 eventually sailed, 240 men deserting prior to embarkation or failing the final medical examination. Of the 2,038 identifiable contractees, no less than 64.7 per cent came from Chihli and 28.7 per cent from Shantung. Of the remaining 6.6 per cent, the largest number came from Shengching (Manchuria) and Honan provinces.[18] This pattern is repeated in more or less equal proportions for every northern shipment throughout the recruiting period under review, November 1904 to November 1906, although the balance between shipments of Chihli and Shantung men was to some extent altered, depending on whether or not the ship called at Chefoo *en route* for Durban. A stop at Chefoo would significantly raise the proportion of Shantung men in a shipment as the port, unlike Chinwangtao, served an almost exclusively Shantung-based labour market. Of the 12,641 men shipped from Chefoo between July 1904 and July 1905, for example, 93.2 per cent came from Shantung province.[19] Nevertheless, despite these changes in detail, the overall picture of recruitment is clear: Shantung and Chihli were the most important provinces in providing recruits to the South African mines, Chihli predominating in a rough ratio of 2.25:1. Of the other provinces which provided emigrants from north China, northern Kiangsu, northern Honan, western Shansi, and southern Shengching were the only areas to do so in significant numbers (see Map 1).

Such a broad definition is helpful in locating the centre of Chinese migration to South Africa but it provides very little help in determining why emigrants went from those areas. A more detailed breakdown does, however, provide some clues. A random selection of contracts from every third shipment from the north reveals a clear predominance of certain prefectures in providing recruits for the mines. A glance at Map 1 will indicate the importance of communications networks in producing this pattern. In Chihli, the most important prefectures (*fu*) and independent departments (*chihli-chou*) for recruiting throughout the two-and-a-half years of the experiment ranged from Yung-ping *fu* and Tsun-hua *chou* in the northeast to Chi *chou* in the south. The heaviest concentrations of emigrants within this broad belt were found in Shun-t'ien *fu*, (Peking), Pao-ting *fu*, and Ho-chien *fu*. In Shantung, Chi-nan *fu*, Wu-ting *fu*, Ts'ao-chou *fu*, and Yen-chou *fu* remained consistently large suppliers of labour. On 10 January 1905, for example, the SS *Sealda* left Chinwangtao for Durban with 2,040 men on board divided into three separate contract groups numbered 40-42. Contract number 40 of 1,905 provided about one-quarter of this, the sixteenth shipment. Chihli men accounted for 62.4 per cent of this contract, Shantung men for about 30.5 per cent. Of the men from Chihli, Shun-t'ien *fu*, T'ien-chin *fu*, Ho-chien *fu*, and Yung-p'ing *fu* provided 26.6, 21.8, 15.3, and 13.5 per cent respectively of all men from the province. Chi-nan *fu* and Wu-ting *fu* provided 43.7 and 24.1 per cent of all men from Shantung province on the same contract.[20] Between July 1904 and July 1905 recruits from Ch'ing-chou *fu* and Chi-nan *fu* provided 18.8 per cent and 15.4 per cent of all recruits going from Shantung to South Africa through Chefoo.[21] Thus it can be seen that the richest recruiting grounds were found in the low plain areas around the metropolitan districts of Chihli, along the line of the Grand Canal, in western Shantung and southern Chihli, in the Yellow River delta, and along the line of the Peking-Mukden railway as far as Ch'inchou-*fu* in Shenching province (see Map 2).

A *fu* or prefecturial analysis brings us closer to the heart of the problem. Yet difficulties still remain, for the size of a *fu* district is such as to leave considerable scope for speculation as to the predominant form of livelihood

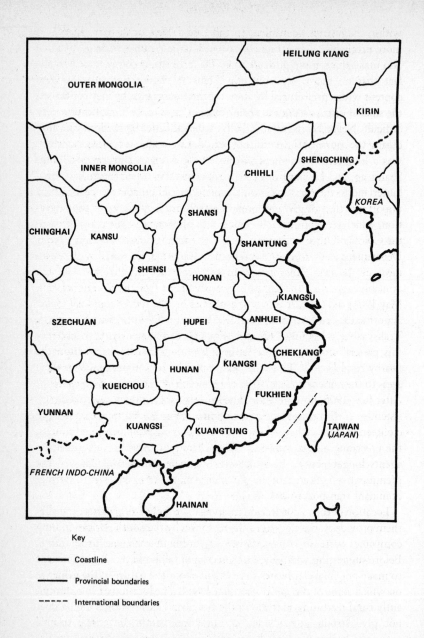

Key

―――――― Coastline

―――――― Provincial boundaries

- - - - - International boundaries

Map 1   China in 1904: main administrative divisions

within the districts identified. In this case a *hsien,* or district, analysis is more profitable. Unfortunately the very large number of *hsien* involved also make this a more difficult task. The problem is compounded by the fact that on many occasions the Transvaal Emigration Agents were content with a prefecturial location for their imigrants, or they romanised the smaller district names in such a manner as to make identification very difficult. Nevertheless certain trends can be identified by random sampling during the course of the recruiting period. Essentially, it appears that there was a long-term movement within all the main prefectures of Chihli, Shantung, and Honan from the urban centres and their immediate rural hinterland to the rural *hsiens* on the prefecturial boundaries. This had the important effect of giving a predominantly rural character to the migration, which is of considerable explanatory importance. Correspondence in the Colonial Office in London, and in the archives of the Foreign Labour Department in Pretoria, indicates quite clearly that the speed with which most of the first emigrants were recruited dictated that most of the available labour for the first southern shipment (per the SS *Tweeddale* in May 1904) and the first two northern ones in July 1904, would have been almost exclusively urban in origin.[22] The high level of demand from the Transvaal between July 1904 and May 1905 to a large extent ensured that this pattern would continue, although recruits quickly came from the nearby rural *hsiens.*[23] This tend was reinforced by the proximity of these areas to the railway and canals or old established communication routes.[24] After June 1905, however, the time lag between shipments increased consistently — 47 per cent of all emigrants being landed in the following eighteen months, whereas 53 per cent of all emigrants had been found in the preceding eleven months.[25] This change in pace allowed recruiting agents longer periods in which to find their labour and removed the premium from the areas of the provincial labour markets closest to the predominant transport routes.[26]

Location of the major recruiting areas and the changing patterns within them provides some clues as to the reasons why the South African mining companies were so conspicuously successful in their recruiting drive. Before suggesting what these reasons might be, however, it is important to make one final clarificatory statement about the nature of the evidence on which some of the speculations are based. The location of a predominantly rural recruiting pattern on the flat plain lands of north China does not give strong grounds for accurate speculation as to the specific economic background of the migrants. The contracts did not require notation of a labourer's social class or occupation in any form whatever.

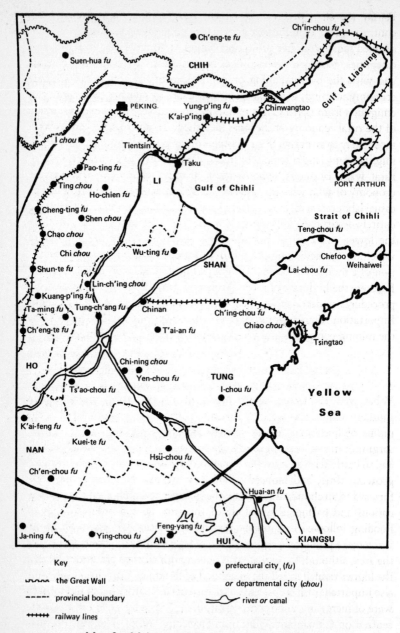

Map 2   Main recruiting areas: North China

Rarely are clues other than straight geographical ones given by the contracts. This is unfortunate for it does not give adequate ground for detailed socio-economic projection; rather, it confines diagnosis to broad categories, based on probabilities. Nevertheless, working on this basis, and with the overwhelming preponderance of peasants in the Chinese economy in mind, it would seem reasonable to say that the majority of emigrants from north China to South Africa came from the lowest strata of the rural economy of the areas identified. That is to say, recruits were most likely to be drawn from members of the poor peasant families (which might occupy land as tenants or freeholders but on a very small scale), from rural wage labourers, who worked directly at times in the farming economy or who were involved in some form of service to it, from urban casual labourers with close rural links of one kind or another, and from the entirely destitute.[27] This supposition that the emigrants were drawn from the lower strata of rural communities is reinforced by the importance which the Chinese Emigration Bureau attached to the proper administration of a monthly allotment system and to its widest possible extension. Further, the high rate of medical rejects during the preliminary selection procedures undertaken at Tienstsin by the Chamber of Mines Labour Importation Agency would suggest both a rigorous standard imposed by the mining companies and a background of considerable distress.[28]

IV

What were the factors which produced this pattern of migration? In southern Chihli and western Shantung agriculture predominated as the means of livelihood. In the former, farmers producing millet, wheat, sorghum, maize, beans, groundnuts, cotton, hemp, fruit, and vegetables had to battle with an intensely dry and cold winter season which restricted growing time, and induced severe dust storms. Nor could they look forward to an abundant rainfall in the summer to supplement these depredations and balance the ecology of the area: all too often drought or flooding followed hard on the unyeilding winter.[29] Western Shantung was a more productive agricultural region, cereals being the main crop of the area, although the climate was only marginally less precarious, in that the higher rainfall raised the likelihood of flooding. Cotton and silk were also important cash crops, and at the turn of the century hemp and tobacco were of increasing importance. Commerce and industry in the area were centred on Chinan and Wuting in Shantung and on Tientsin, Paoting, and Peking in Chihli. Both provinces had rich coal deposits in their northern sectors. Transportation was also an important source of income for many because the Grand Canal passed through the two provinces north as far as Tientsin.

This apparent variety of agricultural pursuit, built as it was upon an unstable ecology, meant that poverty was the omnipresent backdrop against which the South African recruiting companies worked. In 1879 Constance Gordon-Cumming described the province of Chihli as follows:

. . . . it is a wide expanse of grey dust, and the villages are all built of mud. They are all exactly alike, and are all hideous; only some have dark tiled roofs, and the eye rests with thankful relief where occasional gourds or pumpkins form a blessed trail of green in the poor little gardens . . . . In every direction I noticed toilsome methods of irrigation by hand, and only where those are diligently practised has the thirsty earth struggled into greenness.[30]

In 1884 Mark Bell gave a similar picture for Shantung and Chihli:

The villages passed generally varied in area from 30,000 to 10,000 square yards, and consisted of one main street, generally suited for one line of traffic only . . . . The huts are low, one storied, and of mud bricks. The exterior is plastered with mud and chopped straw which is renewed yearly. Roofs are rare that are tiled. There are very few buildings of burnt brick in them (*sic*).[31]

The insufficiency of cash income for the rural population was everywhere apparent, and led the Chinese authorities in the two northern provinces to encourage emigration to South Africa and allow widespread recruiting at a later date. The Commissioner for Weihaiwei, a British leased territory in Shantung, reported to the Colonial Office in 1904 that:

[the] Authorities are anxious for a large scale emigration, because despite a good harvest, starvation looms for large numbers who have been deprived of an additional source of sustenance in Manchuria.[32]

The endemic poverty which these writers describe as the condition of the overwhelming majority of the population, and its location, broadly speaking, in the vast Yellow River delta region from which the majority of the emigrants to South Africa came, point, by implication at least, to flooding and droughts as a major factor in long-term economic decline. By extension, this exposure to natural disaster may be seen as a major causal factor inducing internal and overseas migration. As Yeo Shen-yu has pointed out, in accordance with popular belief, Chihli and Shantung (together with northern Honan) are among the most severely affected flood provinces in all China.[33] Throughout the Ch'ing dynasty Chihli and Shantung consistently recorded a greater propensity to flooding than all other provinces, largely due to the vicissitudes of the Yellow River. Only Hupei province on the Yangtse recorded a greater number of major inundations in the nineteenth century than the provinces on the lower reaches of the Yellow River; the figures being 68 for Hupei, 42 for Chihli, and 31 for Shantung. A similarly grim chronology of droughts is recorded for these provinces: Chihli recorded 41 major droughts in the nineteenth century, as against 38 in Hupei and 34 in Shantung. Nor were the South African migrants taken from an area which had only an historic appreciation of these calamities and their attendant ravages of disease. The effects of the dreadful famines of 1876-79 were evident in Shantung, Chihli, and Shansi as late as the turn of the century. In the three years of this disaster, Wu Wen-hui estimated that nine-and-a-half million people died in Kiangsu, Shantung, Chihli, Shansi, Honan, Anhuei, and Hupei, not to mention the attendant effects on agricultural production in these areas.[34] This population reduction, which had the effect, particularly in Shansi, of making these provinces attractive resettlement areas, exposed these new immigrants to the ravages of an unstable ecology. The failure to control the inundations of the Yellow River or provide sufficient irrigation to overcome drought remained as constant factors in the precarious economic balance of north China, and even intensified at the end of the century. Muramatsu considers that migrations of hungry multitudes into Chihli and Shantung after the famines of 1897-99 in neighbouring provinces exposed these new residents of the delta to the danger of large scale flooding which occurred with disastrous results in August 1898, to be followed in 1899 and 1900 by abnormally dry weather.[35] In fact it appears that the narrowing of the river at Chinan, after the change of course in 1855, made inundations of the river an almost annual occurrence in the later nineteenth century and early twentieth century.[36]

This chronic instability had obvious side effects: rural impoverishment, interregional migration, and ultimately external migration as the pressure of population forced urban wages down. If opportunities for external migration were denied, or were not sufficient to cope with the effects of disaster or population pressure, rural decline was followed by rebellion as in the case of the Boxers. It is no accident that the most successful recruiting grounds for South Africa were exactly those areas which had experienced the greatest intensity of Boxer activity.[37] This connection between emigration and rebellion and banditry was made specifically by the Governor of Shantung in August 1904 in an interview with the secretary to the British Commissioner of Weihaiwei, when he stated that of late:

Some of the Manchurian emigrants have been accustomed to a form of free-lance brigandage (because of the closure of Manchuria during the Russo-Japanese war) which might be turned to effect in Shantung if no alternative outlet can be found. He had a particular desire for peace in the province particularly in the neighbour-hood of the German railway [from Tsingto to Chinan] to avoid the despatch of German troops to 'protect' the entire length of the line . . . . under the guise of Chinese provocation in the form of thieving.[38]

A similar causal connection between the conditions which give rise to banditry and emigration was made by the viceroys of *Liangkuang* in 1904 and *Liangkiang* in 1905 to South African agents.[39]

Yet endemic poverty and chronic ecological instability as causal factors in rebellion and migration have an even closer connection than at first sight may appear. If the alternatives to rural decline for many peasants were flight or rebellion, the number contemplating emigration after suppression of an uprising were significantly increased. The depredations of the Boxer suppression campaign in north China in 1900 are well enough known, but their effects on the propensity to migrate have not been sufficiently emphasised.[40] Widespread looting, loss of life, and com-mandeering of property forced many peasant families on the margins of subsistence below the line of survival. Between 1900 and 1903 the annual migrations from Chefoo into Manchuria were noticeably greater than the immediate pre-rebellion annual totals.[41] Military demobilisation after suppression is also known to have had an aggravating effect on rural dislocation. Many of the *elements déclassés* in the Boxers were made up of demobilised Chinese soldiers disbanded after the modernising of the pro-vincial armies of Honan, Shantung, and Chihli in 1898-99.[42] Echoes of this can be found in the South African migration when Chinese soldiers from the British-organised regiment of Weihaiwei made a substantial contri-bution to the policing of the Transvaal experiment.[43] Nor is the connection between banditry and emigration in this sense necessarily local-ised. The influx of so-called vagabonds from other provinces in the period 1897-99, and 1900-04 had a definitely irritant effect on the political and economic stability of Shantung, Chihli, and Honan.[44] Traces of this process of marginalisation of the peasantry through inter-provincial migration can be found in the South African case also, as recruits from the outlying provinces of Honan, Shansi, Kiangsu, and Shenching found their way to the receiving depots of Chefoo and Chinwangtao in small but persistent numbers.[45]

V

Such large population movements as the colonisation of Manchuria and the indentured migration to South Africa suggest a more fundamental imbalance in the rural economy of north China than can have been the result of natural disasters or rebellions alone, drastic as these were. The persistence of Manchurian emigration from the 1860s onwards, and its ever-increasing volume, indicated a continuing crisis which reached something of a peak in this area in the last years of the nineteenth, and the first years of the twentieth, century.[46] Three major trends can be identified, in addition to those mentioned above, which must have had a definite, if unquantifiable, effect on the volume and pattern of migration: first, an increasingly serious disequilibrium between population and land resources in north China. Second, long-term economic dislocation resulting from the opening up of many new sectors of the Chinese economy to the pressure of the international economy. Last, an increasing direct economic burden on the peasantry as a result of dynastic and social collapse.

   Problems of assessing Chinese population and land resources are notoriously difficult. Statistical information is often sparse as to the sheer size of the population at different times, let alone figures on the all-important relationship of this population to the available cultivable land. Nevertheless certain major features can be identified. As Ho Ping-ti points out, one of the most striking features in the historical changes associated with the geographical distribution of China's population has been the very rapid growth in the numbers inhabiting the low plain provinces of north China in the last hundred years or so.[47] This appears to be associated with a relatively late agricultural development in Chihli, Shantung, and Honan particularly. Historically, the agriculture of these areas has been associated with low yields and a lack of labour-intensive methods of cultivation. A belated revolution in land utilisation associated with the introduction of maize, sweet potatoes, and peanuts seem to have lain behind this population growth.[48] Yet by the end of the nineteenth century is seems that the rate of population growth was beginning to outstrip the capacity of these technical changes to support it. At the turn of the century Shantung was probably the most densely populated province in China with an average density of population in the region of 550 persons per square mile, and a rapidly expanding seasonal and permanent migration to Manchuria.[49] The overall density of population in Chihli was much less, but the concentrations of population in the southern parts of the province indicate that density in these parts was well in excess of the officially recorded figure of 294 persons to the square mile.[50] It was from this southern part that the majority of the South African migrants came. As from Shantung, regular migration on a semi-permanent basis to the northern regions from Chihli was a well-established fact by the beginning of the twentieth century.

This deteriorating situation was reflected in a declining proportion of cultivated land per head in the period under review. This was a general trend throughout the empire between the mid-eighteenth and the end of the nineteenth century, as Chinese population rose, reaching its 1850 peak again somewhere towards the end of the century.[51] Thus Lo Erh-gang estimates that average land available for cultivation throughout the empire decline from 3.86 *mou* (1 *mou* = 733½ square yards; 6.6 *mou* were the equivalent of one acre) per capita of registered land in 1750 to 1.86 *mou* per capita in 1833.[52] By 1875 in Wei-chou in Chihli, the average available was only 1.71 *mou* per capita.[53] A random sample of villages with populations of over 1,000 in Cheng-ting *fu* and Ting *chou* in Chihli in the third and fourth quarters of the nineteenth century reveals an average of 3.01 *mou* per capita, while smaller villages in the same area record a larger average of 9.6 *mou* per capita.[54] This latter situation needs some clarification. The average available for the empire, and considered suitable for maintenance (i.e. 3-4 *mou* per capita), hides significant regional differences in cropping patterns, land utilisation, and growing season. Thus the productive capacity and suitability of 3 *mou* per capita in south China could be very different from that in the north. In fact Lo estimates that these differentials in north China required an average 12-15 *mou* per capita to sustain a livelihood against all vicissitudes.[55] It is a fairly safe conclusion that in the densely populated plain districts of western Shantung and southern Chihli at the turn of the century, the number of households on the margins of subsistence, and therefore particularly vulnerable to natural disasters, was high. Famine, disease, rebellion, and migration became the indices of this trend, and there were marked occurrences of all these between 1896 and 1905.

This general trend of impoverishment and ecological insecurity was intensified by the legal structure of land tenure and the growing tendency towards tenancy in north China at this time. George Jamieson's group investigation into land tenure conditions in north China revealed a growing stratification in the structure of land-holding in three large prefectures of Shantung, with an average tenancy rate of 30 per cent and an average large holding size of 67,000 *mou*. This was compared with an average large holdings size of 400,000 in northern Kiangsu and an 80 per cent tenancy rate.[56] Although the degree of peasant proprietorship in the low plain provinces of north China compares favourably with many southern provinces, it is still apparent that this extent of dependence, especially in view of the other factors mentioned above, could be extremely vexatious and could contribute materially to insecurity and a propensity to migrate. A Chihli district gazetteer at the end of the last century gives the following revealing example.

. . . . the land is not fertile . . . . a slightly bad year drives [tenants] from homes. But wealthy people possess farmsteads and farmland in abundance. In the two hundred villages [of this district; i.e. Hsi-ning] almost one-third of the cultivators are tenants on these farms. They depend on their landlords for their food and clothing. Unscrupulous landlords may collect excessive profits from them, causing them to toil bitterly for an entire year without getting enough to feed and cloth their wives and children.[57]

Generally speaking, consideration of the land question must take account of the fact that most figures are concerned only with registered land which might not represent the total amount of land available for cultivation in a given locality. This factor is off-set, on the other hand, by the fact that, normally inhabitants reported in a locality did not represent all who actually dwelt there. As Hsiao Jung-chuan comments:

It is clear . . . . that the economic situation of small landowners and tenant farmers was by no means attractive, even in normal times; when natural calamities occurred the life of the people in the localities affected became extremely miserable . . . . From the standpoint of the average villager it is difficult to say which of the two situations was the better. In one, the peasants were freer from possible oppression of landlords, but had the disadvantages of an unfriendly economic environment. In the other farmers had to depend upon landlords for their precarious livelihood. In either case the tiller of the soil had little assurance of a decent living for any considerable length of time.[58]

Against this background of endemic poverty and insecurity, many peasant families had developed alternative, or additional, sources of cash income.[59] These usually took the form of domestic handicraft production — in Shantung and Chihli cotton and silk spinning were especially common — porterage, inn-keeping, and the provision of transportation. The latter was a particularly important source of rural income in southwestern Shantung because of the volume of traffic using the Grand Canal. These activities must have had the effect, for many, of staving off indebtedness or even absolute starvation. Yet it is clear that at the end of the nineteenth century these alternatives were being rapidly eliminated by the influx of large quantities of western factory produced goods into the interior of north China. This problem became acute after the treaty of Shimoneseki of 1895 which permitted the establishment of Japanese (and subsequently other western manufactures) in the open ports. The rapid rise of match-wood importation and kerosene (paraffin) had a disruptive effect, but the real disaster for the Shantung and Chihli peasantry was in the introduction of western-produced cotton yarns. As a foreign eye-witness commented in 1901:

In some villages every family has one or more looms, and much of the work is done in underground cellars where the click of the shuttle is heard month in and month out from the middle of the first moon till the closing days of the twelfth. But now the looms are idle and the weaving cellars are falling into ruins. Multitudes who own no loom are able to spin cotton thread, and thus earn a bare support — a most important auxiliary protection against the wolf always near the Chinese door. But lately the phenomenal activity of the mills in Bombay and Japan, and even in Shanghai itself, has inundated the cotton districts of China with yarn so much more even, stronger and withal cheaper than the home-made kind, that the spinning-wheels no longer revolve, and the tiny rill of income for young, the old, the feeble and the helpless is permanently dried up.[60]

Yet the consequences of the intrusion of the international economy into the lives of the northern Chinese peasantry were not confined to cotton, petroleum, or wood by-products. Transport patterns were severely disrupted by the development of steam-dominated coasting traffic in the second half of the nineteenth century. This revolution in water-born transport caused severe damage to the boatmen of the Grand Canal. The completion of the Peking-Hankow railway through Chihli and the Chinan-Tsingtao railway in Shantung likewise threw many small hand carters and porters out of work, and only provided temporary and insufficient employment for unskilled construction labour.[61]

More fundamentally disruptive and economically damaging were the effects of the silver shortage caused by China's increasingly unfavourable balance of foreign trade.[62] The copper-silver exchange rate rose constantly and led to severe hardship for the local peasantry.[63] Hsiao King-Chuan relates an incident in the 1890s in a district city less than one hundred miles from Peking, when the silver-copper rate of exchange was arbitarily doubled by the local magistrate under the guise of the continuing rise in the cost of silver. A new incumbent raised the rate a further 100 per cent in six months, before opposition from the gentry and the populace became overt. When he raised the rate a further 50 per cent as a punishment for such temerity, the official was removed by order from Peking and the exchange rate lowered. The lowered rate was, however, still 100 per cent higher than the officially accepted exchange rate at the beginning of these incidents.[64]

Natural disaster, overpopulation, diminishing land holdings, and vulnerability to the international economy all came to a head and intensified in the 1890s and 1900s and had a direct influence on the Boxer Rebellion, the volume of migration, and the continued unrest in Shantung and Chihli, of which there were numerous reports after the Boxer suppression campaign.[65] Yet this tale of disasters was not yet complete, for, largely as a result of these developments and as an intensification of them, the Imperial regime of the Manchus began to collapse and disintegrate. Between 1894 and 1905 the territory of north China was invaded by foreign powers no less than three times. The Sino-Japanese war of 1894-95 and the Boxer settlement of 1901 affected Chihli and Shantung directly. Both provinces were subject to the ravages of invasion, domestic troop mobilisation, increased taxation, and the direct and indirect effects of huge indemnities. Thus, to the vexatious demands of the land-tax gatherers in these two provinces were added the burdens of frontier defence taxes in 1898 and forced loans for the payment of the Japanese indemnity and for the settlement in 1901 of the Boxer protocol.[66] It is little wonder, therefore, that in 1902 the Governor of Chihli reported that armed peasant gangs in excess of 150,000 men were forcibly resisting taxation demands in his province.[67] At this time also it seems that the burden of the Empire's ordinary taxes shifted unfavourably against the northern provinces, as the increasing inability of the Government to ensure loyalty in the southern provinces delayed tax receipts and thereby enhanced the importance of returns from the north.[68] All these tax payments were made against a declining exchange value for copper against the silver tael, the former being the peasant's normal medium of payment. Symbolic of this crumbling taxation and monetary system was the commutation of the annual tribute payment of rice from the southern provinces in 1900-01, which further undermined the precarious livelihood of the Grand Canal boatmen, porters, and lodging-house-keepers.[69] It may be that the existence of Manchurian emigration, encouraged by Imperial policy after 1860, provided the means of staving off a more formidable anti-dynastic and anti-foreign rebellion than actually occured in the first year of the Boxer uprising. The intensification of these disasters after 1900 meant the continuation of the emigration outlet was imperative for continued socio-economic stability in north China.

VI

It remains to explain how these pressures were actually translated into a large-scale South African migration between 1904 and 1907. The general point of all that has been said is that the insecurity of incomes was widespread in southern Chihli and western Shantung in the ten years preceding the opening up of South African recruiting, and that the existence of cash supplements to these inadequate resources was an imperative for an increasing number of residents of these areas. The deepening crisis may be said to have been reflected in the changing pattern of search for these supplements in Manchuria. Initially at least, migration to the north-east frontier was seasonal and temporary. By the turn of the century, the worsening situation in the northern provinces of China proper and the evident benefits of a permanent settlement in Manchuria were increasing the residuum of seasonal migrants who stayed behind. The trend continued unbroken until the 1920s when the flow became a flood, and seasonal migration had become a full colonising movement.[70] It was during the build-up of this movement that the Russo-Japanese war broke out in Manchuria in 1904. This, the third war on Chinese territory in ten years, brought the annual flow of migrants through Chefoo, Tientsin, and Tsingtao, and along the Peking-Mukden railway, to a virtual halt. The 100,000 reported at Chefoo for the north-east in 1903 was, according to the Commissioner for Weihaiwei, effectively nil in 1904-05. It was at this stage that the Southern African recruiting really got under way. In July 1904 the first shipments left the Taku bar with 4,000 recruits for the Transvaal mines. As the Transvaal Emigration Agent at Chefoo, Wolfe, pointed out in July 1905:

. . . emigration from this province [i.e. Shantung] could hardly have commenced under more favourable auspices. As the area affected by the Russo-Japanese war embraces the whole country to which emigration naturally tended [i.e. Manchuria], an excellent opportunity has arisen for turning it into a new channel. For close on a year coolies have been steadily drafted from this province to South Africa. Local superstition, official opposition and the scepticism of the people have in great measure been overcome. While the war continues it is not unreasonable to suppose that the supply of coolies will be adequate. The great question is how will matters stand when the war is over. Already difficulties are experienced whenever the Japanese require coolies and send a ship to Chefoo to collect them. All able-bodied men are taken, they are paid good wages, there is no medical examination, no questions are asked and coolies are not tied by strict regulations. They are near their homes and can return when they please. Such is the prospect which at present attracts many coolies brought from up-country by the Transvaal recruiters to Manchuria. At the close of the war they will no doubt be encouraged to emigrate there and take up what occupation they prefer.[71]

In the event, Wolfe's fears about the labour supply for the South African mines were to prove well founded, but the full implication of the Manchurian threat was cut short by the Liberal Government's ban on the recognition of further importation licences after November 1906. By then the dependence of the South African Chinese labour supply on conditions prevailing in the regional labour market of north China had been clearly demonstrated.

9

THE POLITICAL ECONOMY OF LABOUR MIGRATION TO SETTLER SOCIETIES: AUSTRALASIA, SOUTHERN AFRICA, AND SOUTHERN SOUTH AMERICA BETWEEN 1890 AND 1914

DONALD DENOON

THIS paper is a segment of a more elaborate work,[1]seeking to define the distinctive features of settler societies in the southern hemisphere. In abbreviated form, the general arguments may prove less persuasive than they should be. I can only apologise for this defect, and throw myself on the reader's mercy for statements which require a more rounded presentation than is possible here. The problem is especially acute in section I which sketches my general position: it is less alarming in sections II (describing the availability of settlers for these societies) and III (reviewing some common explanations for the form and consequences of labour migration). Section IV attempts to relate labour migration to the whole political economy of the societies considered, the most promising avenue for a satisfactory explanation.

I

European exploration and expansion affected none of these societies until after 1500 AD, and at first it affected them very marginally indeed. Nomadic modes — hunting, gathering, fishing, herding — were more common in these temperate regions than in the tropics. Decaying empires provided European adventurers with their richest opportunities, and these were absent from the temperate south. Logically (as well as chronologically) Europeans settled in the temperate regions more slowly and less purposefully then they entered the tropics. Their first settlements — Buenos Aires, Santiago, Cape Town, Botany Bay — were strategic rather than productive in their nature. Production was much more difficult to organise here than in Peru or India, where existing societies could be compelled or enticed to carry on labouring under new management.

Many expedients were tried to guarantee a labour force for these wide lands whose inhabitants so often disappeared at the first whiff of disease, or rallied aggressively to defend their patrimony. Slavery, convicts, 'apprenticeship', and indenture were imperfect techniques, although they were applied ingeniously. As it happens, pastoral production proved to be the most profitable use for much of the conquered land, so long as high shipping costs prohibited the export of bulky foods, and the settler population presented only a narrow domestic market. Hides, wool, and jerked beef made up much of the exports until well into the nineteenth century.

In these circumstances feudal practices were unpromising, slavery beset by difficulties, and capitalist relations of production were rapidly consolidated. *Prazo* estates, or *encomiendas,* which served Iberian purposes very well among peasant producers, were abandoned early on the temperate grasslands. Land was treated mainly as a commodity, and labour, though not perhaps 'free', was more amenable to market pressures than was true in Brazil or the East Indies or Mozambique.

From 1814 to 1914 — the British century — all our societies were profoundly affected by changes radiating from Western Europe. Shipping capacity expanded, railway construction became common, transport costs tumbled, and western Europe could absorb unprecedented volumes of temperate products. If only through a shared expansion and export-led growth, these societies had something in common. The more intriguing thing, however, is that expansion was matched by parallels in social organisation. I suggest that there are sufficient common features to justify the identification of a settler capitalist mode of production.[2]

The common features of this mode may be listed (but not explained) as follows: (i) foundation as garrison outposts of European empires, where regular agrarian production was rare or absent; (ii) land available and labour scarce, leading to periods of reliance on extensive commercial pastoralism; (iii) the new society might include slaves, convicts, and other coerced workers, but it did not accommodate a peasantry; (iv) fully capitalist relations of production established early and thoroughly; (v) 'articulation' with other modes include the complete destruction of hunting, gathering, and herding societies; (vi) when the settler capitalist mode extended to include indigenous agricultural peoples in northern

187

Argentina, southern Chile, New Zealand, the Torres Strait, or eastern South Africa, only a brief period of peasant conditions occurred: within a generation or two, peasantries were broken down into proletarians; (vii) since capitalist relations of production were secure, imperial intervention was rarely necessary in the nineteenth century or after; (viii) however, the rulers of settler capitalist societies used their autonomy in a manner acceptable to foreign investors, and made no serious attempt at diversification or self reliance, at any rate until the 1930s; (ix) formal political life permitted the activity of all social classes committed to export-led and dependent development — but suppressed those social classes which did not share that comitment.

II

The transformation of the economies of these peripheral societies was melodramatic in the generation or two before 1914. Even statistics give some rough impression. Capital investment figures are quite striking, whatever they may mean.[3] Britain was not only the largest net lender of capital, but by a long way the largest investor outside Europe; so British investments overseas provide a rough index of gross overseas investments in this period. By 1913 some £3,780m had been invested, of which £2,000m went outside the empire, including £760m to Latin America. In Latin America, Argentina received £320m (about £40 per capita), and at one stage Uruguay had received £22.5m (about £30 per capita).[4] So much capital was rashly invested in the Platine republics that there was a serious financial crisis in London in 1890[5] but even after that panic investment continued to flow into Argentina and Uruguay from the turn of the century onwards. Chile had £64m by 1913 (£18 per capita).

Britain invested some £1,780m within the Empire, and again the distribution is interesting. The Australasian colonies received £415m (something like £75 per capita), South Africa £370m (£55 per capita), Canada and Newfoundland £515m, and India and Ceylon £380m (£1.2 per capita). A further point to note is that capital was invested and disinvested in great waves. There were periods in the 1890s when Australia, for example, was a net *lender* of capital; and in the aftermath of the Baring crisis the Platine republics received almost no British investment at all, except to service existing debts.[6] Not only did settler colonies receive disproportionate shares of British capital: they received it in erratic floods, so that debt servicing was sometimes an extremely painful matter.

The same disproportion may be discerned in terms of these societies' involvement in international trade. Platt's statistics for 1913 are illuminating here (Table 9.1) These figures[7] do not enable us to estimate equivalent levels of trading commitment for Chile or for Uruguay. Their commitment was less than that of Argentina, but not much less. There must be considerable doubt about the precision of these figures and the meaning to be attached to them but their rough magnitude indicates the nature of these economies by the end of the great burst of expanded production. Much of the investment was devoted to the construction of railways and harbours but it does not seem necessary to parade statistics on this subject. Suffice it to say that the commitment of these societies to international borrowing, to international trade, and to the provision of infrastructure, places them in a category quite different from that of most societies outside Europe in the generation prior to the Great War.

TABLE 9.1: INTERNATIONAL TRADE

	Population (million)	Imports total (£m)	per capita (£)	Exports total (£m)	per capita (£)	Imports and exports total (£m)	per capita (£)
New Zealand	1.1	21.0	19.3	21.8	20.0	42.8	39.3
Australia	4.6	78.2	16.8	79.1	17.0	157.3	33.8
UK	45.6	814.1	17.8	663.8	14.5	1477.9	32.3
Argentina	7.5	77.0	10.3	96.1	12.8	173.1	23.1
South Africa	6.7	39.8	6.0	63.3	9.4	103.1	15.4
Uruguay	1.1	—	—	c 12.0	c 11.0	—	—
Chile	3.3	—	—	c 12.0 +	c 4.0	—	—

Source: D.C.M. Platt, *Latin America and British Trade, 1806-1914* p 107.

As Brindley Thomas[8] suggests, there is commonly a correlation between flows of capital and the migration of workers. In these societies capital was often invested in utilities (especially railways and harbours) serving export production; and labour was required for building transport services as well as harvesting grain, herding beasts, or extracting ore. The correlation is not very reliable however, since some of the capital invested was speculative, and some unsoundly ventured.

We should now try to give some impression of the magnitude of population flows, into and out of our societies. *New Zealand's* white population built up from almost none in 1840, to over a million by 1911 but the massive number came before the 1880s.[9] In the depressed years from 1886 to 1891 more people left New Zealand than arrived, and the population increased because of the recovery of Maoris, and through the great improvement in maternal and child care, in part the result of regulation of breast feeding.[10] The state was more effective as Good Shepherd than as Recruiting Officer — which is only fair, since the economy was reliant on intensive animal husbandry. *The Australian colonies* also experienced huge immigration rates: until the depression of the 1890s, Australian born were usually outnumbered by immigrants. From 1891 immigration almost ceased until 1914, and the natural increase also showed alarming signs of slowing down.[11] The appearance of demographic stability is, however, something of an illusion. The Aboriginal population probably declined seriously in this era; there was a wholesale repatriation of Melanesian labourers from Queensland; and there was a great 'internal' flow of miners from the eastern colonies to the Western Australian gold fields.[12]

Argentine population statistics (like Australian) deal mainly with Europeans but the indigenous population was very small by 1890,[13] so statistics for Europeans probably account for the overwhelming bulk of the population during this period. During the twenty years from 1860 to 1880, Argentina's population may have increased by 111.3 per cent to 2,493,000 (but the estimate excludes the effects of clearing the pampas); during the next forty years the population increased at about 4 per cent to reach 8,510,000 by 1920.[14] At the ports some attempt was made to record migration statistics. The net gains fluctuated greatly: 220,000 in 1889, then a sharp reduction and a long recovery until 1912 when the net gain was 206,000.[15] Even these substantial numbers understate the real population movements. *Golondrinas* (seasonal migrants from Italy) are excluded, and so are immigrants who came overland. Over 100,000 Argentine residents in 1895 had been born elsewhere in South America[16] and there is no reason to suppose that 1895 was an unusual year. *Uruguay's* migrations are more difficult to plot, since many travellers did not use the port of Montevideo. A population of three quarters of a million in 1893 increased, however, to over a million soon after the turn of the century, and there was seasonal migration of some 50,000 to 60,000 in most years.[17]

By contrast, *Chile's total population* remained very stable numerically but the figures conceal two considerable human movements. From the 1860s onwards the state and the central valley landowners completed the conquest of the south, dispossessing the Indians, many of whom emigrated across the Andes to Argentinian Patagonia. The consolidation of *latifundia* in the conquered territory subsequently drove other Chileans into exile.[18] At the same time — the early 1880s — the conquest of the northern nitrate provinces from Peru and Bolivia made it necessary for a new working class to be assembled. In the event, the work force (50,000 by 1914) comprised substantial numbers of Bolivians, Peruvians, and Chinese, as well as former rural labourers from central Chile.[19] Although net immigration rarely exceeded 1,000 per annum between 1891 and 1906, internal movements were of a larger order. So were outward movements: 34,000 Chileans lived in Argentina in 1907, unknown numbers lived elsewhere, often attracted by working opportunities on railways.[20] Of the resident population of some 3,300,000, about 134,000 were foreign-born.

If we define *South Africa* in this era as all of British South Africa south of the Limpopo, including the Transvaal and the Orange Free State, it is still difficult to interpret numbers. Many African workers (both 'internal' and from Mozambique) were allegedly migrants: most white workers were allegedly permanent: the boundaries were rather arbitary; and a major war occurred at the turn of the century. It seems, though, that the white population doubled between 1891 and 1911;[21] the same may have been true of Africans; some 60,000 Chinese arrived and departed; and by 1911 hundreds of thousands of Africans had been initiated into a persistent pattern of contract labour.

These estimates make little sense in isolation. They telescope together all manner of quite distinct migrants, from Prussian military advisers to Mozambiquan miners, Melanesian cane-cutters, and Venetian harvest workers. Foreign technicians were brought in to many of these societies, as academics, engineers, and teachers but these represent small numbers and they were paid for, in the long run, by the much larger numbers of working-class immigrants. Some preliminary comments can be made about the great anonymous mass of labour migrants. First, most of them migrated from rural areas, either because they had been dispossessed through conquest or because rural production systems collapsed. Second, they were deployed in capitalist production systems, whether on land or in the mines, on social terms very different from those they left behind. Third, they were extremely vulnerable to conditions entirely beyond their control: when their labour was no longer required, their immigration could readily be halted, and if they stayed in their place of employment they had no great claim on social welfare. Much like capital and commodities, they swirled around the world in the cheapest of ships. Emigrants from temperate Europe commonly washed up on temperate shores, since most tropical societies could coerce their own peasants into other forms of labour. In societies of recent settlement, then, labour migration was characteristic and crucial.

III

Much of the discussion of migrants in these societies dwells on the migrants themselves, suggesting that migration was an entirely voluntary process, and that new arrivals did little more than attempt to fulfil ambitions fully formed in their societies of origin. In this section, then, we should consider the degree of voluntarism involved, and then ask whether immigrants modified their ambitions on arrival.

When a financial journal in 1890[22] asserted that no migrant would go to the Australasian colonies unbribed, it was asserting that gross numbers of migrants could be explained simply in terms of the supply and demand of employment opportunities, and that migrants themselves were the only decision-makers. That view is, of course, plausible, and not entirely mistaken. In 1910, for instance, 345,000 passengers arrived at ports in the River Plate estuary; in the same year 136,000 departed, 209,000 presumably chose to stay in Argentina or Uruguay, at least temporarily. When World War I dislocated Argentine and Uruguyan production, the trend of migration was reversed. Only half as many arrived, twice as many departed, and there was a net loss of 61,000 people. Throughout our period, there was extensive speculative migration across the Tasman, and between mainland Australian colonies.[23] Many Australian soldiers in the South African War took their discharge in Johannesburg, and settled down to serious agitation. Some European migrants, it would seem, exercised at least some measure of individual choice. By contrast, non-Europeans often exercised much less choice. There is clear evidence of 'management' in such processes as the compulsory repatriation of Melanesian plantation labour from Queensland, the exclusion of Chinese from Australia, the recruiting of Indian, African, and Chinese mining labour in Chile and South Africa, or the dispossession of Indians in Chile or Aboriginals in Australia. At first sight we might suppose that there were two parallel but distinct phenomena: voluntary European migration, and involuntary non-European bulk shipments. These phenomena were not distinct, however. Several cases can be cited to show that migrants themselves did not determine what kind of migration should take place.

The southern states of Brazil were turned over to large-scale coffee production in the second half of the nineteenth century, and the development of coffee coincided with the abolition of slavery. We might expect the coffee barons to employ ex-slaves. In the event, they found that

Italian families imported as coerced share-croppers could be squeezed more thoroughly than former slaves, who were employed mainly as armed guards supervising the Italian share-croppers.[24] The admission of Italians was very clearly a corollory of the exclusion of Brazilian blacks. In Chile and Argentina decisions about the national origin of migrants were consciously made by the state in response to ruling class opinions about the optimum composition of their societies in the future. When the preferred quality of immigrant was temporarily unavailable, sponsored migrant schemes were introduced until such time as market forces remedied the defect.[25] In Australia and South Africa it is abundantly clear that decisions about Chinese and black labour migration were *ipso facto* decisions about white labour migration. While white migrants did indeed make individual choices in response to employment opportunities, they did so in a highly structured context. In effect, the governments of our societies delegated to market forces the provision of white immigrants; when market forces were inadequate, governments intervened. The distinction between 'voluntary' and 'involuntary' migration is not as sharp as it may seem. Any reliance on voluntarism to explain the quantity, quality, and fluctuations of labour migration is unfounded.

It is tempting to see the settler societies as new territories in which migrants could fulfil the aspirations which eluded them at home. This approach reduces the settlers to fragments of the metropolitan society[26] and encourages the assumption that inherited national characteristics were the mainspring of colonial social change. Naturally the colonists were conscious of their metropolitan past and their contemporary links but inherited attitudes do not offer a satisfactory explanation for change in settler societies. Here it must suffice merely to list some events and conditions which are awkward within a fragment-theory approach.

To many Australians and New Zealanders it seems only natural that the working class formed labour parties, entered parliaments, exercised power, and relinquished it on demand; it seems equally natural that women were enfranchised and that no consequence followed from female suffrage. Confronted by evidence that this is not a 'normal' set of developments, some observers attributed such events to the imported British tradition. Yet the working class entered parliamentary politics rather earlier in Australia than in Britain, shared formal power much earlier, and used their power in unchartered ways. It seems perfectly satisfactory to explain the emergence of labour parties in terms of Australian and New Zealand circumstances, as Gollan and Sinclair and their successors have managed to do.[27] Equally, women were enfranchised in the Antipodes a generation earlier than their sisters in Britain, at a time when the only precedent was in Wyoming. No doubt in these cases inherited aspirations may have had some force; but the fact is that these aspirations do not explain particular events, and indeed distract attention from the circumstances in which events took place.

The limitations of arguments based on imported political culture are just as clear in Latin America. Large numbers of immigrants to Argentina (and Uruguay) were Anarchists (and later Syndicalists, and Anarcho-Syndicalists), and they founded local branches of international workers' movements which lasted for generations. Immigrants in Buenos Aires sometimes acted on their imported principles and (for example) organised spontaneous strikes and occasional assassinations; but their sons and daughters more commonly joined the Radical and Socialist parties, whose aspirations were those of J. S. Mill and William Pember Reeves, in so far as they were influenced by foreign political thinkers at all.[28] It was in Chile — lacking sustained contact with Europe political thought — that home-grown anarchist and socialist parties proved more durable and effective.[29] Finally, if imported political culture is to have any explanatory value, then there are inconvenient events to be explained away. Australian workers developed a powerful tradition of hostility towards Chinese and Melanesian competition, manifested in the white Australia policy which was the first preoccupation of the Australian federal parliament. Yet those Australians who migrated to New Zealand found no difficulty in accepting (indeed demanding) the full equality of Maoris in political and economic life; and those Australians who migrated to the Transvaal were insistent on creating and defending a labour aristocracy. The explanation of events, and even of attitudes, requires detailed attention to the whole context in which labour migrants lived and worked.

IV

Labour migration can best be comprehended in the context of the political economies of the host societies, and, for convenience, the six host societies can be treated as three pairs: Australia and Argentina are often compared because of their enormous size and range of climatic conditions;[30] New Zealand and Uruguay were laboratories for social legislation and for comparative history;[31] and I am not the first to compare Chile with South Africa.[32] The justification for such pairing, however, is convenience in presentation rather than ecological determinism.

Rural production must be the starting point of any account of

Argentina and Australia: in good times it was rural production which earned the foreign exchange which financed everything else, although in Australia there were also minerals to be exploited when rural production foundered. Rural relations of production also take us directly to the heart of the contrast between these two societies. In Argentina land was parcelled out in enormous freehold lots, just as soon as the Indians were removed from it. The land was quite freely bought and sold until about 1890, when it was proved to possess durable value.[33] In the far south sheep ran over prodigious expanses; in the far north tropical produce such as sugar and Paraguay tea was grown; but the heart of the economy was the pampas, which mainly produced excellent beef and good wheat. Land was very commonly leased in small lots to tenant farmers, who grew wheat for three years and left the land under alfalfa so that the landowner had instant improved pastures for cattle.[34] Landowners and tenant farmers both employed permanent wage labourers, and during the harvest season they employed annual migrants from Italy at three to six times the ordinary rural wage. There were few interruptions to the exponential growth of rural production. By 1913 Argentine chilled beef earned £10m in Britain, where it monopolised the market for imported chilled beef;[35] nevertheless, the area of land under cultivation expanded from 2.46m hectares in 1888 to ten times that area by 1914, and there was still enough room left over to feed 43,000,000 sheep.[36] Landowners were laughing all the way to the British bank. They faced some social problems, of course. As early as 1893 small farmers rebelled against the great landowners' dominance over the state and in 1912 tenant farmers organised themselves and staged a tenants' strike;[37] but the most numerous rural class of peons never did mobilise themselves. Despite the highly visible disparity between landowner incomes and other rural incomes, and despite the resolute refusal of great landowners to break up their holdings, the latter maintained a firm grip on rural society. At the level of the state, however, they were more seriously threatened. The Baring Crisis coincided with an attempted revolution by disenchanted members of the establishment, and in the first years of the twentieth century the same people led the Unión Cívica Radical (UCR) in an attempt to win power through elections, since revolutionary tactics seemed not to be effective. At the same time anarchist and socialist movements in the cities also threatened landowners' control of the state. In 1912, however, the great landowners altered the electoral system in such a way as to give the Radicals a fair chance of electoral victory, and in this way co-opted large number of ambitious citizens and their leaders into the political system.[38] Whatever may be said of the class composition of the UCR, or of the political substance beneath the populist rhetoric, they acquiesced very readily in the continued dominance of landowners in rural production. They came to power in 1916 and were swept away in 1930 leaving almost no trace. Throughout, and beyond, this period, the landowners enjoyed sufficient control over the state to be called a ruling class.

Squatters in Australia also attempted to seize great expanses of land, and aspired to control the colonial States, but they were prevented from purchasing land cheaply, first by the British administrations before the 1850s and subsequently by the other social classes who dominated the lower houses in the colonial legislatures. Squatters were never secure in their occupancy of the land, nor were they ever a ruling class.[39] By the late nineteenth century also, in contrast to Argentina, Australian rural production was in a state of acute crisis. An eight-year drought (1895-1903) has something to do with it, but in any case the farmers had overrun the ecological boundary of sheep-farming, and there was a structural imbalance in the rural economy which the drought underlined and even helped to correct. Farmers had to diversify their production in order to survive at all and they did so quite effectively. The productive frontier had been reached in most places, and further increases in production required increased labour productivity and greater attention to appropriate product mixes.

More serious than climatic difficulties were farmers' difficulties in the social relations of production. Tenancy was rare, so land holders had no great difficulty on that front; but there was militancy among the rural workers' unions. By 1890 the shearers were so well organised that they had very nearly achieved a closed shop for the whole of eastern Australia. During 1890-91, however, there was a prolonged and often violent battle between shearers on the one hand and sheep farmers and scab labour on the other. The shearers failed, but the failure of industrial action pitch-forked them into parliamentary politics. During the next dozen years or so, Labor Parties briefly held (and often shared) power in several eastern colonies, and even briefly in the new federal parliament.[40] The rise of political Labor coincided (to put it no stronger) with the decline of plantation sugar production, and the establishment of a yeomanry of white sugar farmers in place of Melanesian plantation workers.[41] The political influence of Labor parties, at the very least, added to the pressures for intensification of production methods. Further, the hostility between squatters and all other social classes worked to some extent to the advantage of all rural producers. Australian colonial governments were keen to create opportunities for small-scale rural settlement, and to achieve this objective they invested in railways and in scientific research into agricultural production. The Argentine state, on the other hand, saw no need for agricultural research until the 1950s.[42]

In these very different patterns of class relationships may be found the explanation of the very different patterns of migration. Massive immigration and seasonal migration provided a docile, cheap, and healthy rural work force for the Argentine ruling class. The franchise regulations were such that naturalisation was virtually impossible and the sons and daughters of migrants — citizens by right of birth in Argentina — were more affluent and less militant than their parents. The Socialist Party, whose members were mainly urban and the children of immigrants, sought rural allies among tenant farmers rather than rural workers.[43] The Anarchists, who might have espoused the interests of peons, were isolated from them by language, distance, and culture. Those who ruled Argentina were committed equally to unrestricted exports and to unrestrained migration.

Landed interests never did rule Australia. Self-governing institutions, initiated in the 1850s, included a wide (albeit adult, male, and white) franchise, leaving the squatters a blocking ability in the upper houses of parliament, but enabling urban interests to run affairs in the lower houses. Once Labor Parties formed, they were easily able to form alliances which restricted migration in absolute terms, and by colour. Assisted immigration stopped: so did Chinese migration; and Melanesian sugar workers were largely sent home. The option of cheap, migrant, or coerced labour was simply not available for Australian rural producers.

Although New Zealand and Uruguay share an absurdly large number of common features, it is the difference which demands attention. In 1890 they were the same size in area and population, equally dependent on Britain, equally hopeful of becoming British home-farms, and (unequally) in considerable political and economic distress. By 1914 both had sustained large population increases, both had secured niches in the British food market, and both had enacted social welfare legislation which startled their neighbours and tourists. Yet it is not perverse to emphasise their differences, because similar phenomena had a very different causes and drastically different social consequences.

Great landowners in Uruguay were in much the same condition as their counterparts in Argentina so far as the rural relations of production were concerned but they differed in their relations with the state. To put it in a nutshell, they defied the state at least until 1904, when José Batlle y Ordoñez was President. Batlle had to put down the last of the great *caudillos* in very tense civil war, which ended with the accidental death of the *caudillo* himself. Justifiably nervous of provoking Argentina and Brazil (which intervened in such conflicts through the nineteenth century), Batlle limited his social welfare programme to Montevideo and left rural relations of production severely alone.[44] The resulting political formation has been well described as the landowning bourgeoisie delegating political power to Batlle's petty bourgeois urban followers.[45] Rural production was the beneficiary of favourable international price movements, but the consequence was more extensive rather than more intensive pastoralism. Pastures were not improved, nor was livestock; the great estates were not broken up. In 1908, and in 1915, careful estimates were made of land ownership,[46] and they are worth comparing. (Table 9.2).

TABLE 9.2: LANDOWNERSHIP, 1908 AND 1915

Number of holdings	Size	Percentage of holdings	Area occupied	Percentage of land
1908				
24,433	up to 100 ha	56.05	86,000	0.51
17.765	101 to 2,500	40.75	9,250,000	54.94
1,391	1,501 and over	3.20	7,500,000	44.55
1915				
35,984	up to 100 ha	61.48	1,549,000	8.81
21,033	101 to 2,000	35.94	9,077,000	51.63
1,513	2,001 and over	2.58	6,954,000	39.56

These non-congruent tables do at least suggest the rapid growth of excessively small holdings but an otherwise unchanging structure of landownership, which is evidently what happened. Batlle's populist movement was capable of confounding the growth of urban working-class politics, by creating a large public sector and providing extensive urban social services, but incapable of reaching the rural working class or propelling rural producers towards intensified production. A striking instance of the limited scope of the government is that income tax was introduced only in 1960 — and only 13 returns were filled in![47]

One does not have to be a New Zealander to be tempted towards lyricism. Some writers modestly attribute New Zealand's happy development mainly to economic determinism;[48] but clearly this will not serve the purpose. In different political conditions the owners of the big sheep runs might well have held on to their holdings and held the land-hungry townsmen at bay. In the event 43,777 holdings in 1891 had grown to 73,876 by 1911, while the area of land held individually more than doubled in the same era.[49]. Very likely Maoris gained less than others in the transformation; but, unlike any other peasantry in the countries under review, they were spread (unevenly) throughout the whole social structure, from the professions and individual landownership through to the rural working class, which, like the Australian rural working class, was a relatively skilled and highly paid work force totally unlike the degraded peons of Uruguay's rural slums.[50] These most unusual consequences of rural upheaval must be attributed to the fact that a Liberal and Labour coalition directed events during the period of greatest mobility. The previously dominant coalition of great landowners and Auckland merchants could not conceivably have accomplished the same ends.

Both countries increased their populations at about 3 per cent per annum during the 1900s;[51] but, against the background of very different social changes, these similar statistics must also contain different meanings. In Uruguay immigrants flowed into Montevideo and the countryside as competitors for already scarce employment; in New Zealand they were more rapidly absorbed into a high wage economy as specialist producers or efficient workers in industries ancillary to the rural production system. Militant working-class movements were violently suppressed in this period in both societies;[52] but in New Zealand there was the consolation of employment, compulsory arbitration, and extensive social welfare, while in Uruguay there was only the prospect of emigration. In brief, similar statistical phenomena in migration have very different human meanings, and the differences are to be found in the political economies of the host societies.

Chile and South Africa are, of course, the most difficult cases. To precis an argument developed elsewhere, we may first list the similar features of their political economies in the 1890s. First, there was a landowning bourgeoisie in both societies, and these bourgeoisies had tight control over the machinery of the states. Second, despite earlier participation in the export of agricultural produce, in both societies the landowners showed a pronounced lack of interest in the intensification of rural production. Third, the actual accumulation of capital on a large scale was perceived as depending on mineral production, carried out by companies who raised their capital in Europe. Fourth, the landowning bourgeoisie used the machinery of the State to mobilise and control a large and degraded mining labour force so as to facilitate mineral development, and they did so because they derived more benefit from the profits of mining than from the production of agricultural or pastoral commodities. Rural stability was essential for the survival of the landowning bourgeoisie: rural development was less essential, at least in the short term. At first the landowning bourgeoisie may have believed that mining development would have no more social consequences than the installation of a one-armed bandit in a bar; before long they became apprehensive about the political activities of British capitalists and imperialists, but by that time it was too late because they had come to depend on the revenues yielded by foreign-owned enterprises.

The political institutions of Chile from 1891 until 1920 have been described as those of a parliamentary democracy: elections were held regularly, the electorate was substantial, and votes were dear.[53] After 1891 landowners enjoyed extensive local power through municipal governments, as well as complete dominance in the national forums.[54] At the same time it was necessary to subject to rigorous discipline a large working class which dug out the nitrates, entrained them to the northern ports, and loaded them on the ships: any prolonged interruption of these services risked loss of revenue and the collapse of the edifice of aristocratic living.[55] The dilemma of a degraded work-force which also exercised the franchise could never be entirely resolved, but reliance on foreign workers diminished the risk. The working class itself, united in a common adversity and undifferentiated in terms of skills or incomes, was remarkably free of ethnic tensions.[56] While employers quite naturally preferred foreign labour, other considerations pointed to a local labour force. To sustain a high price for nitrates, producers periodically combined to reduce levels of output, which generally involved dismissing workers until prices recovered.[57] To transport a work force from (say) China in these circumstances would add subsantially to working costs. Peruvians and Bolivians (left behind by the War of the Pacific) could be employed and dismissed with political impunity; for the rest, central and southern Chile had to provide the labour force. The other method of solving the dilemma was to shoot the strikers, to attribute discontent to foreign agitators (implausibly but vehemently), and to ignore their parliamentary representatives. The combination of political and economic pressures prevented the mining industry from relying heavily on immigration, or on Chilean labour, or on resident foreigners, but encouraged a mixture of all these. At the turn of the century there were perhaps 2,000 Chinese, a third of the work force were Bolivians and Peruvians, and the majority were former peasants from central and southern Chile. The total nitrate work force was about 50,000.[58]

Only with hindsight does it seem natural and inevitable that gold mining in South Africa should have developed on the basis of a stabilised and highly rewarded labour aristocracy and an unstable and degraded majority of workers. There is nothing inherent in abstract capital, or in the aspirations of European labour migrants, which required such an arrangement, otherwise we would have found similar arrangements elsewhere. The explanation must lie in the concrete southern African context. There are two dimensions to the same problem: Why did a white labour aristocracy develop? Why did a migrant labour system develop?

Employers of mining labour in the Transvaal had to consider two circumstances which were highly unusual. First, the technical difficulties of getting the ore out of the ground and getting the gold out of the ore required the importation of a considerable number of skilled workers. Only with the passage of twenty years, and the growth of technical education within South Africa, was it conceivable to dispense with immigrant technicians. By that time a great measure of de-skilling had become feasible. Second, unprecedented sums of capital had to be sunk in the mines, situated in a political system which was not committed to industrial capitalism at first and whose leaders were both erratic and ignorant of the technical problems of large-scale mining. These considerations may explain the mine-owners' unusual tolerance of a large and expensive skilled labour force during the first dozen years of mining activity. No attempt was made to reduce the wages of the white miners until 1902, and the skilled miners had no need to form strong unions until that date.[59] This informal alliance stands in stark contrast to the efforts of capitalists to reduce every other element of working costs during the same period; but it has been suggested that alliances of employers and some employees may be characteristic of enclave capitalism.[60] It is sometimes argued that the white working class were really the NCOs of capital. In the 1890s this description may have had a military as well as an industrial dimension.

The consequences of the war of 1899-1902 included a drastic realignment of social classes. The Transvaal became a capitalist state in a sense which had not been true in the 1890s: parliament, executive, and the new bureaucracy were all thoroughly imbued with respect for the logic of capital accumulation. The capitalists' lobbyists in Pretoria could now pack their bags and find alternative employment.[61] It follows that capital no longer depended on the labour aristocracy for political support; it is precisely from 1902 onwards that the earlier alliance broke down. It was succeeded by wage reductions, de-skilling, and the thinning out of the numbers of privileged workers, and inevitably by the formation of more effective unions and the parliamentary representation of the white working class. Among the functions of the labour aristocracy, the supervision of African (and Chinese) labour became more important as against the application of rare mining skills. From the point of view of mine owners, there was no further need for white migrant labour: a sufficient number of supervisors and of skilled employees could now be generated within South Africa itself.

If mine owners' commitment to labour aristocracy diminished over time, the commitment of the landowning bourgeoisie to the preservation of a labour aristocracy increased. The slow development of commercial farming, and the establishment of a real rural police force, rendered large numbers of *bijwoners* redundant. The existence of supervisory jobs in and around mining was a necessary cushion for the cousins of surviving landowners who might otherwise drift into dangerous opposition. What could be more alarming to the comfortable leaders of Afrikaner political movements than a fully enfranchised but economically distressed white lumpenproletariat? In short, for different reasons at different times, a labour aristocracy was sought and protected by the two social classes who held state power at the turn of the century. Without such support it is difficult to imagine that the white working class would have survived.

It is more difficult to account for the evolution of an industrial proletariat disguised as a peasantry. Because of the technical difficulties of mining at deep levels through tough rock,[62] mine owners certainly required cheap labour, and for the first few years dispossessed peasants were the most accessible source of that labour. However, the proving of deep-level mining in the mid 1890s made mining dependent on the constant growth of migrant labour, in response to pressures which the mine owners did not themselves control. The risk inherent in such dependence was shown clearly in the aftermath of the war, when an insufficient supply of African labour was forthcoming. There is also a logical difficulty: cheap labour does not (and did not) necessarily imply short-term migrant labour. It is not clear that mine owners wanted more short-contract labour at all. Serious dilution of the labour aristocracy implied a much more stable semi-skilled labour force. Mine managers seem to have preferred the Mozambiquan workers who spent longer terms of contract in the mines; Chinese miners who came to the Rand on long contracts (like Italians and Moroccans and Indians, who were also considered in 1903-04) could perform a range of mining jobs which was not within the capacity of short-term contract labour.[63] Access to external sources of mining labour might enable the mine owners not merely to pass on the cost of the reproduction of labour but to forget that cost altogether. At any rate there is no indication that mine owners saw short-term quasi-peasant labour as the optimum solution to the labour dilemma.

The landowning bourgeoisie who directed the strategy of Afrikaner nationalism seem not to have held any strong opinions as to the optimum quality of the industrial labour force, except that it should be supervised by a white labour aristocracy and that it should not draw off the labour which maintained rural production. Opposition to Chinese labour in 1904 was re-considered in 1907, when Afrikaner landowners returned to political power.[64] The driving force towards short-term contract labour in the mines does not seem to have been located in the landowning bourgeoisie.

The white labour aristocracy, however, had very powerful reasons for insisting on a permanently unskilled labour force, and the political agitation over the terms on which Chinese miners could be employed makes this quite clear. For reasons which Johnstone elucidates,[65] it was difficult for the post-war white working class to hold a single, clear opinion on most subjects. However, they were not keen to abandon their supervisory function for the perils of direct production, as Creswell wished; and they accepted the need for some kind of degraded labour force, to be supervised by themselves.

Recent research suggests that short-term migrant labour was as much the result of pressures from within African society as of the conscious planning of either capital or the South African state. In the early stages of South Africa's industrial revolution Africans were reluctant to be separated from the land, and the traditional ruling class had every interest in trying to control both the migration out of labour and its return to their chieftaincy. Migrant labour can thus be seen as the result of a complex struggle not simply between different white interests but also between white and black ruling groups over the disposal of the labour power of young men.[66] Even on this showing, however, it is necessary to account for the acquiescence of those social classes which enjoyed access to state power. It is to this question that I wish to direct attention.

Continued reliance on short-term African migrant labour from outside South Africa may best be seen as a strategy which satisfied no important social class completely but gave each what it most required. The labourers came from areas where Afrikaners did not own land, so the labour system did not directly threaten rural relations of production. The labourers were completely disfranchised, so they offered no political threat to capital, to

Afrikaners as they moved into a new role as bureaucratic bourgeoisie, or to the white working class which needed access to the state in order to secure their own position. Being mainly foreign and entirely disfranchised, the migrant labourers were unable to protect themselves from appalling working conditions and steadily eroded wages. As migrants they could only slowly acquire the skills which would have threatened the labour aristocracy and thereby threatened the whole compromise. In short, the development of the migrant labour system was profoundly shaped by the political dispute between the three major social classes who enjoyed access to formal state power.

V

What does this all mean? The experience of six substantial societies, even if we narrow it down to the crucial generation 1890 to 1914, is not easily summarised. By the end of our period so many peculiarly local circumstances have intervened, that a 'settler capitalist' mode is no longer easily visible. Nonetheless some commonalities did persist, and may be worth comment. Despite the idiosyncracies of their experience, one great regularity stands out. In every case a wider governing coalition had been assembled around commitment to export-led growth, and the sanctity of foreign capital. In some cases this coalition was a great majority of the population, while in others it was a great minority: yet the states had unerringly distinguished 'loyal' from 'disloyal' opposition.

Central to this approach is the question of what the state was, and which people it represented. It was the settler state, responsible both to foreign capital and to a local electorate, which must mediate any contradictions between the two masters and which must determine who could safely be admitted within the electoral pale. The settler state (like the settler society) was the product of class struggles and international rivalries focused on the metropolitan homeland. From its inception then, that state confronted the essential and defining problem of serving two masters. In some cases that task was accomplished mainly by coercion, and in other cases by accommodation; but each settler state had to resolve its dilemma in its own way.

This was a dynamic process, not a static or mechanical one. No sooner was an accommodation made than a fresh issue arose. We are confronted by a rather chicken-and-egg puzzle. Why did Labor parties form in eastern Australia from 1890? Partly because the existing civil society already enfranchised white, adult, male workers. Why did it do so? Partly because British authorities wished to constrain a colonial squatter population, and to preserve high land values. Why did British authorities so wish? Essentially because of their own experience, in Britain and elsewhere. And what was that experience . . . ?

If machinery can be conceived as congealed labour power, then perhaps we can conceive settler governmental machinery as the congealed form of earlier class struggles, not only in the settler society itself, but abroad. These governmental institutions could also be dissolved and reshaped — by fresh class struggle — but they could not be wished away. In terms of the law of conservation of matter, transposed to a social situation, we would propose that the founding institutions could never be entirely decomposed, but only reshaped. Thus, however violently the settlers inveighed against their inheritence, they were condemned to do no more than reshape it.

This rather abstruse argument has a very direct bearing on the volume and kind of labour migration which occurred. If we knew nothing of these societies except brute production statistics (that is, if we were economists) we would expect to find very similar kinds of migration to Australia and Argentina, to New Zealand and Uruguay, and to Chile and South Africa. And we would not be entirely mistaken — but we would be no more than partially correct. In each case the state did influence the number and quality of its immigrants, even if the state sometimes delegated that authority to market forces. Since the state did not hover above society, seeking to maximise benefits and to reduce costs, its actions were determined by political processes, and those processes were themselves the product of accumulated historic struggles. In human terms this had a direct bearing on a Solomon Islander's prospects of working in Queensland or going 'home', a Mozambiquan's chances of acquiring skills, a Peruvian's income in Tarapacá, or an Italian's chances of settling in Victoria, Johannesburg, Montevideo, or Valparaíso, or a Chinese worker's expectations in any of these strange environments.

10

THE IMPERIAL WORKPLACE: COMPETITIVE AND COERCED LABOUR SYSTEMS IN NEW ZEALAND, NORTHERN NIGERIA, AND AUSTRALIAN NEW GUINEA

It has been well recognised that labour migrations were an important part of the historical transfer of factors of production from Europe to new markets for manufactures and primary commodities in the nineteenth century, as European countries industrialised and international trade expanded to new levels. The so-called 'regions of recent settlement' (North America, Argentina, Brazil, South Africa, Australia, New Zealand) received by far the largest share of such migrations at the same time as they increased their share of British imports and capital at a faster rate than other markets in Europe or overseas. Historians have been content to concentrate on the problems posed by this phenomenal development and by incorporation into a world trading system. Indeed, the more recent categorisation of the 'regions' listed by Nurkse, McCarty, Denoon, and others draws attention away from factor flows to resource endowment and other endogenous variables as part of a search for a theory of development to account for the relative success or failure of the political economies of settler societies.[1] With the possible exception of Nurkse, the investigators of settler development have paid little attention to those countries of Africa, Asia, or central America which were also affected by the 'forces of growth through trade'[2] and drew their supply of labour in the nineteenth and twentieth centuries from a variety of non-European sources. In short, there has been little comparative treatment of labour mobility throughout the overseas markets that were the objects of British imperial attention or diplomatic and commercial concern.

There are understandable reasons for this division in migration studies.

The scale of capital and labour transfers to the British settlements and the United States resulted in cumulative economic growth which far surpassed the modest investment and technological innovation in the labour intensive tropical colonies. Secondly, earlier staple production in the settlements not only promoted trade and imports, but also helped creat an internal economy with services and infrastructure linking up disparate areas of the region. There are qualifications to be made concerning virtually uninhabitable areas of Canada or Australia, and there are marginal cases of settler economies subordinating as well as incorporating pre-existing subsistence economies. But by and large it is the rapid consolidation of settler economies into single geo-political structures as unitary states or federations which distinguishes the history of the North American colonies and provinces, the Australasian colonies, the old and newly settled areas of Brazil, Chile, Argentina, and the republics and colonies of South Africa.

Elsewhere in the British tropical colonies, imperial consolidation was more apparent than real — even in British India and Malaya, which underwent demographic and political division after independence. In most of tropical Africa the linkages in colonial state economies were very weak between small agricultural and mining enclaves and the subsistence and surplus agriculture and craft production of predominantly rural populations. Nevertheless, labour migration within and across colonial boundaries was a regular feature of staple production for export. Indeed, the export of labour pre-dates much of the external stimulus to West and East African markets, while India and China remained important sources of migrant labour throughout the nineteenth century. But for most of the fragmented colonial states where political economies were of recent construction and governments given to supervisory rather than developmental goals, internal regional migration was relatively unimpeded by state boundaries and provided a transfer of labour factors for temporary or stabilised employment. Such transfers were not essentially different, except in scale, from nineteenth-century Atlantic or other migrations, which often had their origins in rural-urban displacements at an earlier stage of European agricultural and industrial change. Nor was 'oscillation' between wage-earning and rural subsistence or cash farming entirely unknown in the European settler territories, although it was less frequent than seasonal mobility in societies where wage-earning opportunities were limited and land relatively abundant.

If it is agreed that mobility of labour factors accompanied capital investment and trade expansion in all the colonial and post-colonial economies to a greater or lesser degree as part of the industrial growth of north-western Europe, then it is not too far-fetched to look for the causes and consequences of that mobility within a single historical comparative framework. This paper attempts to draw together three patently disparate geographical and socio-political examples of migration to countries of settlement and enclave investment to see what methodological difficulties such a comparison presents.

The common factor of migrant mobility has been a focus of attention, particularly from social scientists with an interest in rural-urban movements in Africa and more recently in Melanesia.[3] Geographical displacement tends to be taken for granted in the literature of migration and group settlement across the North Atlantic and to the British Dominions, in favour of studies of the more immediate 'push' factors and lengthy histories of the incorporation of immigrants into evolving political economies.[4] Mobility is also susceptible to measurement, and this statistical datum has attracted the attention of demographers and economists who have concentrated on the relationship between factor flows, population growth, rural-urban income levels, and (at a greater socio-economic aggregation) levels of public and private investment over long periods of migration. Internal migration, or 'frontier' histories, also provide a counterpart within 'recent settlement' regions to the internal settlement and colonisation patterns of west, central, and southern Africa.[5]

The sophistication of some of the techniques used by social scientists, however, should not obscure two general assumptions which underlie much of the description and measurement of migratory 'flows'. One rests on an elementary notion of equilibrium and human response to supply and demand in terms of price measured in conventional ways or for other expected benefits accompanying displacement. Additional explanation on the supply side includes a variety of social psychology theory derived from behavioural studies of perceived opportunities and response to choices of wage and subsistence occupations, elements of anthropological data on initiation, and, more usefully, discernment of migrant networks between source and receiving areas passing on information and accommodating newcomers.[6] The demand side variables are also qualified and discussed in terms of wages theory, public and private investment patterns, the organisation of plantation and mining industries in terms of capital equipment and labour inputs, and not least the notion of competition and monopsony collusion among employers. Clearly colonial and international labour markets were 'imperfect' in a wide variety of ways, but the notion of market exchange is quite fundamental still in accounts of migration.

The second assumption concerns the correlation of capital flows with migrant settlement and employment. The work of Brinley Thomas and others who have investigated nineteenth-century patterns within the Atlantic economy is well known and need not be described here.[7] While it is a platitude to state that wage employment is accompanied by some investment, it is of importance to measure the rate and incidence of such flows, if any meaningful historical statements are to be made about particular labour migrations. On the whole it is easier to discern such patterns in the aggregated statistics of developed economies than in the very partial records of colonial enclaves. There is moreover, the possibility that certain industries may have reduced labour in proportion to capital investment. But the main qualification to simple correlations between investment and labour recruitment by migration is the fact of disparities within the evolving international economy of the nineteenth century. The three regions of Africa, Melanesia, and Australasia from which examples are taken were marginal to the main flows of British foreign investment and overseas migration in the historical period for which we have reliable statistics. The examples of New Zealand, Nigeria, and New Guinea, moreover, contained employment sectors in competition with each other for wage labour; and while public and private investment undoubtedly took place at important periods of their economic history, the supply of capital could not be taken for granted against the background of British investment opportunities abroad. In these circumstances of comparative disadvantage, it is argued, the role of colonial governments, whether representing settler interests or installed as simple autarchies of the 'Crown Colony' type to uphold the interests of the metropole and a balance of local polities, is correspondingly increased.

One final general point concerns labour migrants. Outside of specialised case studies they are all too often treated as an undifferentiated body of 'factors' and their progress measured in terms of periodic recruitment and turnover. The contribution of detailed cases, however, is that alternative viewpoints are available which suggest differentiation within the wage labour force over long periods of recruitment and employment by occupation and skills, by ethnic and sub-regional sources of supply, and, not least, by entry into the production process itself as entrepreneurs.[8] Employment histories covering a lifetime of job mobility tell us much about the frequency of migration on the scale of a generation of economic activity in wage-earning and farming and about the goals of migrants in terms of housing or other forms of elementary accumulation, including training opportunities for relatives and children.[9] The stabilisation of such a work force, in turn, raises further questions about citizenship within the colonial state and the protection of interests vested in organised groups of employers and workers which colonial governments were called on to answer in response to the consequences of labour migration.

The emphasis in this paper, then, is on three main themes common to each of the examples: administrative intervention in the labour market; the incidence of rate of capital investment to migrant labour recruitment; and the composition of the migrant labour force in terms of origins and occupational skills. It is not intended to provide exhaustive treatment of the cases within the context of their own political economies, and the time depth of the New Zealand case has been restricted to a critical period of investment, although some of the implications of extending that period are discussed in the conclusion.

I. *New Zealand investment and immigration, 1870-1880*

Three decades after annexation the provinces were parochial enclaves in an underdeveloped estate tenuously linked by sea communications. The Maori wars retarded the growth of trade in the North Island, but opened a market for Maori lands. A gold rush stimulated unsystematic colonisation and a pastoral industry in the South. With a population of some three hundred thousand, including an estimated forty thousand Maoris, by the early 1870s, the settlements were nominally a unitary state which formed part of a cluster of Australasian colonies competing for immigrants and capital. From 1869 the central government began to use a relatively advanced banking system and the endowment of confiscated and other public lands to organise a huge programme of investment in infrastructure and settler recruitment. Over the following decade the colony borrowed some £20 million and spent about half this sum during Julius Vogel's period of office as Treasurer and Premier. When he retired in 1875 Vogel became Agent-General in London and continued to supervise the working of the immigration system he had helped to create. The following year the provinces were abolished.

There were heavy *per capita* imports throughout the decade, especially for construction materials; export staples changed from gold and timber to wheat and wool; and there were the beginnings of an industrial manufacturing sector which is reflected in the occupation structure of the population.[10] There was much wastage and much provincial jobbery for contracts. It was also the period of the last and most significant

TABLE 10.1: ASSISTED AND NOMINATED IMMIGRANTS TO NEW ZEALAND

Period (June-July)	Ship arrivals	Assisted	Nominated	Total	Passage money (£)	Net cost of passage
1.11.1871-30.6.1873	33	6,096	1,166	7,585	84,687	71,000
1873-74	63	12,901	1,729	15,012	185,558	148,516
1874-75	95	28,582	3,203	31,785	383,580	377,122
1875-76	56	14,875	1,737	16,612	212,636	208,478
1876-77	25	6,405	1,068	7,473	91,211	not stated
1877-78	29	4,599	1,029	5,628	68,652	,, ,,
1878-79	30	6,394	2,353	8,747	112,686	,, ,,
1879-80	25	2,844	4,569	7,413	90,692	,, ,,
Total	356	82,696	16,854	100,255	1,229,702	

Source: *Appendix to the Journals of the House of Representatives of New Zealand*, Series D, 1872-1881. There are discrepancies in the annual totals, because of the omission of immigrant children from the assisted category. The net cost of passages in the return is arrived at by calculation of monies paid, bills and notes received, and includes representation and recruitment expenses abroad.

demographic gains from immigration, after the period of the gold rush. From 1879 population increase from natural increment exceeded gains from net immigration.

The total number of assisted and nominated immigrants for the period (see Table 10.1) represents about half of total passenger arrivals in New Zealand ports.[11] This number is probably an even greater proportion of the net gain of arrivals over departures for the period (113,079), though there is no certainty that some immigrants assisted from public funds did not move off to the Australian colonies or elsewhere, after a short stay in New Zealand. With the downturn in the New Zealand economy from the early 1880s and a continued favourable trade cycle in Australia before the collapse in 1890, many certainly did transfer their labour to other markets.

Nevertheless, the example is one of state intervention in the organisation of a colonial migrant system. There is ample evidence that both central and provincial governments sought to recruit categories of immigrants considered to be in short supply and essential to the public works programme approved under the immigration and public works acts, 1870-73. Land was dear in comparison with North American prices; wages levels were high, but no higher than in neighbouring Australian colonies, and the additional cost of passages and freight had to be off-set by subsidising recruitment in the United Kingdom. Even after their abolition, the provinces continued to supply a flow of information to a ministry for immigration and to the agent-general to assist selection, and they completed returns on the employment of arrivals. Although Vogel approved total payment of passages, it is clear from correspondence that passage monies were looked on as advances. It is also certain that very little was ever refunded to the provincial superintendents. Apart from fares, there were other direct costs which continued to be borne after the end of the scheme and which included salaries and commissions to agents, advertising (especially in *Reynolds'* and *Lloyds'* weeklies, *The Telegraph* and *Labourers' Union*), upkeep of depots and barracks as reception centres, and gratuities to ships' officers, doctors, and matrons, and port fees.

The agents numbered some hundred and twenty in the United Kingdom and came under the control of the agent-general. They received a bounty at variable rates, according to the age and occupation of immigrants, generally fixed at ten shillings per adult for married couples and single women who were in short supply, and five shillings for a single man. There were special *per capita* fees for Scandinavians and Germans up to a fixed quota of two to three thousand adults. By 1877 the agent-general also used the services of 60 local agents in Ireland, although most intending immigrants applied directly to the New Zealand office in Belfast.[12] One agent reported that some 60 per cent of such applicants embarked each year. Large numbers were also nominated for assisted passages by relatives and employers. Vogel, indeed, preferred this method to bounty immigration. But the returns show very small percentages of such nominations actually arrived, and many of these may be regarded as a search for labour by small businessmen and farmers whose offers were not taken up.

All immigrants were sent under government contracts with a number of shipping companies — Shaw Savill & Company, Albion & Company, P. Henderson & Company, and the New Zealand Shipping Company. Steerage berths cost about £14, a charge which rose steeply to £20 by the 1890s. Contracts were frequently changed, when disputes over rates arose, and there is no evidence of monopsony agreements, though the Conference system began in the Australian trades in the 1880s. On the whole there was fairly strict supervision of conditions of migration through the Passenger Acts: medical and other reports given in the returns from the provinces are detailed and thorough. Awareness of a competitive market in the Atlantic economy encouraged care of the migrants, particularly as the government sought preferred nationalities. These were English, Scots, and Irish, who make up 91 per cent of total assisted immigration, 1870-79, with a few thousand Germans and Scandinavians and a few hundred Italians and French. Introduction of Chinese labour was seriously considered in 1872 and rejected on advice from provincial superintendents that sufficient European and Maori labour would be available for railway construction, particularly after the failure of potato and wheat crops among smallholders in Hawke's Bay Province in the summer of that year.[13]

At the receiving end general labour, rather than land settlement, was the objective of the annual subsidy. There are relatively few agricultural development schemes in the programmes of the 1870s, which contrasts with the usual view of migration as a process of filling 'open spaces'. On the contrary, care was taken, especially in the Otago, Canterbury, and Auckland Provinces, to supervise the arrival of vessels, provide temporary shelter, and circulate information on the immediate openings for tradesmen and labourers in the coastal ports and towns. There is evidence of misdirection of some vessels to provinces particularly in need of labour, but immigrants found themselves in a competitive labour market and could change jobs.

The whole period from 1870 to 1893 can be regarded as a long cycle of

public expenditure in New Zealand, when government debt rose from
£8 million to £38 million and loan expenditure totalled about £32 million.
In the spending spree initiated by Vogel population doubled and over a
thousand miles of railway were opened for traffic. But the boom broke, as
far as immigration was concerned, in 1879 when there was a fall in the
demand for labour, the beginnings of local unemployment in a number of
provinces, and some probing investigations into financial scandals in land
and contracts. The spectacular growth of mortgage banking promoted a
temporary revival, before a sharper and longer recession, a banking crisis in
1893, and withdrawals of British deposits.

Already by 1878 labourers in Nelson Province had petitioned against
further immigration. Assisted immigration stopped, and for the period
1885-89 there was a net loss of migrants and only very small net gains in
the 1890s, before the next period of prosperity, 1900-14.[14] The bounty
system was never revived in a similar form, although small numbers of
farmers were assisted in the 1880s and 1890s by reductions in fares to
compete with Canadian fares.[15] When immigration into New Zealand
from Australia rose to 18,000 a year, during the depressions of 1891-93,
Premier Seddon appealed to the Australian premiers in vain to reduce the
flow. By the end of the next period of investment after 1900 most
immigrants came without assistance from the state.

Occupational differentiation within New Zealand immigration has
never been closely investigated, although the requests of provincial
superintendents and their returns indicate the categories of arrivals.
Auckland and Wellington preferred a large proportion of tradesmen and
mechanics; Canterbury and Otago required greater number of agricultural
labourers and domestic servants.[16] There are no consolidated occupational
returns for the whole period, but for the largest influx, 1874-75, available
statistics show that farm labour, general labour, and servants accounted for
54 per cent of occupational categories.[17] This is a slightly higher
proportion than in the 1871 census, which gives labourers and servants 40
per cent of occupations. But it is also clear from the superintendents'
correspondence that immigrants who declared themselves in one
occupation not infrequently changed occupations after arrival. For
example, a good half of the assisted immigrants to Auckland Province,
1875-76, promoted themselves from general labourers to the more
profitable jobs offering as 'mechanics' and house servants in and near the
city.[18] Much more work would be required on comparative wage levels in
the provinces and the Australian colonies to assess differentials as
inducements to market mobility. There is qualitative evidence that recent

immigrants moved fairly quickly out of poorly paid work at the beginning of the decade and that information readily circulated on the comparative advantages of occupations in different provinces. It should also be remembered that much work was seasonal and movement between public works and agriculture was a structural feature of the New Zealand labour market.[19] There is little evidence, however, of workers' organisations on the supply side, although they begin to appear in some of the skilled trades during the 1880s, and there was a rapid emergence of unions in the depression of the 1890s.[20]

II. *Mining labour on the Jos Plateau, Northern Nigeria, 1902-1945*

Like the Fulani conquest of the early nineteenth century, the British occupation of the Plateau provinces profoundly affected the economic life of the residual agriculturalists of the area. The commercial penetration of the livestock and produce markets of the Niger-Benue confluence in the 1880s and 1890s and the discovery of tin concentrates increased the demand for wage labour, which had already been recruited by the military administration. Between 1902 and 1914 prospecting and mining operations drew on the rural populations of the neighbouring emirates for large numbers of Hausa, Kanuri, and so-called 'pagans' or local Birom from the Jos, Pankshin, and Shendam divisions, where the bulk of concessions were located. Plateau Province was formally constituted in 1925 but already the market centre of Jos had grown into an administrative and commercial centre and the site of temporary migrant camps from which employers and sub-contractors drew their supplies. Early recruitment in the first two decades for prospecting, road-building, and porterage took place in conditions of competition with provincial administration and improved markets for cash crops — groundnuts, shea produce, cassava, and maize — firewood, and livestock which made heavy demands on adult labour at the start of the farming season in March and April. Hausa peasant farmers generally refused wage labour during this season, although there is some evidence that domestic slaves were attracted to the mining camps, and unemployed agricultural labour was regularly mobilised by emirate headmen for government service during the dry season. Particularly severe shortages were experienced by government and private employers between 1909 and 1914 and forced labour contingents of between four and six thousand men were supplied by Zaria, Bauchi, and Nupe emirates for periods of six weeks on public works.[21] Such labour was not supplied to mining companies, however, and the earliest attempt to round up Hausas for the mines in 1918 ended in fiasco when the majority absconded. By that date the annual average of direct and tributers' African labourers was some twenty-one thousand, managed by a hundred and eighty Europeans. The residual Birom of the Plateau Province who bore the brunt of this scattered industrial expansion may have numbered about two hundred thousand at this period. They supplied both labour and food-stuffs, but their precise recruitment and dependence on cash income were not measured by miners or administrators before the 1930s. Similarly, the exact proportions of immigrant Hausa, Kanuri, and others are not known until the earliest census of the mining locations in 1931. The general picture for the first two or three decades of tin mining is one of irregular private recruitment and high turnover in competition with government services and a rising demand for agricultural produce. Relative shortages ended in the 1930s and labour was plentiful and cheap until efforts to increase production during World War II entailed forced recruitment. Each of these three phases in the labour history of the tin mines increased the dependence of local agriculturalists on the main source of cash income and encouraged a stream of labour migration through the central provinces of the northern region of Nigeria.

In the first phase prospecting for, and export of, tin were pioneered by the Royal Niger Company, which had a monopoly of river transport before the completion of the branch railway to the Plateau from the Lagos-Kano line in 1914 and the line from Port Harcourt in 1928. Competition for labour was the cause of a serious dispute between company agents and Lugard's administration. A Master and Servants Ordinance of 1902 was passed to prevent recruitment for work outside provinces where there was a high demand for carriers and public works' labour. The Company refused a monopsony agreement with Lugard and made its own assessment of sources on the Plateau.[22] Its mining engineers recognised the seasonal availability of Birom workers and made an effort to recruit them into casual and short-term employment, while attracting Hausa, Kanuri, and others for positions of stabilised employment based on the mining camps. As the number of companies increased from 1906, they arranged a standard rate of daily pay and formed a Chamber of Mines in 1911. In practice the earliest daily rates on open-cast alluvial mines remained at about 6d (2½p) for a six-hour shift, with a maximum of 9d set by the Chamber. This roughly corresponded with rates for volunteer labour for railway and road construction. The 'political' or coerced labour called out by administrators for three months annually was also paid 6d per day.[23] A very large place was left, however, for mining tributers who leased land and sub-contracted to a company, and these recruited their own gangs of

Hausa and Birom. Indeed, tributing remained one of the few outlets for African mining enterprise, after the prohibition of indigenous mining and smelting on the Plateau, until the formation of small African-owned companies after 1945. As late as 1951, 34 per cent of the African labour force of 57,000 men employed in cassiterite extraction were tributers.[24]

This pattern of standard wages and co-exploitation among a very large number of European companies continued through World War I and the

TABLE 10.2: ANNUAL AVERAGE COSTS, WAGES,
AND AFRICAN LABOUR

	All-in costs per ton (£)	Net Profit per ton (£)	African wages as percentage of output costs	Yearly average of Africans employed
1926	114	91	36	31,206
1927	128	70	42	36,815
1928	123	35	41	39,333
1929	107	30	34	38,333
1930	81	12	31	28,904
1931	74	1	19	20,763
1932	69	20	28	18,089
1933	60	57	32	14,911
1934	75	84	25	20,138
1935	72	86	22	21,829
1936	73	70	23	24,590
1937	85	84	23	36,142
1938	101	31	26	31,865
1939	N/A*	N/A		34,074
1940	N/A	N/A		45,744
1941	N/A	N/A		49,225
1942	N/A	N/A		60,370
1943	N/A	N/A		74,779
1945	N/A	N/A		60,702
1946	N/A	N/A		53,399
1947	N/A	N/A		51,655
1948	N/A	N/A		53,258

*N/A = Not Available

Source: *Annual Reports of the Mines Department, 1921-1949/50;* P.A. Bower in Margery Perham (ed), *Mining, Commerce, and Finance in Nigeria* (London, 1947), pp. 18–19; Souter, 'Colonial Labour Policy and Labour Conditions in Nigeria, 1939–1945', pp. 184-5. Souter's investigation of conscripted labour 1942-44 indicates that the annual averages for these years included 5,272 conscripts for 1942, 13,624 conscripts for 1943, as monthly averages. The gross totals of African labour employed in any year would be greater than the statistical averages of monthly employment used in the official returns. Rates of turnover are not given in any sources.

early 1920s. Employers were obliged to concede higher wages, which doubled to a shilling (5p) or more per day, as the price of imported goods trebled from 1914 to 1918 and as returns from agriculture to peasant farmers producing groundnuts and local food staples made them less dependent on wage labour.[25] The upward trend in wages continued through the temporary recession of 1921, to a weekly average of five or six shillings.

Unfortunately for an assessment of the impact of the depression, statistics of wage rates are not complete in the Nigerian *Blue Books,* and Mines Department reports do not always distinguish between tin mining and other mining labour. But two trends would seem clear. First, the gradual extension of taxation in the 1920s based on a peasant income of £2.5s per annum in Sokoto, Zaria, and Bauchi Provinces included Birom pagans and continued into the depression period when mining labour was cut by half and wages were reduced by about one-third. The fall in tin prices was met by cutting working costs in the most obvious way:

Working costs have been greatly reduced, chiefly by the reduction of native wages. Hausa pick and shovel men are getting about 3s.9d. a week instead of 5s.6d, headpan men about 2s.6d. a week. Pagans are working for as little as 1s.6d. a week. The average price now paid for tribute tin ore is 1½d. a pound.[26]

The yearly average of African labourers, in fact, recovered fairly quickly to pre-1930 levels, but wage rates did not recover and sank to a daily rate of about 8d. or 9d. and remained there well into the 1940s.[27] The general decline of African wages as a percentage of production costs may be seen in Table 10.2.

During World War II there was recourse to forced labour, as the administration conscripted an aggregate of some 14,000 workers between 1924 and 1942 from all of the northern provinces for periods of four months' service.[28] This was well short of the original target required to double the work force and significantly increase the output of tin. The most detailed study of the failure of the conscription emphasises material shortages of housing and foodstuffs, lack of official supervision, numerous desertions, and a high mortality rate, especially among the Tiv of the Benue, which enabled the Colonial Office to prevail against the Ministry of Supply and end conscription in 1944.[29] It was also clear that very low productivity made it unlikely that employers would wish to supplement their labour from this official source, while paying higher costs for direct labour, which rose from 18.3 per cent per cubic yard in 1939 to 52.9 per cubic yard in 1946, compared with falling costs for electro-mechanical and hydraulic techniques.[30] Even so, the tin mines remained relatively labour-intensive because of lack of power supplies and water in a difficult terrain, where tributers handled one-third of lode production until the early 1950s, when there were improved wage rates for a smaller number of direct labourers and some slight increase in electro-mechanical methods of production.

On the whole the history of Nigerian tin mining has been marked by extreme fluctuations in the price of exported cassiterite and in official regulation of output under international control schemes, which in turn have had their repercussions on the recruitment of a migrant and agrarian-based labour force. Prospecting by the Niger Company from 1902 resulted in an extraordinary boom in tin shares on the London market and the rapid formation of numerous small companies. At the height of the boom they numbered one hundred and fifty-two, with a nominal capital of £8 million. This feverish speculation deflated quickly by 1914, when the price of tin fell to under £190 per ton. Thereafter, through the inter-war period, exploitation of the tin fields was characterised by a large number of poorly capitalised firms which were reduced, as a result of the Depression and the tin quota scheme, to some thirty in 1938.[31] Over the same period the estimated issued shares of these firms also declined to £4.8 million.[32] There was a tendency towards concentration with the formation of Amalgamated Tin Mines of Nigeria in 1939, which had a nominal capital of nearly £2 million and produced about half the annual output of the tinfields. But restructuring and holding down wage costs still left the Nigerian tin firms as relatively inefficient and high-cost producers, compared with Malaysia, despite the ways in which the industry 'had off-loaded the major burden of the tin crisis (of the 1930s) onto the Nigerian workers.'[33]

Thus the Plateau labour force was not untypical of other recruits to tropical colonial enclave economies. The major stimulus used by the administration to encourage regular seasonal and short-term employment, whether for agricultural production or wage labour in the northern provinces, lay in native authority taxes. Hausa, Birom, Kanuri, and others were not in equal positions to meet this obligation. Most of the Hausa and Kanuri formed part of a shifting labour force which moved into the middle belt of northern Nigeria in the 1920s and 1930s, together with large members of Africans from tax-paying *cercles* of neighbouring French territories.[34] Like the migrant Zabrama who took the lowest paid jobs in Gold Coast mining, other immigrants from the savannah country of Niger, Chad, Northern Dahomey, and Upper Volta moved to find food and cash. But, unlike the Akim and other Akan of the Gold Coast, who avoided such jobs and had a better alternative in agriculture in the cocoa, kola, and food production of the mining zones, the Nigerian Birom were driven to divide their labour time and compete with the poorest immigrant workers. As local sedentary agriculturalists their lands had been exposed to confiscation for mining leases. They were paid no royalties, unlike proprietors of Gold Coast stool and other lands. And their precious wood and water supplies were steadily diverted for mining production.

In truth, their situation had been recognised as vulnerable from the beginning of tin mining. The Niger Company's chief mining engineer understood that their labour time for cash earnings made inroads on their annual cycle of occupations, which included iron smelting and some tin smelting, before this was prohibited. A high rate of taxation adopted from assessments for the relatively prosperous Hausa groundnut farming provinces varied between 30s. and £30 per annum for different Birom hamlets and could be met only by diverting female labour to the sale of grains and firewood. The African stereotype of under-employment with abundant supplies of seasonal workers had a foundation in the agricultural tasks of many of the Hausa and Kanuri seasonal cycles of production. But the Birom of Jos division worked a variety of soils to produce millet, maize, cassava, and root crops, grazed cattle on swampy ground and grassland and used forest land for hunting and timber supplies. They were mixed farmers on poor and volcanic soils with a wide variety of techniques for terracing and fallow reconstitution, animal husbandry, and elementary crafts, which yielded sufficient to increase their population, once warfare had been stopped, but little surplus for sale. Taxation gradually drove them to the tin mines, and according to the 1931 census the Birom made up 28 per cent of the 15,559 labourers in the Plateau camps. The Hausa made up another 44 per cent, and the remainder where a mixture of Fulani, Kanuri, French Africans, Nupe, and Yoruba from the South.

By the 1940s the Birom predominated among the ranks of the unskilled direct labour and tributers' labourers, as other ethnic groups drifted away in the depression years for marginally higher rates in mining and general labouring for the administration in the southern provinces. This labour displacement of a semi-stabilised migrant force by local agriculturalists became a matter of concern, because of the high incidence of trypano-somiasis among the Birom and the loss of productive land to mining. Most of the semi-skilled occupations around the camps were taken, moreover, by Ibo and Yoruba immigrants. The Birom had little hope of advancement, and their traditional agriculture declined in yields because of shorter fallows. Many hamlets were driven to making cash payments for imported maize, and there was increasing tension between hamlets because of disputes over land rentals and usehold titles. In 1943, reported a District Officer, 'The Bi Rom . . . are dependent on the mines as a source of income, and their welfare is thus bound up with the state of the world tin market'.[35]

Numerically unimportant among the statistics of migrant labour flows in West Africa, the Birom were nevertheless a microcosm of the predicament facing other agriculturalists and pastoralists whose lands were reduced in area and productivity and for whom the existence of wage labour was an alternative which aggravated rather than solved their problems of wresting a livelihood from farming. By the 1950s, when their situation began to improve, it was estimated that their migration in family units to the tin mines was one of the largest annual migrations of wage-earners in Nigeria.[36]

III. *Plantation and Mining Labour in Australian New Guinea, 1914 – 1971*

The Australian Mandate administration inherited a system of labour recruitment for a plantation economy which was extended to all sectors of wage-labour employment. The system had special features which gave the administration a responsibility for supervision through political officers, rather than a labour department, to a much greater degree than the *laisses-faire* policy permitted in Nigeria before the 1940s. Labour indentures for up to two or three years were nearly universal and there was little casual employment in an economy which severely restricted opportunities for Melanesian trading in cash crops. The labour history of New Guinea, in short, is characterised by elaborate regulations, a unique modification of the obligation to pay head taxes, and geographical mobility and wide dispersal of recruits between villages and places of employment. Thousands of New Guinea migrant workers were first introduced to a cash economy through the indentured labour system as it operated in the German and Austrialian periods, although they were numerically only a small percentage of the wholly agricultural populations inhabiting the districts penetrated by the administration. Many thousands more on the New Guinea mainland were never contacted until late in the 1930s and were not incorporated in any sense into the colonial enclave economy until after World War II. Wage labour, therefore, was the widening edge of an industrial wedge driven into a subsistence economy of small villages and gardens in an economic landscape which was almost totally devoid of internal markets, communication networks allowing goods to be moved in bulk, or sources of cash income apart from sale of labour.

TABLE 10.3: EMPLOYMENT OF NEW GUINEA INDENTURED LABOUR

Year (to 30 June)	Plantations	Government	Mining	Domestic service	Shipping	Commerce, industry	Total
1914	17,529	650	—	—	—	—	—
1919	16,700	—	—	—	—	—	—
1922	20,155	—	—	—	—	—	26,619
1923	20,081	—	—	—	—	—	24,701
1924	19,354	—	—	—	—	—	25,164
1925	17,232	—	—	—	—	—	23,421
1926	17,868	—	827[a]	—	—	—	23,569
1927	17,542	—	—	—	—	—	27,002
1928	18,431	—	—	—	—	—	28,253
1929	19,535	—	—	—	—	—	30,325
1930	19,507	1,237	2,000	—	7,386[b]	—	30,130
1931	17,800	900	1,900	—	7,150	—	27,750
1932	15,700	1,160	2,800	—	7,000	—	26,606
1933	16,999	1,116	3,875	2,283	685	3,284	28,242
1934	17,369	1,020	5,142	2,487	568	4,009	30,595
1935	17,269	1,066	6,369	3,139	700	5,450	33,993
1936	18,773	1,210	6,816	3,677	843	5,608	36,927
1937	19,760	1,577	7,394	4,225	7,220		40,176
1938	20,855	1,747	7,189	4,477	7,511		41,779
1939	20,657	2,190	7,162	4,498	7,107		41,614
1940	20,477	1,956	7,105	3,385	6,238		39,161

[a]Commonwealth Archives Office, CRS A518, A458/8 and Q840/1/3 for Mining Wardens' reports.

[b]For 1930, 1931 and 1932 official totals include domestic service, shipping, and commerce and industry.

Sources: *Statistics, which are incomplete for all years before 1930, are from Reports to the League of Nations on the Administration of the Territory of New Guinea, 1921/22 – 1940/41*; Commonwealth of Australia, *Report on Expropriated Properties and Businesses*, 1924. For the background, see Heather Radi, 'New Guinea under Mandate 1921 – 1941', in W.J. Hudson (ed) *Australia and Papua New Guinea* (1971).

The distribution of the indentured labour force in different sectors of the territorial economy was sufficient to account for almost all non-white occupations in the inter-war period, as is shown in Table 10.3 In a sense, therefore, the Australian military and civil occupation had simply followed the pattern begun by the Germans, who created a coerced labour exchange through regulation, some forced recruitment, by taxation and by measures to secure the production of export staples. German plantations and merchant stores were expropriated and sold off by auction, together with those of their resident labourers who stayed on between 1921 and 1928. The Expropriation Board and private recruiters endeavoured to provide planters and businessmen with a long-term and docile labour force to continue the major industry on which both settlers and the administration depended for a return on investment and support costs. At the same time the Australian administration made annual reports to the League Mandates Commission which emphasised the regulation of the pace of European contact with partially known and isolated communities. Both for humanitarian and for economic reasons much of the New Guinea mainland was kept in 'reserve', while the commercially developed archipelago of plantations and ports employed a migrant labour force which was not permitted to stabilise in the towns and was periodically returned to island and mainland villages after long periods of service.

The regulatory controls were applied through two Labour Ordinances of 1922 and 1936 which embodied all the main features of the system. Periods of indenture were carefully recorded, although they could be extended beyond the statutory three years for males. There were regular repatriations and a fairly constant turnover with a large incidence of inter-district mobility, helped by prohibition of casual labour more than twenty miles away from home villages. More important, the head taxes of the German period became a fixed sum of 10s. for all males over twelve years, although it was never collected universally. Certain administrative auxiliaries and all males already under labour contracts were exempted. Wages were fixed first at 5s., then 10s., a month for males with elaborate scales of rations, clothing, elementary equipment, housing, and health standards and procedures for signing on and off. Breaches of contracts by employers or labourers — desertion was the most usual offence — were punished as criminal offences by fines, imprisonment (with forced labour), and by adding to length of service. Regulations on recruiting were particularly detailed — an indication of the difficulty of supervising a practice undertaken by professional agents, by employers, and frequently by their employees. Villages were 'opened' or 'closed' when population levels were thought to be adversely affected by absence of males, although there is ample evidence that recruiters ignored these provisions in the 1920s, when there were several notorious incidents and court cases. On the whole the patrol officers themselves did not lend their services in recruiting for private employers, but they called regularly on the manpower of villages when on tour and recruited for administrative departments in the towns.

The capitalisation of the plantations derived mainly from German investment increased by restrictions on the export of profits during the war, when German planters and firms continued to operate under army supervision. Much of this extension of plantations came to fruition during the 1920s and required increased amounts of plantation labour, which levelled off at some 20,000 workers a year. The plantations and stores were sold off at inflated prices, before the collapse of copra on world markets, and had a book value of some £3 million supplied in the form of mortgages for a few hundred planters by the Commonwealth Bank, and more particularly by the merchant shipping firms of Burns, Philp and Company and W.R. Carpenter and Company. Ultimate title was held by the Custodian of Expropriated Properties, which gave the Commonwealth government an interest in seeing that capital and charges were repaid by settler-planters, many of whom were politically vociferous returned servicemen. As mortgage debt and working costs increased and profit margins narrowed to extinction during the 1930s, the economic fate of the territory was identified by planters as dependent on plantation production and the system of indentured labour. The one could not stand without the other and the Legislative Council gave political sanction to revision and elaboration of the labour regulations and set limits on the beginnings of New Guinean ventures into produce marketing. The administration was obliged to support this sectional viewpoint, and for a variety of reasons regarded a casual labour market and rural-urban migration with a suspicion which was rationalised into an argument for protection of the interests of New Guinea villagers. Officials did, however, begin to support schemes for New Guinean copra drying without disbanding the restrictions which required such entrepreneurs to market copra through planters' and merchants' stores and which prohibited indentured workers from trading in copra.

As revenue from copra exports declined, gold mining, which had been developed very slowly from German times, employed small numbers of recruited and indentured labour and expanded dramatically from 1930. Major capital investments were made in the Morobe district by New Guinea Goldfields Limited which eventually called up £4.5 million, and by Bulolo Gold Dredging Limited, which had a capital of $4 million. Both enterprises relied heavily on carriers and Guinea Airways. Indentured labour for the mining industry and ancillary services was recruited on exactly the same terms as plantation labour and suffered severely from working at high altitudes, particularly on the Wau Edie fields over three thousand feet. The industry supported about a quarter of administration revenues in the form of royalties and other charges and the total wages bill of both the principal companies tended to rise as a percentage of working costs, because of the importation of expensive skilled Australian labour. Gold prices also rose, although the Commonwealth government imposed a heavy gold tax in 1939.[37] New Guinea Goldfields made a considerable effort to reduce working costs by recruiting indentured labour for semi-skilled positions, a move which resulted in a series of strikes by white miners and Commonwealth intervention to impose an arbitration award in 1941.

The most striking feature of recruitment, however, is not occupational mobility but constant physical transfers between districts where villages constituted a reserve for enclaves of employment, including administrative services and the police who were also under contracts of indenture. The percentage of total labour moving between districts, 1923 – 1940, rose from 31.1 per cent of the annual total to 40.2 per cent. There were wide variations between district recruitment totals and in general the Sepik, as the most underdeveloped region, served as a reservoir for all other districts, while the more developed district of New Britain tended to receive rather than export labour. About half Morobe's contract labour for mining and carrying came from outside the district, mostly from the Sepik.

A second feature of this closely regulated labour force is the narrow occupational range of standard wage employment for migrants. Even Guinea Airways used indentured labour, as did all the merchant firms. After a strike at Rabaul in 1929, started by the highest paid workers in the police and shipping services, planters and administrators were extremely sensitive to any suggestion of reform of the system and resisted the establishment of white unions on the goldfields becasue of their possible demonstration effect.

The period of the war aggravated the worst features of indenture, which became a forced recruitment and labour system for armies in the field and for the Australian administrative service engaged in supplying forward bases and in reconstruction after 1944. Following the cancellation of all contracts of service in 1945, labour deserted *en masse*. The contract system was not abolished, however, although penal sanctions were, and by 1958 ordinances permitted the beginnings of a stabilised urban work force. Migrant labour has remained a structural feature of the New Guinea economy, although workers' associations were given legal status in 1962. The urban minimum wage began to outstrip the rural wage, encouraging further urban 'drift', and at the same time new opportunites for income from cash crops created a new set of wage differentials in the rural districts.

The formal end of the migrant labour system by amendments to the Native Employment Ordinance in 1971 stopped compulsory repatriation to villages, while income disparities opened the way for squatter settlements at Moresby, Rabaul, and Madang and the beginnings of urban unemployment as a permanent feature of enclave development.

Conclusion

There are obvious problems of comparability in a survey of migrant systems drawn from historial examples of different stages of economic growth. Apart from the quality of the historical data, it may be objected that the category of 'settler' implies a freedom of mobility and location which was absent from plantation and industrial labourers in the imperial tropics. Such a distinction ignores the large proportion of colonial state assistance for white settlers, as well as indentured labour, in the nineteenth century, and the constraints on choice apparent in the market mechanisms of passage brokers, limited capital and personal savings, and sheer ignorance of conditions of settlement and employment in overseas territories in North America, Australasia, and Africa. It ignores, too, the large amount of internal rural-urban migration and settlement within the imperial tropics not subject to administrative control.

A more useful distinction in migrant categories lies, rather, between those whose conditions of work and levels of skills allowed them to enjoy a measure of vertical mobility and a participation in the organisation of a political economy, and those whose entry into such economies was partial, peripheral, and without political influence on the organisation of the state. Some colonial states contained both categories of immigrant worker, as, for example, in New Guinea where white settlers were in a minority, or Queensland, where Melanesian labourers were in a minority. In Nigeria there was little participation by either migrant workers or urban and rural communities in the institutions of colonial administration, except through traditional and subordinate authority structures, until the beginnings of urban representation in the 1920s and regional representation after 1945. But it could not be said that the condition of foreign immigrants in Nigeria or other West African countries with large settler communities has been improved by such constitutional integration. Indeed (like Melanesians in Queensland) they have found themselves the object of resentment and discriminatory legislation in Ghana and ethnic persecution and expulsion in Nigeria.[38]

Apart from differences in degree of participation in the organisation of a political economy, the examples also present the historian with the difficulty of accounting for migrant flows in conventional supply and demand terms in economies where cycles of investment gave rise to employment of both skilled and unskilled workers, and where seasonal patterns of rural agriculture or unfamiliarity with the disciplines of industrial wage labour discouraged stabilised recruitment at the early stages of commercial and industrial production. There is also a different chronology for incorporation of staple-producing enclaves and settler economies within the developing structures of world markets in the nineteenth and twentieth centuries, although primary producers were all adversely affected and suffered unemployment in the depression of the 1930s. A common theme between the examples, however, is the regulatory role of the colonial state in conditions of competition and shortage of migrant labour.

In New Zealand, as in the Australian colonies, the initiative for government intervention in determining the type and numbers of immigrants was secured from the imperial power at a relatively early stage of internal political autonomy, although settler economies remained heavily dependent on capital imports and overseas markets for staples. Between 1860 and 1919 the Australian colonies, which had already ended convict transportation to the eastern settlements and prohibited this type of forced labour from entering South Australia, gave financial assistance to some 1.25 million immigrants (or roughly half of total immigration) by selection, nomination, and land orders.[39] Similarly, New Zealand during the 1870s had relatively easier access to sources of capital than either New Guinea or Nigeria in the inter-war period. But loans, capital equipment, and sales of timber, wool, wheat, and other produce in distant markets were far from guaranteed, and the colonial agents and the government had to compete with other investment portfolios. Paradoxically, New Zealand had also to compete for immigrants, as neighbouring Australian colonial governments increased the choices for British settlers by lowering fares to the most distant markets. A second important influence of the colonial state on immigration, after the positive financial assistance of the 1870s, lay in the racially selective and restrictive policies which were adopted, particularly for Asian immigration in the 1880s, and were given statutory form by 1920.

Sectoral competiton for labour, rather than international competition, was a feature of investment both in New Guinea plantations and Nigerian mining. In New Guinea, investment was from sources of private capital in two phases in the 1890s and the late 1920s and early 1930s, while merchant and mining investment in Nigeria was accompanied by an important underwriting of colonial loans for port and railway development covering the period from the late 1890s to the 1920s. German, Australian, and British administrations were all required to support the costs of military conquest and peacetime patrols. They were also major employers of labour, particularly during public works programmes.

On the whole such public and private investment created enclaves in predominantly subsistence economies. New Guinea plantations had their counterparts in the Cameroons, but commercial agriculture in Nigeria rested on a broad base of indigenous cash crop production which was also a major employer of rural labour. But it should be remembered that as late as 1938 agriculture, mining, the public sector, commerce, and industry in Nigeria had a wage labour force of only 230,000 workers, or some 4 per cent of the economically active male population.[40] New Guinea's 40,000 workers represented hardly more than 8 per cent of the total enumerated adult population in the late 1930s, which was, moreover, underestimated at that period.

In both territories, therefore, the economic sectors employing migrant labour were very narrow and specific to particular modes of production. Rail, road, and river communications did something to serve these sectors in Nigeria, but in New Guinea there were no roads or railways at all. Terms such as the New Guinean or Nigerian 'economy' prior to political unification and massive increases in sources of expenditure after World War II beg a whole series of questions about linkages which were elementary or absent and services and manufactures which were little in evidence and did not enter any system of national accounts. If the New Zealand example, like that of other Pacific territories, had been examined for the period before the 1860s, production for export would have been characterised by similar experiments in resource exploitation with limited capital and wage labour, before company investment in land sales, immigration from the Australian colonies and elsewhere, political annexation, and the construction of a state-wide economy.

One conclusion, therefore, might be that the colonial government was required to make greater efforts to assist recruitment and control wage labour in conditions of limited enclave development and relative disaggregation of regional economies in the colonial state. Compared with New Guinea, Northern Nigeria would appear to be an intermediate case with only spasmodic intervention, no conventional labour administration until after World War II, but with a consistently expansive taxation of agricultural populations which encouraged temporary migration for cash income where this could not be found in commercial agriculture. Coercion was tried more directly for brief periods in 1918 and the 1940s for the benefit of mining production, and the administration itself used such labour for its own services. Seasonal migration and some urbanisation in the mining centres provided the bulk of labour, but resident agriculturalists in the specific case of the Birom suffered further coercion from loss of land to the new industry and had a narrower range of occupations than other migrant workers. By contrast, New Guinea provides an example of severe constraint on choice, a fixed cash wage which was kept low, a disciplined indenture system, and a lack of alternatives from commercial agriculture. It was essentially a coercive sytem by indirect means and formal controls, and direct forced labour was employed in World War II.

The New Guinea case also provides evidence of restriction, as well as regulation, of mobility. The urbanisation which is a feature of market and industrial development in Africa and elsewhere in the Pacific was deliberately discouraged by settlers and officials through curfew enforcement, labour lines in specific areas, and regular return of labour to rural villages. In the longer term our view of specific examples of wage labour migration to limited sectors of a colonial economy may have to take into account the broader dimensions of rural-urban drift which has become a major feature of European, North American, and Australasian population movements from the nineteenth century. Given the economic importance of the agricultural sector in New Zealand, it is remarkable that the percentage of the population directly engaged in farming and farm labouring remained under 15 per cent and that there was a steady shift between 1871 and 1900 away from the country hamlets and counties to the cities and boroughs.[41] Rural-urban migration has remained the dominant feature of West African migrations from the savannah to the towns and ports of the forest belt, with a net gain of some 1.6 millions, 1965-1975, or 45 per cent of total urban growth in eight of the region's states.[42] New Guinea has now clearly been drawn into the same pattern of internal migration and would probably have done so earlier without the controls on mobility which arrested urban settlement by wage labourers or, indeed, by Asian or migrants other than Australian and European settlers.

A more general point from the three examples is that it is possible to analyse labour migration without making a rigid distinction between movements of 'people' and movements of 'labour', as emphasised in S. Amin's general survey of West African cases.[43] Such a distiction telescopes much of the early economic history of 'recent settlement' colonies and regards them as 'structured and complete' from the beginnings of colonisation. On the contrary, North America, Australasia, and New Zealand provide good examples of mercantile enclave development, forced labour, slavery, and indenture, along with assisted immigration and investment by settler families. Even within the West African region, the distinction between migrant farmers and labourers in groundnut, cocoa, and cotton production has not been hard and fast and can be interpreted as prospection of a variety of opportunities in response to the demands of an overseas staple economy on lands broken in for commercial agriculture. Such movements of traders and settlers were, in any case, not new in the history of kola and cattle production and marketing. Like European migration, colonisation of Nigeria's middle belt, the foundation of new ethnic wards in Nigeria's towns and mining camps, and the exodus of Nigerians to Ghana, can be regarded as a shift in human resources including know-how, personal capital, and elementary social structures. Wage labour was a significant element in such shifts into capitalist modes of production, because enclaves with low-level technology were labour intensive.

But migration was not restricted to wage labour for such enclaves. A more important consideration than typological distinctions between migrants is the dynamics of their contribution to capitalist investment and production in enclaves and structured colonies after one or two generations of labour inputs from mobile workers. The question is whether the division of labour present from the beginnings of incorporation of overseas territories into world markets entailed occupational stratification which prevented or delayed migrants' vertical mobility within the developing political economy. If explored in greater depth and brought up to date, the New Zealand case suggests that the rural Maori population, despite some notable professional and political advances in the late nineteenth century, remained as smallholders and migrant agricultural workers, until their movement into urban services and industries from the 1940s.[44] From different rural backgrounds, other Pacific islands' migrants to New Zealand have followed a similar delayed entry into the pattern of urbanisation set by European and Australian immigrants over a longer time-scale.

A clearer case of occupational differentiation among labour migrants can be seen in the history of New Guinea's Chinese community, introduced in the German period for general services and supervisory roles on plantations. These were quickly changed for commerce, crafts, and operation of the copra-purchasing stores from which New Guinea entrepreneurs were excluded until the late 1930s. Apart from the obvious example of Australian settler and mineworker stratification in New Guinea, there have been more recent group differences in the rural and urban workforce according to acceptance of migratory work contract schemes for the Highlands in the 1960s, compared with a preference for casual urban work in Port Moresby for Papuans and more specialised industrial mine work on Bougainville for workers from Buka.[45]

This kind of group or ethnic specialisation among unskilled migrants is not unknown in the earlier history of labour in Nigeria, where local communities supplied most of the labour for the Enugu colliery, and where Benin and Warri plantations and timber concessions drew regularly on Ishan workers from the north of Benin province.[46] It would not be too much to conclude that the Birom had become structurally dependent on the tin mines for cash income by the 1940s, although other peasant farming communities subject to conscription at that period were not.[47] Few, if any, of the seasonal casual workers rose to positions as foremen or gang supervisors, who were mainly Hausa and Kanuri, many of whom had experience in other fields of mining and public works, while Ibo and Yoruba occupied the minor administrative and clerical posts of the mining companies.[48]

But for most of the colonial period it would be accurate to state that in Melanesian and Northern Nigerian societies the upper limits of occupational skills were fairly soon reached by migrant workers, remembering that only a small percentage of the economically active population was engaged in wage-earning at all. It is an open question how far this impediment to occupational mobility simply resulted from lack of skills or from forms of job preservation and was compounded by the temporary or seasonal recruitment of labourers. But lack of job mobility is a further constraint on choice, particularly in societies on the edge of enclave economies. In New Zealand by the 1870s the range of occupations had expanded rapidly, and it was the seasonal migrant worker, rather than whole ethnic groups, who remained on the edge of the wage-earning sectors of the economy. The possible exception to this contrast with the sectoral enclaves of New Guinea and Nigeria lies in the case of the rural Maori farmers and wage-earners whose position within the development of New Zealand's economy has not been studied. It may be possible to look on them, however, as part of a 'reserve' which was drawn on at a late date when manpower was in short supply in the 1940s. Such reserves were, of course, tapped in Melanesia and Africa earlier in the nineteenth century in conditions of specific competition for particular modes of production.[49]

Such competition on an international level was also present for settler labour, but in general the coercive and restrictive regulation of recruitment which was a feature of some Melanesian and African labour systems at times of a high labour supply price was not required, and, indeed, would have been resisted as settlers participated in the representative institutions of the political economy.

NOTES

INTRODUCTION

1   E. J. Hobsbawm, *The Age of Capital, 1848-1875* (London, 1977), p.228.
2   B. Thomas, 'Migration. II. Economic Aspects' in *The International Encyclopaedia of the Social Sciences,* Vol. 10 (London, 1968), p. 229.
3   C. Newbury, 'Labour Migration in the Imperial Phase: an essay in interpretation', *Journal of Imperial and Commonwealth History, iii (1975), p. 235.*
4   *Ibid.,* p. 236.
5   See below, pp. 16-18
6   S. Amin (ed), *Modern Migrations in Western Africa* (London, 1974), pp. 85, 89.
7   History Task Force, Centro de Estudios Puertorriquenos, *Labor Migration under Capitalism: the Puerto Rican experience* (New York and London, 1979), pp. 21-2.
8   K. Marx, *Grundrisse* (Harmondsworth, 1973), p. 100.
9   For a discussion of the dualist model, see G. Standing, 'Migration and Modes of Exploitation: the social origins of immobility and mobility', *Population and Employment Working Paper No 72* (Geneva, ILO, 1979). For the debate over the 'backward sloping curve of labour supply' in the South African mining industry, see S. van der Horst, *Native Labour in South Africa* London, 1942, reprinted 1971). pp. 197-9.
10 E. P. Thompson, *The Poverty of Theory* (London, 1978), p. 280. For a fine discussion of the problems involved in Thompson's notion of human 'agency' and the wider issues raised, see P. Anderson, *Arguments within English Marxism* (London, 1980), chapter 2.
11 B. Thomas, *Migration and Economic Growth: a study of Great Britain and the Atlantic economy* (Cambridge, 2nd edition, 1973), p. 26.
12 Amin, *op. cit.,* p. 89.
13 C. Murray, 'Explaining Migration: the tradition in Eastern and Southern Africa', unpublished paper, Seminar on Labour Migration in the Empire/Commonwealth Studies (hereafter Labour Migration Seminar), 6 November 1979, p. 2.
14 See below, pp. 27-8.
15 See below, p. 183.
16 See below, pp. 32-3
17 See below, p. 175.
18 See below, pp. 118-24.
19 See, for example, R. Palmer and N. Parsons (eds), *The Roots of Rural Poverty in Central and Southern Africa* (London, 1977) and the chapters by Guy, Harries, Kimble, and Shillington in S. Marks and R. Rathbone (eds), *Industrial and Social Change in South Africa: African class formation, culture and consciousness 1870-1930* (London, 1982).
20 See below, pp. 30, 32.
21 B. Thomas, 'Migration and International Investment' in A. R. Hall (ed), *The Export of Capital from Britain* (London, 1968), pp. 47, 49.
22 See N. Harris, 'The New Untouchables: the international migration of labour', *International Socialism, ii (1980), p.37.*
23 P. Corrigan, 'Feudal Relics or Capitalist Monuments? Notes on the sociology of unfree labour', *Sociology, xi (1977), p. 445.*

24 See below, p. 226.

25 See below, p. 30.

26 See below, pp. 34-46, esp. 46.

27 Joy Parr, *Labouring Children: British immigrant apprentices to Canada 1869-1924* (Toronto, 1980).

28 Corrigan, *op cit.*

29 See below, p. 193.

30 See below, p. 226.

31 By Graves, Emmer, Tinker, Richardson, Legassick and de Clercq, and Burke.

32 See below, pp. 62-5.

33 See, for example, Palmer and Parsons, *op cit;* H. Wolpe, 'Capitalism and Cheap Labour Power in South Africa: from segregation to apartheid', *Economy and Society,* i (1972), pp. 425-56; and the chapter by Legassick and de Clercq in this collection.

34 Hobsbawm, *op. cit., p. 235.*

35 See below, pp. 129-33.

36 See below, pp. 48-56.

37 W. Ashworth, *A Short History of the International Economy since 1850* (London, 3rd edition, 1975), p. 196.

38 R. Cohen, 'Habituating Migrant Agricultural Workers in the US: the role of the state and the growers', unpublished paper, Labour Migration Seminar, 19 May 1981.

39 See below, p. 209.

40 See below pp. 143-5.

41 See the introduction to Marks and Rathbone, *op. cit.*

42 K. Marx, *Capital,* Vol. I (Harmondsworth, 1976), p. 939.

43 See below, pp. 24-8, 74, 133-5, 176-7.

44 See below, pp. 71.

45 G. Standing, 'Migration and Proletarianisation', unpublished paper, Labour Migration Seminar, 13 January 1981, p. 19.

46 For a recent stimulating comparison between South Africa and Israel in this respect, see S. Greenberg, *Order and the Ethnic State: developing markets and labor control in Israel and South Africa* (forthcoming).

47 Standing, 'Migration and Proletarianisation', p. 19.

48 *Ibid.*

49 D. Hemson, 'Dockworkers, Labour Circulation and Class Struggles in Durban, 1940-1959', *Journal of Southern African Studies,* iv (1977), pp. 88-124.

50 E. Laclau, *Politics and Ideology in Marxist Theory* (London, 1977), p. 157.

51 Standing, 'Migration and Proletarianisation', p. 7.

52 The earliest work was probably G. Wilson's *An Essay on the Economics of Detribalization in Northern Rhodesia,* Parts 1 and 2 (Livingstone, Rhodes-Livingstone Institute, 1941-2), followed by I. Schapera, *Migrant Labour and Tribal Life* (London, 1947). The literature is, however, too vast to cite here.

53 By ideology, we mean: 'A whole *system* of thought, or co-ordinated beliefs and ideas, which form a framework, or higher-level group of related concepts, for more specific and particular notions, analyses, applications and conclusions. As such it will be generally related to certain activities and policies, but not necessarily in any simple and obvious or direct manner; and for those who conduct discussion at the

higher (or more general) level the relation may not always be fully conscious, still less explicit. At its most general, an ideology constitutes or implies a philosophical standpoint. . . . provided that this is not given too formal or methodological a connotation'. (M. Dobb, *Theories of Value and Distribution since Adam Smith: ideology and economic theory* (Cambridge, 1973), p. 1.)

54 Marx, *Grundrisse*, p. 100. For the full quotation see above, p. 4.

55 W. Freund, 'Labour Migration to the Nigerian Tin Mines in the Colonial Era, 1900-1960', paper, Labour Migration Seminar, 12 February 1980, published in *Journal of African History*, xxii (1981), as 'Labour Migration to the Northern Nigerian Tin Mines, 1903-45.'

56 Murray, 'Explaining Migration', p.21.

57 G. Standing, 'Migration and Modes of Exploitation: the social origins of mobility and immobility', *Journal of Peasant Studies*, viii (1981), p. 80.

1. ENGLISH INDENTURED SERVANTS AND THE TRANSATLANTIC COLONIAL ECONOMY

1 Norfolk Record Office (hereafter RO), AYL 535, William Doughty to Robert Doughty, 20 December 1667.

2 Norfolk RO, AYL 535, William Doughty to Robert Doughty, 28 January 1668.

3 Norfolk RO, AYL 535, will of William Doughty proved in 1686; R. S. Dunn, *Sugar and Slaves: the rise of the planter class in the English West Indies, 1627-1713* (London, 1973).

4 The most extended accounts of transatlantic indentured servant movement are in A. E. Smith, *Colonists in Bondage* (Chapel Hill, 1947), and D. W. Galenson, *White Servitude in Colonial America* (Cambridge, 1981).

5 Hugh Tinker, *A New System of Slavery: the export of Indian labour overseas 1830-1920* (Oxford, 1974).

6 This essay is a synthesis of recent work on indentured servitude and the English colonial economies. My particular aim is to specify more closely the determination of the flow of migrants from the point of view of the sending economy and the likely interrelationship with structures of demand for labour. I am grateful to the Institute of Commonwealth Studies seminar series and to the Organization of American Historians for giving me the opportunity to develop some of these thoughts.

7 C. Reynel, *The True English Interest* (London, 1674), p. 59.

8 H. A. Gemery, 'Emigration from the British Isles to the New World 1630-1700: inferences from colonial populations', *Research in Economic History*, v (1980), pp. 179-231.

9 *Ibid.*, p. 215. These are Gemery's preferred estimates, although he does present a lower series based on even less optimistic demographic conditions for the Caribbean.

10 Recent analyses of this movement, depending upon socio-economic analysis rather than hagiography, are T. H. Breen and S. Foster, 'Moving to the New World: the character of early Massachusetts immigration', *William and Mary Quarterly*, 3rd series (WMQ), xxx (1973), pp. 189-222; A. Salerno, 'The Social Background of Seventeenth-Century Emigration to America', *Journal of British Studies*, x (1979-80), pp. 31-52.

11 E. A. Wrigley and R. S. Schofield, *The Population History of England 1541-1871: a reconstruction* (London, 1981), esp. pp. 185-8, 200-02, 219-28.

12 *Ibid.,* p. 219.

13 A similar chronology, although on nothing like the same scale, may be seen to have operated in seventeenth-century France: H. Charbonneau, *Vie et Mort de Nos Ancêtres* (Montreal, 1975), pp. 35-8.

14 Dunn, *op. cit.,* pp. 300-04; D. B. Smith, 'Mortality and Family in the Colonial Chesapeake', *Journal of Interdisciplinary History,* viii (1977-78), pp. 403-27.

15 Smith, *op. cit.* In the registrations of indentured servants leaving Bristol for the years 1654-62, only thirty, 0.6 per cent of the total, were indentured for New England (Bristol RO, 04220 (1)); D. Souden, ' "Rogues, Whores, and Vagabonds"? Indentured servant emigrants to North America, and the case of mid-seventeenth-century Bristol', *Social History,* iii (1978), pp. 23-41, esp. p. 37.

16 Dunn, *op. cit.,* pp. 53-6; W. F. Craven, *White, Red, and Black: the seventeenth-century Virginian* (Charlottesville, 1971), p. 5; L. G. Carr and R. R. Menard, 'Immigration and Opportunity: the freedman in early colonial Maryland' in T. W. Tate and D. L. Ammerman (eds), *The Chesapeake in the Seventeenth Century: essays on Anglo-American society* (Chapel Hill, 1979), pp. 206-52, esp. pp. 206-7; Gemery, *op. cit.,* p. 217.

17 A. S. Kussmaul, *Servants in Husbandry in Early Modern England* (Cambridge, 1981).

18 D. W. Galenson and R. R. Menard, 'Approaches to the Analysis of Economic Growth in Colonial British America', *Historical Methods,* xiii (1980-81), pp. 3-18, esp. p. 11.

19 D. W. Galenson, 'The Market Evaluation of Human Capital: the case of indentured servitude', *Journal of Political Economy,* lxxxix (1981), pp. 446-67.

20 Souden, *op. cit.,* pp. 26-7, 37; Wrigley and Schofield, *op. cit.,* p. 202.

21 Souden, *op. cit.,* pp. 27-8.

22 G. Gardyner, *A Description of the New World, or, America Islands and Continent . . . .* (London, 1651), introduction and p. 8.

23 R. Wodenoth, *A Perfect Description of Virginia* (London, 1649), p. 8.

24 J. Hammond, *Leah and Rachel, or, The Two Fruitful Sisters Virginia and Maryland . . . .* (London, 1656), p. 12.

25 R. Ligon, *A True and Exact History of the Island of Barbados* (London, 1657), pp. 43-6, 109-16.

26 See K. G. Davies, *The North Atlantic World in the Seventeenth Century* (Minneapolis, 1974), and R. Davis, *The Rise of the Atlantic Economies* (London, 1973), for general treatments.

27 G. Debien, 'Les Engagés pour les Antilles 1634-1715', *Revue d'Histoire des Colonies,* xxxviii (1951).

28 L. Bourrachot, J.-P. Poussou, and C. Huetz de Lemps, 'Les Départs de Passagers Pyrénéens par Bordeaux au XVIIIe Siècle', *Bulletin de la Société des Sciences, Lettres et Arts de Pau,* 4e série, iii (1968), pp. 133-62.

29 Much of this discussion is drawn from D. C. Souden, 'Pre-industrial English Local Migration Fields' (unpublished PhD thesis, University of Cambridge, 1981).

30 Wrigley and Schofield, *op. cit.,* pp. 207-10, 642-3.

31 J. Thirsk and J. P. Cooper (eds), *Seventeenth Century Economic Documents* (Oxford, 1972), pp. 713-50.

32 Reynel, *op. cit.,* p. 54.

Notes

33 Thirsk and Cooper, *op. cit.*, p. 80.

34 M. Spufford, *Contrasting Communities: English villagers in the sixteenth and seventeenth centuries* (Cambridge, 1974), esp. pp. 121-64.

35 Bristol RO, 04220 (1), 04220 (2), 04355 (6), 04356 (1).

36 Souden, 'Rogues, Whores and Vagabonds', pp. 32-4.

37 Salerno, *op. cit.*, pp. 34-7.

38 Souden, 'Pre-industrial English Local Migration', pp. 141-9.

39 Bristol RO, 04356 (1).

40 M. Ghirelli (ed), *A List of Emigrants from England to America 1682-1692* (Baltimore, 1968); C. D. P. Nicholson, 'Some Early Emigrants to America', *Genealogists' Magazine,* xii (1955-58) and xiii (1959-62), *passim;* J. Wareing, 'Some Early Emigrants to America, 1683-1684: a supplementary list', *ibid.*, xviii (1975-76), pp. 239-46. See J. Horn, 'Servant Emigration to the Chesapeake in the Seventeenth Century' in Tate and Ammerman, *op. cit.*, pp. 51-95.

41 M. Campbell, 'Social Origins of Some Early Americans' in J. M. Smith (ed), *Seventeenth Century America* (Chapel Hill, 1959), pp. 63-89; D. W. Galenson, '"Middling People" or "Common Sort"? the social origins of some early Americans reexamined', *WMQ,* xxxv (1978), pp. 499-524, with 'Debate', *ibid.*, pp. 525-42, *WMQ,* xxxvi (1979), pp. 264-86; Souden, 'Rogues, Whores and Vagabonds', pp. 26-7.

42 D. W. Galenson, 'Literacy and the Social Origins of Some Early Americans', *Historical Journal,* xxii (1979), pp. 75-91. Compare, however, the very high illiteracy of the servants leaving Lyme Regis 1683-89, Dorset RO, B7/M9/1-28.

43 Also Kussmaul, *op. cit.*, esp. chapter 5; K. D. M. Snell, 'Agricultural Seasonal Unemployment, the Standard of Living, and Women's Work in the South and East, 1690-1860', *Economic History Review,* 2nd Series, xxxiv (1981), pp. 407-37.

44 L. G. Carr and L. S. Walsh, 'The Planter's Wife: the experience of white women in seventeenth-century Maryland', *WMQ,* xxxiv (1977), pp. 542-71; Horn, *op. cit.*, p. 63; PRO, HCA 30/635-36; J. and M. Kaminkow (eds), *A List of Emigrants from England to America, 1718-1759* (Baltimore, 1964). Also Galenson, 'Market Evaluation', p. 454.

45 Wrigley and Schofield, *op. cit.;* on p. 228 they calculate that 58 per cent of the fall in total numbers in the third quarter of the seventeenth century is 'attributable' to emigration.

46 J. Child, *A New Discourse of Trade* (1694 edition), p. 72.

47 Much recent research is exemplified in L. G. Carr, A. C. Land, and E. G. Papenfuse (eds), *Law, Society, and Politics in Early Maryland* (Baltimore, 1977); Tate and Ammerman, *op. cit.;* E. S. Morgan, *American Slavery, American Freedom,* (New York, 1975).

48 J. Lorimer, 'The English Contraband Trade from Trinidad and Guiana, 1590-1617' in K. R. Andrews, N. P. Canny, and P. E. H. Hair (eds), *The Westward Enterprise: English activities in Ireland, the Atlantic, and America 1480-1650* (Liverpool, 1978), pp. 124-50; Morgan, *op. cit.*, pp. 82-8; R. C. Batie, 'Why Sugar? economic cycles and the changing of staples on the English and French Antilles 1624-54', *Journal of Caribbean History,* viii (1976), pp. 1-41, esp. pp. 1-9; Dunn, *op. cit.*, pp. 3-59.

49 Letter of John Pory, in S. M. Kingsbury (ed), *Records of the Virginia Company of London* (Washington, DC, 1933), iii, p. 221.

50 A. L. Beier, 'Social Problems in Elizabethan London', *Journal of Interdisciplinary History*, ix (1978-79), pp. 203-21, esp. p. 219.

51 PRO, HCA 30/635-636. See also Souden, 'Rogues, Whores, and Vagabonds', esp. pp. 26-8. For the general basis of New World trading, see R. Brenner, 'The Social Basis of English Commercial Expansion, 1550-1650', *Journal of Economic History*, xxxii (1972), pp. 361-84.

52 This cyclical pattern is elegantly analysed in R. R. Menard, 'The Tobacco Industry in the Chesapeake Colonies, 1617-1730: an interpretation', *Research in Economic History*, v (1980), pp. 109-77. See the short-run variation in numbers of *engagés* for the French Antilles at the same times in Debien, *op. cit.*, pp. 248-9.

53 PRO C78/735/13; Southampton Civic RO, SC9/3/12, folios 65v-69v; Bristol RO, 0447 (1), folio 141.

54 Batie, *op. cit.;* Dunn, *op. cit.*, pp. 46-83.

55 Souden, 'Rogues, Whores and Vagabonds', pp. 35-6; W. A. Claypole and D. J. Buisseret, 'Trade-Patterns in Early English Jamaica', *Journal of Caribbean History*, v (1972), pp. 1-19, provide data on the relative levels of continued white immigration and Negro importation into Port Royal.

56 Carr and Menard, *op. cit.;* P. G. E. Clemens, *The Atlantic Economy and Colonial Maryland's Eastern Shore: from tobacco to grain* (Ithaca, 1980), pp. 48-53.

57 *Ibid.*, pp. 52-5.

58 R. R. Menard, 'From Servants to Slaves: the transformation of the Chesapeake labor system', *Southern Studies*, xvi (1977), pp. 354-90.

59 D. W. Galenson, 'White Servitude and the Growth of Black Slavery in Colonial America', *Journal of Economic History*, xli (1981), pp. 39-47; see e.g. J. H. Bennett, 'Cary Helyar, Merchant and Planter of Seventeenth-Century Jamaica', *WMQ*, xxi (1964), pp. 53-76, esp. pp. 70-73; R. B. Davis (ed), *William Fitzhugh and his Chesapeake World 1676-1712* (Chapel Hill, 1963), esp. pp. 15, 92, 202-5.

60 Smith, *op. cit.*

61 R. Gray and B. Wood, 'The Transition from Indentured to Involuntary Servitude in Colonial Georgia', *Explorations in Economic History*, xiii (1976), pp. 353-70.

62 Menard, 'From Servants to Slaves'; H. A. Gemery and J. S. Hogendorn, 'The Atlantic Slave Trade: a tentative economic model', *Journal of African History*, xv (1974), pp. 223-46.

63 P. Clark, 'The Migrant in Kentish Towns 1580-1640' in P. Clark and P. Slack (eds), *Crisis and Order in English Towns 1500-1700* (London, 1972), pp. 117-63.

64 Child, *op. cit.*, p.183.

65 Morgan, *op. cit.*, chapters 3-5, is a classic example of failure to control for the inherent biases in employers' views of their employees, and vice versa.

2. WHY DID CONTRACT LABOUR NOT WORK IN THE NINETEENTH CENTURY UNITED STATES?

1 John Franklin Jameson, *The American Revolution Considered as a Social Movement* (Princeton, 1926), pp. 29-30.

2 A Federal Act prohibiting peonage was passed in 1867.

3 Dennis Clark, 'Babes in Bondage: indentured Irish children in Philadelphia in the nineteenth century', *Pennsylvania Magazine of History and Biography*, ci (1977), pp. 484-5, James Motley, 'Apprenticeship in American Trade Unions', *Johns Hopkins University Studies in History and Political Science*, xxv (1907), pp. 15-17.

4   In 1793 the Supreme Court of Pennsylvania decided that a minor could not be bound as a servant although he or she might be apprenticed to a trade. However, 'The custom as it applied to immigrants included children as well as adults, and was thought a necessity, as practiced. [The Court] affirmed (it) to be mutually beneficial to the state and the immigrant'. (Cheeseman A. Herrick, *White Servitude in Pennsylvania* [Philadelphia, 1926], p. 6, citing Dallas Reports, II, 198, 199).

5   Karl Frederick Geiser, 'Redemptioners and Indentured Servants in the Colony and Commonwealth of Pennsylvania', *Yale Review* (August 1901), pp. 2-3: Richard B. Morris, *Government and Labor in Early America* (New York, 1946), pp. 344-5; Phineas Bond, Philadelphia, 16 November 1778, to Lord Carmarthen, *Annual Report of the American Historical Association for 1896* (Washington, 1897), I, 582-3. Galenson's preliminary work suggests that binding after arrival 'according to the custom of the country' did not bring significantly longer indentures than those entered into in Britain. They could not have been shorter or servants would have had no incentive to bind themselves before departure (David W. Galenson, 'British Servants and the Colonial Indenture System in the Eighteenth Century', *Journal of Southern History*, xliv [1978], pp. 59-65).

6   'The Diary of John Harrower, 1773-6, *American Historical Review*, vi (1900), p. 368; Geiser, *op. cit.*, p. 54; Bond, 16 November 1788, *loc. cit.*, p. 583; Morris, *op. cit.*, p. 432.

7   Morris, *op. cit.*, p. 437.

8   Robert O. Heavner, 'Indentured Servitude: the Philadelphia Market, 1771-1773', *Journal of Economic History*, xxviii (1978), p. 712. Galenson, 'British Servants and the Colonial Indenture System', pp. 57-8.

9   E. I. McCormac, 'White Servitude in Maryland, 1634-1820', *Johns Hopkins University Studies in Historical and Political Science*, xxii (1904), p. 107.

10   William Miller, 'Effects of Revolution on Indentured Servitude', *Pennsylvania History*, vii (1940), p. 138.

11   Bond, November 1789, *loc.cit.*, p. 642; Miller, *op. cit.*, pp. 139-40; Herrick, *op. cit.*, p. 254. It was 'never revived with any great vigour' in Maryland, however (McCormac, *op. cit.*, p. 108).

12   William Miller wrote with respect to the law of master and servant in Pennsylvania between 1775 and 1789 that 'no changes were made in the rights of either party or in the obligations of one to the other. Certainly not in statutory law nor apparently in custom either, was there any departure from colonial practice.' (Miller, *op. cit.*, p. 133. See also pp. 134-6); Samuel McKee, Jr, *Labor in Colonial New York* (New York, 1935), pp. 176-8; Geiser, *op. cit.*, pp. 67-8; Morris, *op. cit.*, p. 322; Louis Hartz, *Economic Policy and Democratic Thought, Pennsylvania, 1776-1860* (Cambridge Mass., 1948), p. 185.

13   What was actually proposed was that the cargo of servants be liberated by a subscription to pay their passages 'repaying themselves by a small rateable deduction out of the wages of such Servants' *(Independent Gazette, 24 January 1784, quoted in McKee, *op. cit.*, p. 176).

14   Geiser, *op. cit.*, p. 41; Herrick, *op. cit.*, pp. 256-9.

15   Morris, *op. cit.*, p. 408.

16   Herrick, *op. cit.*, pp. 265-6.

17   Miller, *op. cit.*, pp. 131-2.

18   Maldwyn A. Jones,'The Background to Emigration from Great Britain in the Nineteenth Century', *Perspectives in American History*, vii (1973), p. 12; Herrick,

op. cit., pp. 254, 259; David Jeremy, 'Damning the Flood: British Government efforts to check the outflow of technicians and machinery, 1780-1843', *Business History Review,* li (1977), 1-34. Estimates of foreign immigration to the United States during the French Revolutionary Wars vary considerably. In 1793 Thomas Cooper stated that 10,000 a year were arriving from Britain, Ireland, and Germany (Thomas Cooper, *Some Information Respecting America* [Dublin, 1794], p. 66). After that the outbreak of war, the danger of impressment, and the certainty of employment in the armed forces of men who might otherwise have emigrated as indentured servants must have reduced the flow. In 1804 Samuel Blodgett asserted that immigration had averaged 4,000 a year during the previous ten years. At the close of the wars Dr. Adam Seybert estimated that immigration could not have averaged more than 6,000 a year during the two decades after 1790 *(Statistical Annals . . . of the United States of America* (Phildelphia, 1818), p. 28). But George Tucker thought this estimate too low by half *(Progress of the United States in Population and Wealth in Fifty Years* (Boston, 1843), p. 20). Contemporary newspapers placed the immigration through Philadelphia alone as high as 14,000 in 1807, however (Herrick, *op. cit.,* p. 259). If one takes the largest, and probably wildly exaggerated, assertion of 30,000 a year in the 1800-10 decade, bound immigrant servants might have accounted for 11 per cent of the non-slave labour force in 1800. The percentage was certainly much less than this, especially in that not all immigrants were indentured servants or redemptioners. (Henry Wansey, *The Journal of an Excursion to the United States of North America in the Summer of 1794* (Salisbury, 1796), p. 204; *Niles Weekly Register* (Baltimore), 18 May 1812, p. 184; 30 November 1811, p. 239). The proportion of immigrants who were indentured is no less difficult to ascertain than the total numbers. For evidence that servants were still coming in during the wars, however, see William Priest, *Travels in the United States of America* (London, 1802), pp. 81-7; Geiser, *op. cit.,* p. 41; Wansey, *op. cit.,* p. 183.

19   The 1810 law in Pennsylvania required masters to give six weeks' schooling each year to children under indenture. In 1818 extra charges for landing were prohibited; husband and wife could not be sold out of state against their will. (Herrick, *op. cit.,* p. 263; McCormac, *op. cit.,* pp. 47, 77).

20   Bond, 10 September 1791, to Lord Grenville, *loc. cit.,* p. 488.

21   McCormac, *op. cit.,* pp. 109-10. For early British passenger legislation, see Oliver McDonagh, *A Pattern of Government Growth* (London, 1961), pp. 54-73.

22   Morris, *op. cit.,* p. 514.

23   Geiser, *op. cit.,* p. 42. His views are repeated by Herrick, *op. cit.,* p. 266; Morris, *op. cit.,* p. 363; Hartz, *op. cit.,* pp. 220, 223, 186; and Heavner, *op. cit.,* pp. 701-2. On abolition of imprisonment for debt, see Walter Hugins, *Jacksonian Democracy and the Working Class: a study of the New York workingmen's movement, 1829-37* (Stanford, 1960), pp. 136-8; F. T. Carlton, 'Abolition of Imprisonment for Debt', *Yale Review,* xvii (1908-9), pp. 339-45; Arthur Mayer Schlesinger, Jr, *The Age of Jackson* (Boston, 1945), pp. 134-6.

24   William Cohen, 'Negro Involuntary Servitude in the South, 1865-1940: a preliminary analysis', *Journal of Southern History,* xlii (1976), pp. 31-60. Pete Daniel, *'The Shadow of Slavery: peonage in the South, 1901-69* (Urbana, 1972); Morris, *op. cit.,* p. 433.

25   Jones, *op cit.,* pp. 16, 18. Richard Morris estimated fares and other costs of

emigration at £20 for an adult on the eve of the Revolution (*op. cit.*, p. 319). Geiser put it even higher, at £22 (*op. cit.*, p. 45). See also Herrick, *op. cit.*, p. 265; McCormac, *op. cit.*, p. 108.

26 Morris, *op. cit.*, p. 445.

27 Heavner, *op. cit.*, pp. 710-11.

28 Geiser, *op. cit.*, p. 54.

29 Morris *op. cit.*, p. 460.

30 Extract from a letter to George Washington from Valentine Crawford, 1774, *Documentary History of American Industrial Society*, I, pp. 344-5.

31 Geiser, *op. cit.*, p. 7.

32 McCormac, *op. cit.*, p. 39.

33 David Jeremy, 'British Textile Technology Transmission to the United States: the Philadelphia region experience 1770-1820', *Business History Review*, (1973), pp. 24-52. Charlotte Erickson, *American Industry and the European Immigrant, 1860-85* (Cambridge Mass., 1957), pp. 1-3, and references on pp. 199-200.

34 Erickson, *op. cit.*, pp. 36-42. See also Charlotte Erickson, *Invisible Immigrants* (London 1972), pp. 265-7.

35 Herrick, *op. cit.*, p. 201.

36 *Niles Weekly Register*, 31 October 1829, p. 150.

37 'By the mid-nineteenth century criminal persecutions for enticing a servant had become virtually non-existent, and civil cases were rare.' (Cohen, *op. cit.*, p. 35.)

38 James Bagley Clements, *History of Irwin County, Georgia* (Atlanta, 1932), pp. 415-17. This type of occurrence led Workingmen's Associations to seek protection for creditors in Mechanics Lien Laws as well as for themselves as debtors. Other evidence of the relative ease of securing labour for railways and canal construction in the South is to be found in company papers. 'Messrs. Johnson & Blissett can command any force which may be required . . .' (R. B. R. Blanch, Chief Engineer, Roanoke Valley Railroad, to Charles B. Fisk of Covington and Ohio Railroad, 28 November 1853. BR Box 194 (12) Huntington Library). One man was recommended as a contractor because he had settled for a long time in a village near the proposed construction site in Virginia and 'His intimate acquaintance with the agriculturalists of certain villages will be of Service to other Contractors, who are Entire Strangers . . .' (Thomas Mathius, Lewisburg, Va., 23 December 1853, to Fisk, BR Box 194 (20)). Another contractor noted in such an application '. . . we will put a negro force upon it which has been in our employment during the last five or six years and are now well used to the business . . .' J. Hunter, Central Railroad, Va., 25 April 1856, to Fisk, BR Box 194 (27)).

39 For information relating to these two contractors I am indebted to my former student, Mrs. Mary Fleming. See also Charles M. Scanlon, 'History of the Irish in Wisconsin', *Journal of the American Irish Historical Society*, xiii (1914), pp. 238, 250. Rev. Henry J. Browne, 'Archbishop Hughes and Western Colonisation' *Catholic Historical Review*, xxxvi (1950), pp. 258-9; Erickson, *American Industry*, p. 70.

40 Albert Fishlow, *American Railroads and the Transformation of the Ante-Bellum Economy* (Cambridge Mass., 1965).

41 H. Ross, Scotch Settlement, Ohio, 2 February 1830. Reference work available on the Erie Canal in letter from John Richards, Johnsburg, Warren County, NY, 3 November 1817. (2722E, National Library of Wales).

42 Charles T. Harvey to John F. Seymour, nd. (This and subsequent references are

from St. Mary's Falls Ship Canal Company Papers, Cornell Collection of Regional History).

43 Letter to Stockholders of the St Mary's Falls Ship Canal Company, 13 October 1854.

44 Harvey to Hon Erastus Corning, President, 1 January 1855.

45 *Memorandum of Agreement* signed by John F. Seymour for St Mary's Falls Ship Canal Company and John Richardson for Michigan Central Line. See also Erickson, *American Industry*, pp. 70-71.

46 D.E. Whitmund, St Mary's Falls Ship Canal Company Land Office, Detroit, to Seymour, 28 September 1854. See also J.N. Brooks, Sault Ste Marie, to Seymour, Utica NY, 30 September 1854.

47 See for example Rev Alexander J. Peyton, *Emigrant's Friend* (Cork, 1853), pp. 17-19. Carl Wittke, *We Who Built America* (New York, 1940) p. 136.

48 Harvey to Corning, 3 February 1855.

49 'The main cause was the influence of the grog shop keepers . . . one of whom I had arrested and kept in jail till he asked forgiveness with due humility.' (Harvey to Seymour, 1 August 1853).

50 Harvey to Seymour, 15 April 1854.

51 Paul W. Gates, *The Illinois Central Railroad and Its Colonization Work* (Cambridge Mass., 1934); David Lightner, *Labour on the Illinois Central Railroad, 1852-1900: the evolution of an industrial environment* (Arno, NY, 1977); Erickson, *American Industry*, pp. 71-2.

52 Roswell B. Mason, Chicago, to W.P. Burrall, 4 July 1853. For low fares arranged by the agent sent to New Orleans, see Mason to Robert Schuyler, President of the Illinois Central, 14 March 1853 (1 M3.1, Newberry Library). Similarly, when the Covington and Ohio Railway was under construction in Virginia, arrangements were made to transport labourers at a special low rate if as many as fifty travelled at the same time. (D.H. Whitcomb, Jacksons River, to Fisk, 30 June 1860 (BR Box 195 (55)).

53 Mason to Burrall, treasurer of the Illinois Central, 6 August 1853 (1 M3.1). His letter of 9 August 1853 makes similar assertions.

54 Lightner, *op. cit.,* p. 287.

55 Mason, Bloomington, to Schuyler, 19 April 1853 (1 M3.1).

56 Lewis Broad to Mason, 19 May 1856 (Illinois Central papers held in the company's offices). On upward pressure on wages, see also Central Military Tract Railroad Company, *Report,* 2 April 1855, p. 3 (Newberry Library, Chicago).

57 In addition to references cited in Erickson, *American Industry,* pp. 6-7, 19-22, 200n, see Whitcomb, General Superintendent, Virginia Central Railroad, to Governor of Virginia, John Letcher, 16 July 1861, (Brock Collection, BR200 (56), Huntington Library).

58 The American Emigrant Company is discussed in my *American Industry,* chapter 1. What follows is based on manuscripts in the Huntington Library which I had not then seen. Henry Ward Beecher, Brooklyn, NY, to Thomas Haines Dudley, 13 February 1865, (DU 179, Huntington Library). See also John Williams, AEC, to Dudley, 25 March 1865, (DU 4365); 24 September 1864 (DU 4363); 2 September 1864, (DU 4362).

59 Thos Matheson, Newcastle-upon-Tyne, to Dudley, 30 May 1864, (DU2845). Also Henry Bates, Oldham, Lancs, to Dudley, 20 June 1854 (DU158).

60 Bert J. Lowenberg, 'Efforts of the South to Encourage Immigration, 1865-1900', *The South Atlantic Quarterly,* xxxiii (1934), p. 367. George E. Pozetta, 'Foreigners in Florida: a study of immigration promotion, 1865-1910', *Florida Historical Quarterly,* liii (1974, p. 166. R.H. Woody, 'The Labor and Immigration Problem of South Carolina During Reconstruction', *Mississippi Valley Historical Review,* xviii (1931), p. 210. E. Russ Williams, Jr, 'Louisiana's Public and Private Immigration Endeavours: 1866-1893', *Louisiana History,* xv (1974).

61 Erickson, *American Industry,* chapters 8-9.

62 Charlotte Erickson, *Emigration from Europe, 1815-1914* (London, 1976), pp. 187-95. Amy Zahl Gottlieb, 'The Regulation of Coal-Mining Industry in Illinois with special reference to the influence of British miners and British precedents, 1870-1911' (unpublished PhD dissertation, University of London, 1975), pp. 36-44.

63 Erickson, *American Industry,* pp. 52-60. An early example of such efforts was the response of the New York Typographical Association in 1833 to news of advertising for workers in Scotland: they addressed a circular to the printers of the United Kingdom, (Motley, *op. cit.,* p. 19).

64 For evidence of the way in which workers from Britain tended to emigrate in trade networks, see Erickson, *Invisible Immigrants,* pp. 243-5.

65 Erickson, *American Industry,* pp. 47, 51-52, and 'The Recruitment of European Immigrant Labor by American Industry, 1860-85' (unpublished PhD thesis, Cornell University, 1951, pp. 231-3).

66 William B. Gates, *Michigan Copper and Boston Dollars,* Cambridge Mass., (1951), p. 97. John Rowe, *The Hard Rock Men: Cornish immigrants on the North American mining frontier* (New York, 1974), pp. 62-95. Erickson, *American Industry,* pp. 43-4, 48.

67 John Harris Foster, 'War Times in the Copper Mines', *Michigan Pioneer Historical Society Collections,* xviii (1892), p. 380.

68 Most of the former Confederate States did enact legislation against contract-breaking in the Black Codes of 1865-67. These laws were repealed or unused until after the end of Radical Reconstruction (Cohen, *op, cit.,* pp. 42-3).

69 For example, see draft of letter to Editor of the *Mining Journal,* nd (187?) (John Daniell Papers, Huntington Library, Vol 3, p. 25). Daniell cited wages for miners on contract at $65 to $100 a month with board costing only $20. The quotation is from Daniell to Michael Harrison, 16 April 1886 (Daniell Papers, Vol 17, p. 288). For brief details of Daniell's carrer, see Rowe, *op. cit.,* pp. 88-9.

70 Michael Harrison, 65 Craddock St, Spennymoor, County Durham, 16 March 1886 (Daniell Papers, Box 1). See also letter from John Fawcett, West Hartlepool, County Durham, 26 March 1886; W.M. McIntosh, Gateshead, Durham, 15 March 1886 (Daniell Papers, Box 1).

71 Daniell to Harrison, 16 April 1886, (Daniell Papers, Vol 17, p. 288).

72 Erickson, *American Industry,* p. 80.

73 Claude P. Smith, 'Official Efforts by the State of Mississippi to Encourage Immigration, 1868-1886', *Journal of Mississippi History,* xxxii (1970), pp. 327-9. Woody, *op. cit.,* p. 204.

74 Smith, *op. cit.,* pp. 339-40. Woody, *op. cit.,* p. 204.

75 *Ibid.,* p. 207.

76 *Ibid.,* p. 212. See also Erickson, *American Industry,* pp. 27, 73.

77   *Ibid.*, p. 70.

78   *Amerika* (Gothenberg), 2 May 1870, p. 7.

79   Humbert S. Nelli, *Italians in Chicago, 1880-1930* (New York, 1970), p. 64.

80   Erickson, *Emigration from Europe*, pp. 217-28.

81   Nelli, *op. cit.*, pp. 64-6. George A. Pozetta, 'A Padrone Looks at Florida: Labour recruiting and Florida East Coast Railroad', *Florida Historical Quarterly*, liv (1975), pp. 77-8. For cases of deportation of aliens for having been lent passage money by *padroni*, sometimes allegedly on the security of a mortgage in the old country, see *Annual Report of the Commissioner General for Immigration, 1908*, pp. 131-2 (Bulgarians, Turks, Macedonians); for *1911*, pp. 119-21, 129-30 (Greeks).

82   V. Palumbo to R.J. Goff, General Superintendent of the Florida East Coast Railway, St Augustin, 3 February 1901, in Pozetta, *op. cit.*, p. 82.

83   Carlton J. Corliss, 'Building the Overseas Railway to Key West', *Tequesta*, xiii (1953), pp. 15-16; Henry S. Marks, 'Labour Problems of the Florida East Coast Railway Extension from Homestead to Key West, 1905-1907', *Tequesta*, xxxii (1972), p. 78; Pozetta, *op. cit.*, p. 78.

84   Irwin Yellowitz, *Labor and the Progressive Movement in New York State,* (Ithaca, 1966). Illinois, *Tenth Annual Report of the Bureau of Labor Statistics*, 1898, part II, p. 96. John Mitchell, former President of the United Mine Workers, noted ruefully that labour agencies served immigrants, but that there was no such network for the native-born (*American Federationist*, November 1911).

85   Illinois Free Employment Office, *7th Annual Report*, 1905, p. 3; *9th Annual Report*, 1907, p. 71; New York, *First Annual Report of the Commissioner of Labor*, p. 25; *Third Annual Report*, 1903, p. 183. New York's free Bureau was abolished in May 1906 because it served only the market for domestic workers (*Fifth Annual Report*, 1905, I, Part I, pp; 14-17); E.L. Bogart, 'Public Employment Offices', *Quarterly Journal of Economics*, xix (1900), pp. 351-3.

86   Illinois Free Employment Office, *13th Annual Report*, 1911, pp. 8-9; New York Commissioner of Labor, *Fourth Annual Report*, 1904, I, Part II, pp. 47-50; J.E. Connor, 'Free Public Employment Offices in the United States', United States Bureau of Labour, *Bulletin*, xiv (1907), p. 34.

87   Illinois Free Employment Office, *6th Annual Report*, 1904, p. 4.

88   Illinois Free Employment Office, *13th Annual Report*, 1911, pp. 109-10.

89   Illinois Free Employment Office, *13th Annual Report*, 1911, p. 8; *14th Annual Report*, 1912, p. 5; Grace Abbott, 'The Chicago Employment Agency and the Immigrant Worker', *American Journal of Sociology*, xiv (1908), p. 294.

90   Gunther Barth, *Bitter Strength* (Cambridge Mass., 1964), pp. 55-8, 88-93, 117-18.

91   *The Merchant's Magazine and Commercial Review*, August 1870, p. 99.

3. THE CORNISH DIASPORA OF THE NINETEENTH CENTURY

1   The Cost Book system was a form of company organisation peculiar to Cornish mining. Its main features were unlimited liability, an absence of fixed capital, and the right to transfer shares or relinquish interest simply by written notice.

2   Newbury, 'Labour Migration in the Imperial Phase'.

3   M. Nikolinakos, 'Notes Towards a General Theory of Migration in Late Capitalism', *Race and Class*, xvii (1975), pp 5-17.

4   Hobsbawm, *Age of Capital*, p. 236.

Notes

5   Erickson, *Invisible Immigrants*, pp 22-3.

6   C. van Onselen, 'Black Workers in Central African Industry: a critical essay on the historiography and sociology of Rhodesia', *Journal of Southern African Studies*, i (1975), pp 229-46.

7   Corrigan, 'Feudal Relics or Capitalist Monuments?'.

8   Rowe, *Hard Rock Men*, p. 44.

9   C. B. Glasscock, *The War of the Copper Kings* (New York, 1938), pp 74, 114, 133-4.

10   *Ibid.*, p. 114.

11   G. Blainey, *The Rush That Never Ended: a history of Australian mining* (Melbourne, 1968), pp 45, 77, 121-5, 129, 295-6.

12   O. Pryor, *Australia's Little Cornwall* (Adelaide, 1962).

13   Transvaal, *The Miners' Phthisis Commission, 1902-1903* (Pretoria, 1904), para 10.

14   C. J. Hunt, *The Lead Mines of the Northern Pennines* (Manchester, 1970). Also R. Burt, 'The Lead Industry of England and Wales 1700-1880' (unpublished PhD thesis, University of London, 1971) and *John Taylor* (Buxton, 1977), pp 23, 26, 56.

15   R. Palmer, *A Touch on the Times: songs of social change 1770-1914* (London, 1974), p. 130.

16   A. Todd, *The Cornish Miner in America* (Truro, 1967), p. 20.

17   M. D. Bernstein, *The Mexican Mining Industry 1890-1950* (New York, 1974), and A. Todd, *The Search for Silver: Cornish miners in Mexico 1824-1947* (Padstow, 1977), pp 47-8.

18   W. F. C. Purser, *Metal Mining in Peru* (New York, 1971), p. 83.

19   Letter from Trevithick, quoted in E. Vale, *The Harveys of Hayle* (Truro, 1966), p. 155.

20   *Ibid.*

21   *BPP*, 1884-85, xxx, C 4402, *Royal Commission on the Housing of the Working Classes*, First Report, paras 7943-54.

22   *BPP*, 1904, xiii, Cd 2091, *Report on the Health of Cornish Miners, 1904*, Appendix III.

23   G. Blainey, 'A Theory of Mineral Discovery: Australia in the nineteenth century', *Economic History Review*, xxiii (1970), pp 298-313.

24   C. Spence, *British Investments and the American Mining Frontier, 1860-1901* (New York, 1958), p. 73.

25   *Ibid.*

26   *The Economist*, 18 June 1881, p. 756.

27   *BPP*, 1850, xl, 1163, *Papers Relating to the Australian Colonies: Report on Immigrants by the Ship 'Lysander', 1849*.

28   R. L. Stevenson, *Across the Plains, with other Memories and Essays* (London, 1925), p. 60.

29   G. Burke, 'The Poor Law and the Relief of Distress: West Cornwall, 1870-1880', *Journal of the Royal Institution of Cornwall*, viii (1979), pp. 148-59.

30   *Daily News*, 8 January 1879, p. 6.

31   W. H. Hudson, *The Land's End: a naturalist's impression of West Cornwall* (London, 1923), p. 176.

32   *BPP*, 1912-13, xix Cd 6480, *Report of the Royal Commission on Divorce and Matrimonial Proceedings, Evidence, Vol. II*, para 12838.

33   *Health of Cornish Miners*, Appendix III.

34   For example, H. D. Lowry, *Women's Tragedies* (London, 1896), and H. Harris, *The Luck of Wheal Vor* (Truro, 1901). Also R. R. Blewett, 'The village of St Day in the Parish of Gwennap', paper given at the Board of Education Short Course for Teachers in Public Elementary Schools on 'The Citizen in the Modern World', held at Selwyn College, Cambridge, 13-27 July 1935.

35   *Health of Cornish Miners,* Appendix II.

36   *Ibid.*

37   *Ibid.,* Case No 71.

38   *Ibid.*

39   *BPP,* 1893-94, cvi, C 7222, *General Census of England and Wales, 1891,* Vol. IV *General Report,* p. 27.

40   R. Duncan, 'Case Studies in Emigration: Cornwall, Gloucestershire and New South Wales', *Economic History Review,* xvi (1963-64), pp. 272-89.

41   *BPP,* 1864, xxiv, C 3389, *Report of the Commissioners Appointed to Enquire into the Condition of All Mines in Great Britain to which the Provisions of the Acts 23 & 24 Vict Cap 115 do not Apply,* paras 8806, 10287-91.

42   *The Cornishman* (Penzance), 11 September 1913, p. 6.

43   Marx, *Capital,* Vol. I (Harmondsworth, 1976), p. 818.

44   S. and B. Webb, *A History of Trade Unionism in Britain* (London, 1911), p. 421.

45   J. Taylor, *On the Economy of Mining* (1814), reprinted in R. Burt (ed), *Cornish Mining: essays on the organisation of Cornish mines and the Cornish mining economy* (Newton Abbot, 1969), pp 31-48.

46   A. L. Rowse, *The Cornish in America* (London, 1969), p. 16.

47   A. K. Hamilton Jenkin, *The Cornish Miner* (London, 1927), p. 332.

48   Todd, *Cornish Miner in America,* p. 24; also T. R. Harris, *Methodism and the Cornish Miner* (Cornish Methodist Historical Association Occasional Publication No 1, 1960).

49   J. Rule, 'The Tribute System and the Weakness of Trade Unionism in the Cornish Mines', *Bulletin of the Society for the Study of Labour History,* xxi (1970), p. 28.

50   See, for example R. Gregory, *The Miners in British Politics 1906-1914* (Oxford, 1968), pp 1-3.

51   R. Harrison (ed), *Independent Collier: the coal miner as archetypal proletarian reassessed* (Sussex, 1978). Also R. Moore, 'Religion as a Source of Variation in Working-class Images of Society' in M. Bulmer (ed), *Working Class Images of Society* (London, 1977), pp 35-55.

52   Rule, *op. cit.,* p. 25.

53   G. Burke, 'The Cornish Miner and the Cornish Mining Industry 1870-1921' (unpublished PhD thesis, University of London, 1982), esp. pp. 359-62.

54   E. Gitsham and J. Trembath, *A First Account of Labour Organisation in South Africa* (Durban, 1926), pp. 25-6, 66, 160.

55   Pryor, *op. cit.;* also P. Payton, 'The Cornish Radical Tradition: its background in Cornwall and its development in South Australia' (unpublished paper, University of Adelaide, 1977).

56   R. Lingenfelter, *The Hard Rock Miners: a history of the mining labour movement in the American West 1863-1893* (Berkeley and Los Angeles, 1974), pp. 6 *et seq;* also Rowe, *op. cit.*

57   G. Burke and P. Richardson, 'The Decline and Fall of the Cost Book System in the Cornish Mining Industry 1895-1914', *Journal of Business History,* xiii (1981),

pp. 4-18. Also R. Samuel (ed), *Miners, Saltworkers and Quarrymen* (London, 1977), pp. 1-98.

58 J. Rule, 'The Labouring Miner in Cornwall: 1740-1870' (unpublished PhD thesis, University of Warwick, 1971), pp. 381-2.

59 *Western Daily Mercury*, 5 March 1866, p. 2.

60 *Ibid.*

61 *Ibid.*

62 *Ibid.*, p. 3. Also 10 March 1866, p. 5.

63 *Ibid.*, 14 March 1866, p. 3.

64 *Ibid.*, 10 March 1866, p. 5.

65 *BPP*, 1909, xxxix, Cd 4265, *Royal Commission on the Poor Laws*, Vol 1, paras 4450-51.

66 *HC Debates*, Vol. 123, 15-23 December 1919, p. 855, 4. Also Vol. 125, 10-27 February 1920, p. 1682-56.

67 *Royal Cornwall Gazette*, 3 March 1920, p. 9.

68 *Gold Hill Daily News*, 16 September 1864, p. 29. Quoted in Lingenfelter, *op. cit.*, p. 40.

69 'The Scabby Cousin Jack', in S.P. Stenger, 'Protest Songs from the Butte Mines, *Western Folklore*, xxvi (1967), pp. 157-67.

70 Rowe, *op. cit.*, p. 246.

71 *Ibid.*, p. 247.

72 Lingenfelter, *op. cit.*, p. 62.

73 Pryor, *op. cit.*, Also Payton, *op. cit.*, quoting the *South Australian Register*, April 1914.

74 Pryor, *op. cit.*, pp. 123-38.

75 J.R. Harris, 'Skills, Coal and British Industry in the 18th Century', *History*, lxi (1976), p. 182.

76 Harrison, *op. cit.*, p. 6.

77 *The Beehive*, 10 January 1974, p. 9, and 28 February 1874, p. 2.

78 *Ibid.*, 10 January 1874.

79 *Redruth Times and Camborne Advertiser*, 23 January 1974, p. 2.

80 C. Fisher and J. Smethurst, 'War on the Law of Supply and Demand: the Amalgamated Association of Miners and the Forest of Dean colliers 1869-1975', in Harrison, *op. cit.*, pp. 114-55.

81 *Ibid.*, pp. 141-4.

82 *Redruth Times and Camborne Advertiser*, 16 January 1874, p. 2.

83 *Ibid.*, 1 May 1874, p. 2.

84 *The Beehive*, 10 January 1874, p. 9.

85 *The Cornishman*, 15 January 1914, p. 1.

86 G. Burke and P. Richardson, 'The Profits of Death: a comparative study of miners' phthisis in Cornwall and the Transvaal 1876-1918', *Journal of Southern African Studies*, iv (1978), pp. 147-71.

4. INTO SERVITUDE: INDIAN LABOUR IN THE SUGAR INDUSTRY, 1833-1970

1 *BPP*, 1944-45, Cmd 6607, vi, *Report of the West India Royal Commission* (printed and distributed in 1940, but publication delayed until 1945).

2   Tinker, *New System of Slavery,* represents the present writer's more extended statement about the subject of this paper. A chapter in a later work, 'Independent, but Still Colonised', Chapter 3 of *The Banyan Tree: overseas emigrants from India, Pakistan and Bangladesh* (London, 1977), is a rather brief account of present-day conditions with more emphasis on the political framework than on the plantation.

3   Elsa V. Goveia, *Slave Society in the British Leeward Islands at the end of the Eighteenth Century* (New Haven, 1965), p. 238.

4   Tinker, *New System of Slavery,* p. 15.

5   The specially designed emigrant ships were also employed as troop transports, but the facilities laid down for the coolies were, on paper, superior to those provided for British soldiers.

6   See Tinker, *New System of Slavery,* Chapter 5, 'The Passage'.

7   It was possible, in 1978, to find a few small, remote estates in both Mauritius and Guyana where the old barracoons were still occupied by estate workers.

8   *BPP,* 1910, xxvii, Cmd 5192, *Report of the Commission on Emigration from India to the Crown Colonies and Protectorates.*

9   Tinker, *New System of Slavery,* p. 219. By an unfortunate coincidence, the word *kuli* in the Fijian language means dog.

10   See Hugh Tinker, 'Odd Man Out: the loneliness of the Indian colonial politician — the career of Manilal Doctor', *Journal of Imperial and Commonwealth History,* ii (1974).

11   See Hugh Tinker, *The Ordeal of Love: C.F. Andrews and India,* (London, 1979).

12   See K.L. Gillion, *The Fiji Indians: challenge to European dominance, 1920-1946* (Canberra, 1977), Chapters II and III.

13   In the mid-1930s the BGLU still had under 500 members. A statue to Critchlow was set up outside the parliament building in Georgetown, Guyana, by order of Cheddi Jagan. Similarly, a statue of Manilal Doctor was erected in Port Louis. It is sad that the liberation story has to depend on such ersatz heroes. The man on the statue ought to be the tattered Indian field-worker.

14   See the present writer's *Separate and Unequal: India and the Indians in the British Commonwealth, 1920-1950* (London, 1976), p. 164.

15   *Ibid.,* pp. 214-7.

16   See Gillion, *op. cit.,* Chapter IX.

17   Much of the material in this section is based on a paper by Robin Cohen, 'The Politics of Unemployment in Mauritius', *Manpower and Unemployment Research* (Montreal, 1978).

18   The relative importance of sugar to the four economies under review may be expressed in terms of the percentage of total exports which sugar represents: 5.1% for Trinidad; 27.3% for Guyana, 51.1% for Fiji; and 90% for Mauritius.

19   Probably the best picture of life of the contemporary Indian sugar worker is contained in the novels of Samuel Selvon, particularly in his *Tiger* novels, also in *The Plains of Caroni.* Perhaps Selvon makes his sugar workers too much masters of their own fate, as individuals.

5. THE IMPORTATION OF BRITISH INDIANS INTO SURINAM (DUTCH GUIANA), 1873-1916

1   S. van Praag, *De zogenaamde immigratie van koelies, het verderf dier kolonie en haar*

negerbevolking; redevoering gehouden in de zittingen der Koloniale Staten van Suriname van 2 en 5 februarij 1874 en 11 en 14 december 1876 (Amsterdam, 1877), p. 26.

2   Jay R. Mandle, *The Plantation Economy: population and economic change in Guyana, 1838-1960* (Philadelphia, 1973), pp. 20-24.

3   R.M.N. Panday, *Agriculture in Surinam, 1650-1950: an enquiry into the cause of its decline* (Amsterdam, 1959) pp. 45-95.

4   *Ibid.*, pp. 126, 177, 179.

5   Glen Willemsen, *Koloniale Politiek en Transformatieprocessen in een plantage-economie, Suriname 1873-1940* (Amsterdam, 1980), pp. 57-9.

6   B. Heldring, 'De toekomst van Suriname', *De Gids*, i (1876), p. 226.

7   George A. Gierson, 'Report on Colonial Migration from the Bengal Presidency', India Office Records (IOR), Emigration Proceedings (EP), vol. 2058 (July-December 1883), pp. 1005-139.

8   IOR, EP 1863 (1882), 24 February 1882, pp. 525-57.

9   L.J.M. de Klerk, *De immigratie der Hindustanen in Suriname* (Amsterdam, 1953), p. 68 (one example).

10   R.A.J. van Lier, *Frontier Society: a social analysis of the history of Surinam* (The Hague, 1971), p. 126.

11   *BPP*, 1877, lxxviii, C 1861, *Slave Trade, No. 3 (1877): Reports respecting the Condition of Coolies in Surinam*, p. 19.

12   IOR, EP, 932 (1877), p. 34.

13   IOR, EP, 932 (1877), appendix August, A, p. 7.

14   De Klerk, *op. cit.*, pp. 62-3.

15   C 1861, *Slave Trade*, pp. 54-5.

16   IOR, Files J + P/2/64, numbers 27/12, Consul to FO, 19 July 1873.

17   Panday, *op. cit.*, pp. 136-7.

18   IOR, EP, 2278 (1884), p. 31, Consul to FO, 21 July 1883.

19   IOR, EP, 2058 (1883), p. 1305, Consul to FO, 20 February 1883.
     IOR, EP, 2510 (1897), pp. 1277-82, Consul to FO, 8 October 1897.

20   De Klerk, *op. cit.*, p. 88.

21   *Ibid.*, p. 127.

22   Richard N. Bean and Robert P. Thomas, 'The Adoption of Slave Labor in British America', in Henry A. Gemery and Jan S. Hogendorn (eds), *The Uncommon Market: essays in the economic history of the Atlantic slave trade* (New York, 1979), p. 383.

23   De Klerk, *op. cit.*, p. 132, and D.W.D. Comins, *Diary of a Tour in Surinam or Dutch Guiana* (Calcutta, 1892), p. xxx.

24   IOR, EP, vol. 694 (1875), pp. 315-376, Consul to FO, 2 March 1875.

25   IOR, EP, vol. 2278 (1884), p. 32.

26   IOR, EP, vol. 932 (1877), Appendix C, October 1877, p. 1.

27   C 1861, *Slave Trade*, pp. 39-40.

28   IOR, EP, vol. 694 (1875), January 1875.

29   James McNeil and Chiman Lal, *Report to the Governor of India on the Conditions of Indian Immigrants in Four British Colonies and Surinam* (London, 1915), p. 153. and D.W.D. Comins, *Note on the Emigration from the East Indies to Surinam or Dutch Guiana*, (Calcutta, 1892).

30   Comins, *Note on the Emigration*, p. 33, and IOR, EP, Vol. 962 (1877), pp. 237-39, Consul to FO, 21 June 1877.

31   Chandra Jayawerdena, *Conflict and Solidarity in a Guianese Plantation* (London, 1963).

32   IOR, EP, vol. 2278 (1884), p. 21, and Coumins, *Diary of a Tour,* p. xxvi.

33   C 1861, *Slave Trade,* p. 19.

34   IOR, EP, vol. 1171 (1878), p. 87 (August).

35   IOR, EP, vol. 2278 (1884), p. 34, and Comins, *Note on Emigration,* p. 34.

36   C 1861, *Slave Trade,* p. 56.

37   De Klerk, *op, cit.,* pp. 136-37.

38   C 1861, *Slave Trade,* p. 58.

39   IOR, Files L/J + P/6/77, file 1105.

40   E. van den Boogaart and P.C. Emmer, 'Plantation Slavery in Surinam in the last decade before Emancipation: the case of Catharina Sophia', in Vera Rubin and Arthur Tuden (eds), *Comparative Perspectives on Slavery in New World Plantation Societies* (New York, 1977), p. 216.

41   Comins, *Note on Emigration,* p. 31.

42   Comins, *Diary of a Tour,* p. v.

43   Van den Boogaart and Emmer, *op. cit.,* p. 216.

44   Public Record Office, London, FO 37 vol. 597, Indian Government to India Office, 22 July 1878.

45   C 1861, *Slave Trade,* pp. 14-15.

46   *Ibid.,* pp. 28-29.

47   *Ibid.,* p. 59.

48   *BPP,* 1910, xxvii, Cd 5192-4, *Report of the Commission on Emigration from India to the Crown Colonies and Protectorates* (Sanderson Report), question 4934, p. 181.

49   Michael Craton, *Sinews of Empire: a short history of British slavery* (London, 1974), pp. 194-5.

50   De Klerk, *op. cit.,* pp. 125-6.

51   C 1861, *Slave Trade,* p. 46.

52   *Ibid.,* p. 21.

53   Van den Boogaart and Emmer, *op. cit.,* p. 216, table 6A.

54   Comins, *Note on the Emigration,* p. 22.

55   De Klerk, *op. cit.,* pp. 123-4.

56   Van den Boogaart and Emmer, *op. cit.,* p. 223, note 20.

57   IOR, EP, vol. 2278 (1884), p. 31.

58   IOR, EP, vol. 2278 (1884), p. 528.

59   IOR, EP, vol. 932 (1877), p. 340, Consul to FO, 3 March 1876.

60   IOR, EP, vol. 1171 (1878), pp. 93-96.

61   IOR, EP, vol. 932 (1877), pp. 147-8.

62   C 1861, *Slave Trade,* pp. 17-18.

63   IOR, EP, vol. 2058 (1883), p. 1307.

64   Benjamin S. Mistrasingh and R. Matilal Marké, *Mathura, Ramanjee en Raygaroo: verzet tegen uitbuiting en onderdrukking in Suriname* (The Hague, 1978).

65   Comins, *Note on the Emmigration,* p. 23.

66   C 1861, *Slave Trade,* p. 78, and IOR, EP, vol. 932 (1877), August, Appendix A, pp. 13-14.

67   IOR, EP, vol 2278 (1884), pp. 1221-41.

68   Comins, *Note on the Emigration,* p. 33, and the yearly abstracts of the Migration Department.

69   Comins, *Note on the Emigration*, p. 25.

70   *Ibid.*, p. 25.

71   *Ibid.*, p. 17.

72   IOR, EP, vol. 2058 (1883), p. 1503.

6. THE NATURE AND ORIGINS OF PACIFIC ISLANDS LABOUR MIGRATION TO QUEENSLAND, 1863-1906

1   The concept of the labour reserve used in this essay is that which has been elaborated upon by Meillassoux and others. The labour reserve is an under-developed region comprising agricultural self-sustaining communities from which labour is drawn to work in capitalist production. Most importantly, it is the labour reserve which bears the cost of the reproduction of the labourers in this situation. 'The cheap cost of the labour in these countries' writes Meillassoux, 'comes from the super exploitation, not only of the wage earner but also of the labour of his kin group' (pp. 101-3). In this sense, the labour reserve is not separate from but an organic component of capitalist production. C. Meillassoux, 'From Reproduction to Production', *Economy and Society*, i (1972), pp. 93-105; and *Maidens, Meal and Money* (Cambridge, 1981). The concept has been most developed by historians of Southern Africa. See especially G. Arrighi, 'Labour Supplies in Historical Perspective: A Study of the Proletarianization of the African Peasantry in Rhodesia', *Journal of Development Studies*, vi (1970), pp. 197-234; Wolpe, 'Capitalism and Cheap Labour Power in South Africa. See also Legassick and de Clercq's chapter in this volume.

2   For a recent estimate of the volume of labour migration in the South-west Pacific between 1840 and 1915 see Colin Newbury, 'The Melanesian Labor Reserve: Some Reflections on Pacific Labor Markets in the Nineteenth Century', *Pacific Studies*, iv (1980), pp. 1-25.

3   For recent examples, see Hector Holthouse, *Cannibal Cargoes* (Adelaide, 1969), E.W. Docker, *The Blackbirders* (Sydney, 1970), and Faith Bandler, *Wacvie* (Adelaide, 1977). See also T.M. MacCallum, *Adrift in the South Seas Including Adventures with Robert Louis Stevenson* (Los Angeles, 1934) and T.D. Dunbabin, *Slavers of the South Seas* (Sydney, 1935).

4   J.M. Wood, *British Policy in the South Pacific 1786-1893* (Sydney, 1948); W.P. Morrell, *Britain in the Pacific Islands* (Oxford, 1960); O.W. Parnaby, *Britain and the Labor Trade in the Southwest Pacific* (Durham NC, 1964).

5   For recent examples see C.M.H. Clark, *A History of Australia* (Melbourne, 1978), pp. 355-6; R.A. Huttenback, *Racism and Empire*, (Ithaca, 1976), p. 42.

6   P. Corris, review of Holthouse, *op. cit.*, and Docker, *op. cit.*, in *Journal of Pacific History* (afterwards JPH), viii (1972), pp. 239-40. For an earlier expression of this view see D. Scarr, *Fragments of Empire*, (Canberra, 1967) p. 139.

7   J. A. Bennet, review of J. D. Melvin, *The Cruise of the Helena*, edited by P. Corris (Melbourne, 1977), *JPH*, xiv (1979), pp. 234-6.

8   R. M. Keesing, review of P. Corris, *Passage, Port and Plantation* (Melbourne, 1973), *JPH*, ix (1974), pp. 215-17.

9   Parnaby, *op. cit.*, p. 72.

10   Corris, *Passage*, p. 54.

11   R. Bedford, 'A transition in circular mobility' in H. Brookfield (ed), *The Pacific in Transition* (London, 1973), p. 215.

12 P. Corris, *Passage*, p.2 and Chapter 3. See also Bedford, *op. cit.*, p. 196: D. Scarr, Introduction to W. E. Giles, *A Cruize in a Queensland Labour Vessel to the South Seas*, edited by D. Scarr, (London, 1968), p.23.

13 Corris, *Passage*, p. 29; D. Scarr, 'Recruits and Recruiters', *JPH*, ii (1967), p. 7, and 'Recruits and Recruiters' in J. W. Davidson and D. Scarr (eds), *Pacific Islands Portraits* (Canberra, 1970), p. 228.

14 Peter Worsley, *The Trumpet Shall Sound* (London, 1970), p.49. It should perhaps be stressed here that there is an historiography which lies somewhere between the popular and revisionist positions. I refer to those studies which are content to describe in detail the methods of the labour traders, especially their use of force and fraud, and yet admit of a voluntarist element in the migration process. Prominent examples of this can be found in the works of O.W. Parnaby, Deryck Scarr, and Kay Saunders. In these works, however, as in much Pacific historiography, the narrative method fails to come to terms with the problem of historical explanation. Even the pseudo-scientific paradigm of recruiting developed by Saunders, with its three phases of 'Commencement', 'Transition', and 'Maturity', is descriptive rather than analytical. In concentrating on the activities of the recruiters, moreover, and in their treatment of voluntarism, these studies ignore the mainsprings of the migratory process which begins with the history of the migrants themselves. (Parnaby, *op. cit.*; Scarr, 'Recruits and Recruiters' and Introduction to *Cruize in a Queensland Labour Vessel*; K. Saunders, 'Uncertain Bondage: An Analysis of Indentured Labour in Queensland to 1907, with particular reference to Melanesian servants' (unpublished Phd thesis, University of Queensland, 1974), Chapter 3.

15 Bennet, *op. cit.*, pp. 234-6.

16 Newbury, *op. cit.*, This important article deserves closer critical attention than space permits here. Of particular interest to the essay is Newbury's use of the term 'labour reserve' which he appreciates as a spatial concept. This is a quite different meaning of the term as it is applied in the southern African literature to which he refers. (See above note 1) The importance of Newbury's article lies in his recognition that the origins of labour migration cannot be dissociated from the operation of the regional economy or from the growth of the world economy. Although this distinguishes his essay from other revisionist literature, it is still a neo-classical economic engine which drives Newbury's model of Pacific migration. In addition to the general weaknesses of neo-classical economic theory suggested here, Newbury's analysis is undermined by the inapplicability of neo-classical concepts to precapitalist economic forms. At the same time, the subtlety and comprehensiveness of Newbury's neo-classical perspective should be contrasted with the fundamentalist 'libertarian' economic approach of R. Shlomowitz. See especially his 'Markets for Indentured and Time Expired Melanesian Labour in Queensland, 1863-1906' *JPH*, ii (1982), pp. 70-91.

17 Saunders, 'Uncertain Bondage', p. 85 and Peter Corris, '"Blackbirding" in New Guinea waters, 1883-84', *JPH*, iii (1968), p. 87.

18 For a more detailed criticism of neo-classical economic theory applied to labour migration and other references see the Editors' introduction to this volume.

19 See Scarr, 'Recruits and Recruiters', pp. 15-16; Corris, *Passage*, pp. 52-3.

20 *Ibid*, Chapter 4 and 'Kwaisulia of Ada Gege' in Davidson and Scarr, *op. cit.*,

Chapter II. Deryck Scarr described Kwaisulia's activities well before his student, Corris, elaborated on the passage master's career. See especially Scarr, 'Recruits and Recruiters', pp. 17-18.

21 'The proletarianisation of workers', writes O. C. Cox, 'may be thought of as the "commoditisation" of their capacity to labor; that is to say, the transformation of the major human element in production into a mass of persons mainly dependent upon the vicissitudes of a labor market. In this way labor is freed — indeed, as mercilessly freed as an inanimate commodity.' O. C. Cox, *Caste, Class and Race: a study in social dynamics* (New York 1970, first published 1948), p. 180.

22 For a comprehensive examination of the economic history of Queensland's sugar industry in this period see A. A. Graves, 'Pacific Island Labour in the Queensland Sugar Industry, 1862-1906' (D. Phil Thesis, University of Oxford, 1979), to be published as *The Political Economy of the Queensland Sugar Industry, 1862-1906* (London, Royal Historical Society, forthcoming), Chapters 2, 3, 4, and 5.

23 The following is based on my detailed study of the economics and organisation of the recruiting industry in *ibid*, Chapter 7.

24 Tinker, *New System of Slavery*, p. 39.

25 T. A. Coghlan, *Labour and Industry in Australia* (London, 1918), I, p. 277. For a study of the early sealing industry see D. R. Hainsworth, 'Exploiting the Pacific Frontier: The New South Wales Sealing Industry, 1800-1821', *JPH*, ii (1967), pp. 59-76.

26 D. Shineburg, *They Came for Sandalwood: a study of the sandalwood trade in the South West Pacific, 1830-1865* (Melbourne, 1967).

27 R. G. Ward, 'The Pacific *Beche-de-Mer* Trade with Special Reference to Fiji', in R. G. Ward (ed), *Man in the Pacific Islands: essays in geographical change in the Pacific Islands* (Oxford, 1972), pp. 91-123.

28 By September 1883 the CCNH had purchased 245,000 hectares in various parts of the region. By 1905 the company's land holdings had been increased to 776,843 hectares or 5,700 square miles. E. Daville, *La Colonie Francais aux Nouvelles Hebrides* (Paris, 1895), cited in C. S. Belshaw, *Changing Melanesia: social economics of culture contact* (Melbourne, 1954), p. 45.

29 The history of the cash crop in the Western Pacific has yet to be written. Its importance lies not only in the contribution of peasant agriculture to the regional economy but in its connection with proletarianisation. Recent research in Southern Africa and other comparable regions demonstrate that there is a close relationship between the emergence of a peasantry and labour migration. See, for examples, Arrighi's 'Labour Supplies in Historical Perspective' and C. Bundy's *The Rise and Fall of the South African Peasantry* (London, 1979).

30 H. E. Maude and I. Leeson, 'The Coconut Oil Trade of the Gilbert Islands' in H. E. Maude (ed), *Of Islands and Men* (Melbourne, 1968), pp. 233-83. For an insight into the relationship between copra production and labour migration see Newbury, *op. cit.*, pp. 10-11 and 24.

31 R. G. Crocombe, 'Land Tenure in the South Pacific', in Ward, *op. cit.*, pp. 219-51.

32 See, for example, Ward, *op. cit.*, p. 94. Ward also estimates that 500,000 feet of stacked firewood was burnt by the *beche-de-mer* trade in Fiji alone between 1827 and 1835 (p. 118). This does not take into account the timber burnt during other intensive periods of the trade (pp. 118-9).

33   For an account of this process as it occurred later in New Guinea, see H. C. Brookfield and P. Brown, *Struggle for Land: agriculture and the struggle for land among the Chimbu of the New Guinea Highlands* (Melbourne, 1963).

34   This process is illustrated well in the tables compiled by C. A. Price and E. Baker in 'Origins of Pacific Island Labourers in Queensland', *JPH*, xi (1967), pp. 114-6.

35   This process was not unique to the south-west Pacific. See Hobsbawm, *Age of Capital*, Chapters 7 and 8, for other examples.

36   In 1893, for example, the labour history of 1037 recruits prior to their contracting for Queensland was as follows: 244 had previously worked in Queensland, 20 in Fiji, 35 in Noumea, 11 in the Sandwich Islands, 9 in Honolulu, 2 in New Britain, 1 in Vila, and 710 were new recruits. (Immigration Agent to Principle Under-Secretary, Queensland State Archives [afterwards QSA], Col. A/776; 94/8069).

37   Compare this with an orthodox view that missionaries were a bulwark against the labour trade, Parnaby, *op. cit.,* pp. 76-7.

38   For studies of the missionaries in the south-west Pacific see N. Goodall, *A History of the London Missionary Society* (Oxford, 1954); J. D. Resby, 'British Missionaries in the South West Pacific, 1842-1900', (unpublished B. Litt thesis, University of Oxford, 1964); D. L. Hilliard, 'Protestant Missions in the Solomon Islands, 1849-1942' (unpublished PhD thesis Australian National University, 1966). Useful contemporary accounts include E. S. Armstrong, *History of the Melanesian Mission* (London, 1900); H. H. Montgomery, *The Light of Melanesia* (London, 1904); J. G. Paton, *J. G. Paton, Missionary of the New Hebrides* (London, 1899).

39   Belshaw, *op. cit.,* pp. 48-9; F. Rhodes, *Pageant of the Pacific,* 2 vols. (Sydney, c1938), II, p. 235.

40   Paton to Service, nd *BPP*, 1883, xlvii, C 3814, *Correspondence Respecting New Guinea, the New Hebrides and Other Islands in the Pacific,* p. 29.

41   M. R. Allen, 'The Establishment of Christianity and Cash Cropping in a New Hebridean Community', *JPH,* iii (1968), pp. 25-46; Belshaw, *op. cit.*

42   Evidence (afterwards Ev.) McIntyre, *Queensland Parliamentary Papers* (hereafter *QPP*), 1906, II, 635, Q. 5766; T. Harrison, *Savage Civilisation* (London, 1937), pp. 153-5.

43   See for example, Ev. Gardiner, *Queensland Votes and Proceedings* (afterwards *QVP*), 1876, III, 68, Q. 144; Attorney-General to Governor of Queensland, 13 April 1869, QSA, GOV. A/3.

44   For examples of the ideology see Rhodes, *op. cit.,* II, p. 236; Paton, *op. cit., passim;* H. C. Gratton, *The South West Pacific to 1900* (Michigan, 1963), p. 194.

45   Rev D. Macdonald, 'The Historical and Commercial Aspects of the New Hebrides', *Royal Geographical Society of Australasia,* (Victoria), ii (1889), pp. 49-55.

46   Scarr, *Fragments of Empire,* p. 204.

47   Governor of New Zealand to Thurston, 12 August 1890, with minutes of the mission synod and remarks by Thurston, Western Pacific High Commission, *Inward Correspondence,* No 246 of 1890, cited in Scarr, *Fragments of Empire, p. 204.*

48   Horrocks to Immigration Agent, 6 July 1877, *QVP*, 1877, II, 12226; *QVP*, 1885, II, 824-5; Norman to Ripon, 1 October 1892, *BPP*, 1893-94, lxi, C 7000, *Further Correspondence Relating to Polynesian Labour in the Colony of Queensland,* p. 33; D. Macdonald, *The Labour Trade Versus Christianity in the South Sea Islands* (Melbourne, 1878), p. 30.

49   Lilley to Governor of Queensland, 13 April 1869, *QSA,* GOV. A/3.

50 See, for example, the views of Bishop Selwyn in the *Manchester Guardian,* 4 May 1892; 'Report of A. C. Smith to the Women's Presbyterian Mission Union', enclosed in Norman to Ripon, 8 October 1894, in *BPP*, 1895, lxx, C 7912, *Further Correspondence Relating to Polynesian Labour in the Colony of Queensland,* pp. 159-60; Bishop Wilson to Griffith, 23 May 1895 in *ibid.,* p. 310; Rose to Colonial Office, 18 May 1892, in *BPP*, 1892, lvi, C 6808, *Further Correspondence Relating to Polynesian Labour in the Colony of Queensland,* pp. 2-7.

51 M. McGillvray, 'The Commerce of the New Hebrides', *Royal Geographical Society of Australasia* (Victoria), ix (1891), p. 48.

52 Immigration Agent to Colonial Secretary, 9 September 1867, QSA, Col. A/94; 67/2324.

53 Ev. Sheridan, *QVP*, 1876, III, 103, Qs 1127-30.

54 Marcel Mauss, 'Essai sur le Don', *Année sociologique,* seconde serie, (1923-24). Republished as *Sociologie et anthropologie* (Paris, 1950). Translated as *The Gift,* by Ian Cunnison, with an introduction by E. E. Evans-Pritchard (London, 1954). References in this essay are based on the 1969 reprint of the English edition.

55 The contributions of the main participants in this debate are critically surveyed by C. Meillassoux in 'The "Economy" in Agricultural Self-sustaining Societies: a gift exchange is analogous to modern legal forms of trade. Meillassoux, ('The "Economy". . .', p. 132. Theory of the History of Exchange', *ibid.,* pp. 171-208.

56 Mauss, *op. cit.,* pp. 11 and 12, 70. The use by Mauss of modern legal language, 'rights' for example, is criticised by Meillassoux on the grounds that it assumes that gift exchange is analogous to modern legal forms of trade. Meillassoux, (The Economy. . . .', p. 132.

57 C. Levi-Strauss, *Sociologie et anthropologie* (Paris, 1950), p. 139.

58 Mauss, *op. cit.,* pp. 10-11.

59 K. Polyani, M. Arensburg, W. H. Pearson, (eds), *Trade and Markets in the Early Empires* (Glencoe, 1957).

60 The following is based especially on Meillassoux, 'The"Economy". . .', and 'The Social Organisation of the Peasantry: The Economic Basis of Kinship', in Seddon, *op. cit.,* pp. 161-9. See also Dupre and Rey, *op. cit.,* and C. A. Gregory, 'Gifts and Commodities: a critique of the theory of "Traditional" and "Modern" goods with particular reference to Papua New Guinea' (unpublished PhD Thesis, Cambridge University, 1980). I am grateful to Dr Gregory for his advice on this section of the essay in particular.

61 Meillassoux, 'The "Economy". . .', pp. 140-1.

62 K. Marx, *Pre-capitalist Economic Formations* edited by E. J. Hobsbawm, (London, 1964), p. 94.

63 For a recent discussion of this process with particular reference to Papua New Guinea, see, Gregory, *op. cit.,* Chapters 6 and 7. See also C. A. Gregory, 'Gifts to Men and Gifts to God: gift exchange and capital accumulation in contemporary Papua', *Man* (NS), xv (1980), pp. 626-52.

64 R. F. Salisbury, *From Stone to Steel* (Melbourne, 1962), Chapter 4. Salisbury calls 'elite goods', 'prestige tokens'.

65 *Ibid.* See also C. S. Belshaw, *In Search of Wealth* (Memoir No 80, American Anthropological Association, 1955) and *The Great Village* (London, 1957).

66 Parnaby, *op. cit.,* Figure 4, p. 146; Table CXXI, *QVP*, 1882, I, 1148; Horrocks to

Colonial Secretary, 8 February 1878, QSA, Col. A/253; 78/624; W. T. Wawn; *The South Sea Islands and the Queensland Labour Trade* edited by P. Corris (Canberra, 1973), p. 17. Detailed figures published annually by the Queensland Registrar-General suggest that females constituted only 6.21 per cent of the Pacific Islands population which entered Queensland between 1869 and 1904.

67   Figures drawn from the Annual Reports of the Queensland Registrar-General suggest that approximately 92 per cent of Pacific Islanders who entered Queensland between 1863 and 1906 either died in Queensland or returned home. This figure should be qualified by the following comments: (i) a small proportion of repatriated workers were not landed at their own villages; (ii) the Registrar-General constantly referred to the inaccuracy of the mortality figures since deaths of Pacific Islanders were not always recorded in Queensland; (iii) a very small number of immigrants moved to other colonies in Australia, principally northern New South Wales; (iv) approximately 2,500 Islanders remained in Queensland following the repatriation of the immigrants in 1906.

68   W. G. Ivens, *Island Builders of the Pacific* (London, 1930), pp. 46-7. See also C. M. Woodford, 'Notes on the Manufacture of the Malaita Shell Bead Money of the Solomon Group', *Man*, Viii (1908), p. 83; N. C. Deck to the Editor of *Oceania*, 24 August 1934, *Oceania*, v (1934), p. 243; Corris, *Passage*, p. 114.

69   *Ibid.*

70   The economic and social functions of Pacific Island workers' consumption of colonial commodities is studied in detail in A. A. Graves, 'From Truck to Gifts: the trade box system in a colonial economy', paper presented to the conference on 'Colonialism and Migration: Indentured Labour Before and After Slavery' Leiden, Centre for the History of European Expansion, 21-23 April 1982.

71   Price and Baker, *op. cit.*

72   Log of the Barque *Alfred*, 1828-9, Royal Commonwealth Society, London, Mss.9.

73   C. M. Woodforde, 'Notes on the Manufacture of the Malaita Shell Bead Money of the Solomon Group', *Man*, viii (1908), p. 81.

74   A. I. Hopkins, 'Depopulation in the Solomon Islands', in W. H. Rivers, (ed), *Essays in the Depopulation of Melanesia* (Cambridge, 1922), p. 62.

75   Other passage masters in the Solomon Islands included Tamiu of Bukulun, Laughlin Islands; Soga of a Thousand Ships Bay, Ysabel; Sambui, a chief in the Logu district of the west coast of Guadalcanal; and a number of chiefs on San Cristobal. The Malaita list is, however, especially long and in addition to those already mentioned included Dahe and Raha of the Maramsike Passage, Muldo and Eriga of Ataa Cove, 'Billy Bina' of Bina Island in Alite Bay, Tafetemau of Sinerango, and Wate of Port Adam. Corris, *Passage*, p. 61; R Fowler, 'McMurdo of the Schooner Stanley', *Queensland Heritage*, i (1968) p. 5.

76   For detailed studies of Kwaisulia and other passage masters in the Solomons see, Corris, *Passage*, Chapter 4; and Corris 'Kwaisulia of Ada Gege', pp. 253-66; Docker, *op. cit.*, pp. 129-38, 159, 249-54, 272. The following biographical details are based on these works.

77   Report of the Government Agent of *Bobtail Nag*, 11 December 1875, QSA, Col. A/218; 75/465.

78   Corris, 'Kwaisulia of Ada Gege', p. 258.

79   See above, pp. For a more detailed study of this aspect of leadership in Melanesia see E. Prokosche, 'Economics of Leadership in Some Melanesian Societies'

(unpublished MA thesis, University of London, 1965). For a discussion of the characteristics of big men or chiefs in the Solomons, see N. D. Sahlins, 'Poor Man, Rich Man, Chief', in I. Hogbin and L. R. Hiatt (eds), *Readings in Australian and Pacific Anthropology* (Melbourne, 1966), pp. 164-7.

80 Buttanshaw to Attorney-General, 10 November 1883, QSA, Col. A/673; 83/5957.

81 Corris, 'Kwaisulia of Ada Gege', p. 258.

82 Kwaisulia was paid by the labour recruiters in arms and ammunition, dynamite, kerosene, arsenic, strychnine, axes, crowbars, fencing, wire, iron spikes, dogs, and building materials. Docker, *op. cit.*, p. 136.

83 Ev. Young, QPP, 1906, II, 517, Q. 1703; Rannie, *op. cit.*, pp. 183-7.

84 *Ibid.*, p. 259.

85 Corris, *Passage*, pp. 33-7; Scarr, *Fragments of Empire*, p. 142.

86 *Ibid.*

87 Immigration Agent to Principal Under Home Secretary, 9 March 1896, QSA, Col. A/804; 96/3334.

88 Again, compare Corris, 'Kwaisulia of Ada Gege', p. 258.

89 E. Mandel, *Marxist Economic Theory* (London, 1968), Chapter 11.

90 For example, see R. C. Thomson, 'Natives and Settlers on the New Hebrides Frontier', (unpublished seminar paper, Institute of Commonwealth Studies, University of London: 9 November 1976), p. 4. For detailed examinations of the ecology and geography of the south-west Pacific see K. B. Cumberland, *South West Pacific* (Christchurch, 1954), Chapter 1; or H. C. Brookfield and D. Hart, *Melanesia* (London, 1971), Part I.

91 A. G. Price, *Western Invasions of the Pacific and its Continents* (Oxford, 1963), esp Chapter 6; Belshaw, *Changing Melanesia*, pp. 5 and 188-9; Harrisson, *op. cit.*, p. 56; A. M. Kamarck, *The Tropics and Economic Development* (Baltimore, 1976), Chapter 7; L. Doyal and I. Pennell, 'Pox Britannica; health, medicine and underdevelopment' in *Race and Class*, xviii (1967), pp. 155-72; R. H. Black, 'The Epidemiology of Malaria in the South West Pacific: changes associated with increasing European contact', *Oceania*, xxvii, (1956-57), pp. 136-42.

92 Ev. Campbell, QVP, 1869, II, Q.86. For other examples of the direct link between starvation and Queensland labour recruiting, see Goodall to Immigration Agent, 5 March 1874, QSA, CPS, 10/B/G1; Ev. Sandeman, QVP, 1876, III, 148, Q.2103; Note by Brenan on a report of the Government Agent of the recruiting vessel *Sybil*, 5 April 1895, in BPP, 1895, lxx, C 7912, p. 281; Letter by J. R. Selwyn in *Guardian* (Manchester), 4 May 1892; Ev. Young, QPP, 1906, II, 519, Qd. 1705-8; Ev. Hammond, QPP, 1906, II, 522, Qs. 1798-1801 and 1887-1893. For specific references to drought or water shortages and Queensland labour recruiting see Report of the Government Agent of the recruiting vessel *Lytonna*, 24 May 1871, in Gibson to Immigration Agent, 24 May 1871, QSA. Col. A/156; 71/1482; W. Coote, *The Western Pacific* (London, 1883), p. 79; Report of the Bishop of Tasmania's trip to Melanesia, in Norman to Ripon, 16 August 1892, in C 7000, p. 19; Thurston to Ripon, 23 March 1895, in C 7912, pp. 197-8; Report of the Government Agent of the recruiting vessel *May*, and supplementary report, 27 February 1895, in Norman to Ripon, 28 February 1895, in *ibid.*, pp. 202-5.

93 Ev. Sandeman, QVP, 1876, III, 147, Q.2065; Ev. Rome, QVP, 1876, III, Qs.168 and 1279; Ev. Langdon, QVP, 1889, IV, 124, Q.956; D. Rannie, *My Adventures*

Among South Sea Cannibals (London, 1912), pp. 98-9. Ev. Macdonald, *QVP*, 1885, II, 881, Q.1656; see also the reports of medical inspections of immigrants on recruiting vessels between 30 May 1892 and 9 October 1894 which are printed in C 7000, *passim*, and C 7192, *passim*.

94   Rhodes, *op. cit.*, II, pp. 19-25.

95   *Ibid.*

96   *Ibid.*

97   J. L. A. Hope, *In Quest of Coolies* (London, 1872), p. 72.

98   *BPP*, 1883, xlvii, C 3641, *Correspondence Respecting the Natives of the Western Pacific and the Labour Traffic*, p. 93.

99   Neame to Colonial Secretary, 30 January 1878, QSA, Col. A/253; 78/611; Mackay District Planters' Association to Colonial Secretary, 22 January 1878, QSA, Col. A/252; 78/342.

100   W. G. Ivens, *Dictionary and Grammar of the Language of Sa'a and Ulawa, Solomon Islands* (Washington, 1918), p.225.

101   Bridge to Erskine, 27 July 1882, *BPP*, 1883, xlvii, C 3641, p. 149.

102   *Presbyterian Review and Monthly Recorder* (Melbourne), March 1878, p. 55; *Christian Review and Messenger* (Melbourne), October, 1871, p. 13.

103   Belshaw, *Changing Melanesia*, p. 4.

104   See for example Thompson, *op. cit.*, pp.2 and 5.

105   HM Schooners, *Sandfly, Beagle Conflict, Renard,* and *Alacrity*. For further details see Scarr, *Fragments of Empire*, p. 37. Compare the following with the view that the British Navy performed a humanitarian role in the south-west Pacific. See, for example, D. K. Fieldhouse, *Economics and Empire* (London, 1973), p. 246, and J. Bach 'The Royal Navy in the Pacific Islands', *JPH*, iii (1968), pp. 3-20.

106   For example, see Scarr, *Fragments of Empire*, pp. 167-75.

107   See, for example, Secretary of the Admiralty to Hoskins, 6 June 1878, in *BPP*, 1878, xlix, *Further Papers Relating to the Execution of a Native of Tanna Onboard HMS Beagle* (Sessional Paper No 293), pp. 536-8. As a result of questions asked in the British Parliament *HC Debates*, Vol. 264, c. 1027, a Bill was drafted in 1882 in an attempt to control statutorily the Navy's arbitrary use of force against Pacific Islanders. The Liberal Premier, Gladstone, objected to the Bill because it involved 'the assumption of too heavy an administrative and financial responsibility', Scarr, *Fragments of Empire*, pp. 168-71; Parnaby, *op. cit.*, pp. 171-2.

108   Rhodes, *op. cit.*, II, pp. 200 and 254.

109   Macdonald, *op. cit.*, p. 12.

110   *Ibid.*, p. 19. See also Corris, *Passage*, pp. 57-8.

111   W. H. R. Rivers (ed), *Essays in the Depopulation of Melanesia;* Bridge to High Commissioner, *Western Pacific High Commission,* 9 August 1882, C 3641, p. 155; Ev. Reynolds, *QPP*, 1906, II, 515, Qs. 1627-52.

112   Graves, 'Pacific Islands Labour in the Queensland Sugar Industry', pp. 179-84.

113   *Ibid.*

7. CAPITALISM AND MIGRANT LABOUR IN SOUTHERN AFRICA

1   *Report of the Economic and Wage Commission* (Clay Report) (UG 14/1926), paras. 128-31.

2   *Report of the Commission on the Socio-Economic Development of the Bantu Areas Within*

South Africa (Tomlinson Commission) (UG 61, 1955), p. 41.

3   Until relatively recently the most comprehensive treatment of the development of a system of labour migration in southern Africa around the needs of capital in South Africa was Sheila van der Horst's *Native Labour in South Africa*. More recently available was F. Wilson, *Labour in the South African Gold Mines* (Cambridge, 1972).

4   S.X. (F. Perry), 'The Transvaal Labour Problem', *African Monthly*, 1 December 1906.

5   On the position of coloured labour, see van der Horst, *op. cit.*

6   For a discussion of the findings of the 1970 census in relation to foreign-born Africans in South Africa see D. Clarke, 'Foreign African Labour Inflows to South Africa and Unemployment in Southern Africa, in C. Simkins and D. Clarke (eds), *Structural Unemployment in South Africa*, Natal University Development Studies Research Group (Pietermaritzburg, 1977).

7   K. Marx, *Capital*, Vol. I (London, 1954), p. 630.

8   *Ibid.*, pp. 632-3, 639.

9   *Van der Horst, op. cit.*, was the earliest work on the nineteenth-century origins of migrancy; see also M. Legassick, 'South Africa: capital accumulation and violence', *Economy and Society*, iii (1974); C. D. L. Hemson, 'The Class Consciousness of Migrant Workers: the dock workers of Durban' (unpublished PhD thesis, University of Warwick, 1981), discusses the *togt* system. Recent work which examines the impact of the burgeoning colonial capitalist economy on various regional and rural African societies in the second half of the nineteenth century is now being published. See, for example, P. Delius, 'Migrant Labour and the Pedi, 1840-80' in S. Marks and A. Atmore (eds), *Economy and Society in Pre-Industrial South Africa* (London, 1980), and the chapters by Shillington, Kimble, Guy, and Harries in Marks and Rathbone, *Industrialization and Social Change in South Africa*.

10   See F. Johnstone, *Class, Race and Gold: a study of class relations and racial discrimination in South Africa* (London, 1976); M. Williams, 'An Analysis of South African Capitalism', *Bulletin of the Conference for Socialist Economists*, iv (1975); also his *South Africa: the crisis of world capitalism and the apartheid economy* (London, AAM 1976).

11   See van der Horst, *op. cit.*, pp. 160-72, 186-232; on Mozambican migrant miners, see the historical section of R. First, *The Mozambican Miner* (Brighton, 1983), and Harries in Marks and Rathbone, *op. cit.*

12   On the lengths of contracts, see van der Horst, *op. cit.*, pp. 210-15.

13   The new mining technology and consequent reorganisation of the labour process is discussed in Duncan Innes, 'Monopoly Capital and Imperialism in Southern Africa: the role of the Anglo-American group' (unpublished PhD, University of Sussex, 1980).

14   Van der Horst, *op. cit.*, p. 222.

15   *Ibid.*, p. 218.

16   H. Wolpe, 'Capitalism and Cheap Labour Power in South Africa'. Wolpe's article emphasised the need to understand the transition which affected the reserves in the 1930s and 1940s. Marion Lacey's recent book, *Working for Boroko: the origins of a coercive labour system in South Africa* (Johannesburg, 1981), also sheds light on this.

17   For the background to state policy after World War II, see M. Legassick, 'Legislation, Ideology and Economy in Post-1948 South Africa', *Journal of Southern*

African Studies, i (1974).

18   *Report of the Native Laws Commission, 1946-48* (Fagan Commission) (UG 28, 1948), p. 18.

19   Tomlinson Commission, pp. 75-87.

20   *Foreign Africans: summary of the report of the Froneman Commission by Ken Owen,* SAIRR (Johannesburg, 1963), pp. 2-5.

21   On the generation of surplus population, see C. Simkins, 'Measuring and Predicting Unemployment in South Africa, 1960-77' in Simkins and Clarke, *op. cit.*

22   See D. Clarke, 'Foreign African Labour Inflows'; also his 'Foreign African Labour and the Internationalization of Labour Reserves in South Africa, 1970-77', section d. of *Foreign Migrant Labour in South Africa: studies on accumulation in the labour reserves, demand determinants and supply relationships,* ILO (Geneva, 1977) F. Wilson, *Internation Migration in Southern Africa,* SALDRU Working Paper No 1 (Cape Town, 1976).

23   ·A brief updated comment on the strategies open to southern African migrant workers may be found in Legassick's forthcoming review of W. R. Bohning (ed), *Black Migration to South Africa,* ILO (Geneva, 1981), in the *Journal of Development Studies.*

8. COOLIES, PEASANTS, AND PROLETARIANS

1   D. Denoon, 'The Transvaal Labour Crisis, 1901-1906', *Journal of African History,* vii (1967), pp. 481-94.

2   P. C. Campbell, *Chinese Coolie Emigration to Countries within the British Empire* (London, 1923), pp. 161-216.

3   Johnstone, *Class, Race and Gold,* pp. 32-4.

4   W. B. Worsfold, *The Reconstruction of the New Colonies under Lord Milner,* 2 vols (London, 1913); Campbell, *op. cit.,* I. M. Meyer, 'Chinese arbeidvraagstuk van die Witwatersrandse goudveld, 1903-1910' (unpublished PhD thesis, University of Pretoria, 1946); J. A. Reeves, 'Chinese Labour in South Africa, 1901-1910' (unpublished MA thesis, University of the Witwatersrand, 1954); D. Denoon, A Grand Illusion: the failure of imperial policy in the Transvaal Colony during the period of reconstruction, 1901-1905 (London, 1973), pp. 127-58.

5   Wolpe, 'Capitalism and Cheap Labour in South Africa'; Arrighi, 'Labour Supplies in Historical Perspective'; C. Perrings, *Black Mineworkers in Central Africa: industrial strategies and the evolution of an African proletariat in the Copperbelt, 1911-1941* (London, 1979).

6   Ta Chen, *Chinese Migrations, with special reference to Labour Conditions* (Washington, DC, 1923).

7   China, *Year Book, 1920-1* (Peking, 1922), p. 91.

8   Statement by the Colonial Secretary (Lyttelton), House of Commons, 27 February 1904, in PRO/CO 291/75/10687.

9   P. Richardson, *Chinese Mine Labour in the Transvaal* (London, 1982), Table A:2, p. 192.

10   A. P. Jones, 'Britain's Search for Chinese Co-operation in the First World War' (unpublished PhD thesis, University of London, 1977), pp. 120-1.

11   Ho Ping-ti, *Studies in the Population of China, 1368-1953* (Cambridge, Mass, 1959),

pp. 158-63.

12 See, for example, J. Davids (ed), *The Coolie Trade and Chinese Emigration. Vol. 17 of American Diplomatic and Public Papers: the United States and China, 1842-1860* (Delaware, 1973).

13 These contracts are in the Archives of the Foreign Labour Department of the Transvaal Government (hereafter FLD), housed in the Transvaal Archives Depot, Pretoria, Republic of South Africa (hereafter TAD); the contracts are to be found in TAD/FLD 343-53.

14 The full text of the Anglo-Chinese Labour Convention, dated 13 May 1904, the Importation Ordinance of the Transvaal Colony, and the Contract of Service can be found in Transvaal, *Handbook of Ordinances, Proclamations, Regulations and Instructions Connected with the Importation of Foreign Labour into the Transvaal* (Pretoria, 1906).

15 For a description of the main features of the local government structure under the Ch'ing, see Ch'u T'ung-tsu, *Local Government in China under the Ch'ing* (Stanford, 1969), pp. 1-13.

16 For a full discussion of the difficulties of this source material, see P. Richardson, 'The Provision of Chinese Indentured Labour for the Transvaal Gold Mines, 1903-1908' (unpublished PhD thesis, University of London, 1978), pp. 236-8.

17 Richardson, *Chinese Mine Labour in the Transvaal,* p. 253, n. 89.

18 TAD/FLD 344, Contract nos 23-6 of 1904.

19 TAD/FLD, f.11/-, Report on a journey through Shantung Province with special reference to South African emigration by E. D. C. Wolfe, Transvaal Emigration Agent, Chefoo, July 1905.

20 TAD/FLD 345-6, Contract nos 40-42 of 1905.

21 TAD/FLD 83, f.11/-, Report by Wolfe on Shantung, July 1905, see note 19.

22 TAD/FLD 405; for the origin of the northern shipments, see PRO/CO 879/85/755, Walter to Lyttelton, 20 July 1904.

23 See TAD/FLD 343/7, Contract nos 16-54 of 1904-05.

24 For details of these at the time, see L. Richard, *A Comprehensive Geography of the Chinese Empire* (Shanghai, 1908), passim.

25 Archives of the Chamber of Mines of South Africa (ACMSA), Chinese Labour File (Ch) 66, Shipping returns of the Chamber of Mines Labour Importation Agency (CMLIA), 1904-7, in CMLIA Circular to Members, 8 February 1907.

26 *Transvaal Administration Reports, Annual Report of the Foreign Labour Department for 1905-6,* p. 11.

27 ACMSA/Ch. 19, Report on Recruiting Work in China by G. Baldwin, 11 October 1906.

28 ACMSA/"G" Letters from China, Brazier to Bagot, 8 April 1905.

29 Information in this paragraph is based on Richard, *op. cit.,* pp. 66-78, 79-89.

30 C. F. Gordon-Cumming, *Wanderings in China, 2 vols (London, 1886), I, p. 134.*

31 M. S. Bell, *China. Being a Military Report on the North-Eastern Portions of the Provinces of Chihli and Shuntung; Nanking and its Approaches; etc. Together with an Account of the Chinese Civil, Naval and Military Administration,* 2 vols (Simla, 1884), I, p. 162.

32 PRO/CO 879/85/755, Lockart to Lyttelton, 13 September 1904.

33 Yao Shen-yu, 'The Geographical Distribution of Floods and Droughts in Chinese History', *Far Eastern Quarterly,* ii (1943), pp. 357-80.

34 Wu Wen-hui, 'Tsai-huang hsia Chung-kuo nung-ts'un jen-k'ou yü ching-chi

chih tung-t'ai', *Quarterly Review of the Sun Yat-sen Institute for the Advancement of Culture and Education,* iv (1931), pp. 43-59.

35   Y. Muramatsu, 'The Boxers in 1898-1899', *Annals of the Hitotsubashi Academy,* iii (1953), pp. 236-61.

36   V. Purcell, *The Boxer Uprising* (London, 1963), pp. 177-8.

37   For a foreign estimate of these areas, see the list of areas barred for Imperial examination, in *BPP,* 1902, Cd 1005, *Chinese Plenipotentiaries to the Doyen of the Diplomatic Body,* 13 June 1901, enclosure 9 in Satow to Lansdowne, 22 June 1901.

38   PRO/CO 879/85/755, Johnstone to Lockhart, 29 August 1904, enclosed in Lockhart to Lyttelton, 13 September 1904.

39   PRO/FO 228/1547, Campbell to Satow, 16 September 1904; PRO/CO 291/90/23254, Report of an Interview between the Viceroy at Nanking and the British Military Attache, Yangtze Valley, 7 April 1905, enclosed in FO to CO, 3 July 1905.

40   Purcell, *op. cit.,* p. 247, n. 1.

41   The figures for these years were on average 3.4 times higher than in 1896: see Imperial Maritime Customs Service, *Returns of Trade and Trade Reports for 1896* (Shanghai, 1897), p. 52; *BPP,* 1901, Cd 429, *Annual Trade Reports for Chefoo for 1900; BPP,* 1903, Cd 1386, *Annual Trade Reports for Chefoo for 1902.*

42   Purcell, *op. cit.,* p. 176.

43   *Report of the Special Committee Appointed to Inquire into Present Conditions in Regard to Control of Chinese Indentured Labourers in the Witwatersrand District, with minutes of evidence, procedure and appendices* (Johannesburg, 1906), evidence of J. Morris, p. 92; in Shantung, 1898-1914 (Cambridge Mass, 1967); P. Billingsley, 'Peasant Insurgency in China: Bai Lung, the White Wolf', unpublished paper presented to

44   Muramatsu, *op. cit.;* J. E. Schrecker, *Imperialism and Chinese Nationalism: Germany in Shantung, 1898-1914* (Cambridge Mass, 1967); P. Billingsley, "Peasant Insurgency in China: Bai Lung, the White Wolf", unpublished paper presented to the Peasants Seminar, Centre of International and Area Studies, University of London, 18 January 1974.

45   See, for example, TAD/FLD 349, Contract nos 18-9 of 1905, for shipment no 24 per the SS *Ikbal,* arrived Durban 7 July 1905.

46   Ho, *op. cit.,* p. 162.

47   *Ibid.,* pp. 283-8.

48   *Ibid.,* see also M. Elvin, *The Pattern of the Chinese Past* (London, 1973), p.309.

49   Ta Chen, *op. cit.,* pp. 24-5.

50   *Ibid.*

51   Ho, *op. cit.,* pp. 283-8.

52   Lo Erh-gang, 'T'ai-p'ing t'ien-kuo ke-ming ch'ien ti-jen-k'ou yen-p'o wen-ti', *Chung-kuo chin-tai shih lun-ts'ung* (Taipei, 1958), 2nd ts'e, pp. 16-87.

53   Hsiao Kung-chuan, *Rural China: Imperial Control in the Nineteenth Century* (Seattle, 1960), p. 380.

54   *Ibid.,* pp. 17-20.

55   Lo Erh-gang, *op. cit.*

56   G. Jamieson et al., 'The Tenure of Land in China and the Conditions of the Rural Population', *Journal of the North China Branch of the Royal Asiatic Society,* new series, xxiii (1888), pp. 59-174.

57   Hsiao, *op. cit.,* p. 385.

58   *Ibid.*, pp. 382-4.

59   Ho, *op. cit.*, p. 224

60   A. H. Smith, *China in Convulsion,* 2 vols. (New York, 1901), I, pp. 90-1.

61   Purcell, *op. cit.*, pp. 173-4.

62   A. Feuerwerker, *The Chinese Economy, 1870-1911* (Michigan, 1969), *passim.*

63   There was a net outflow of silver from China every year from 1902 to 1908: Imperial Maritime Customs Service, *Decennial Trade Reports, 1902-1911* (Shanghai, 1913), App: Trade Statistics, Table V — Treasure, pp. 352-3; the question of silver in the Chinese economy at this time is extremely complicated, for in addition to a shortage of silver caused by this outflow there was a long-term decline in the sterling value of the Hwaikwan tael from £0-6-7.75 in 1872 to £0-2-8 in 1911 (Imperial Maritime Customs Service, *Decennial Trade Reports, 1902-1911* App: Trade Statistics, Table II, No. 7, Value Tables of 40 Years: Value of Principal Articles of Foreign Importation, pp. 336-7). This decline was accompanied by a fall in the purchasing power of silver as against other commodities in China of over 50 per cent between 1880 and 1910 (China, *Silver and Prices in China: Report of the Committee for the Study of Silver Values* and Commodity Prices (Shanghai, 1935), pp. 6-7. Thus it seems that the rural economy would have been subject to the economic effects of hoarding due to shortage, rising commodity prices due to silver depreciation relative to other commodity prices, and rising costs of foreign exchange for the purchase of foreign manufactured goods and foodstuffs, which was becoming widespread at the beginning of the twentieth century (Ho, *op. cit.*, App III, pp. 289-91). It is one of the less obvious ironies of the employment of Chinese labourers in the Transvaal gold mines that it was in part made possible by the development and consolidation of the gold standard, and that this emigration was required to maintain the expansion of the world's gold stock, which in turn ensured the continued erosion of silver values: Richardson, *Chinese Mine Labour in the Transvaal*, p. 110.

64   Hsiao, *op. cit.*, pp. 443-4.

65   J. Chesneaux, *Peasant Revolts in China, 1840-1949* (London, 1973), p. 55.

66   M. Bastid, M.-C. Bergère, and J. Chesneaux, *Histoire de la Chine. 2: De la guerre franco-chinoise à la fondation du parti communiste chinois, 1885-1921* (Paris, 1972), pp. 77-8.

67   Chesneaux, *op. cit.*, p. 55.

68   Bastid, Bergère, and Chesneaux, *op. cit.*, pp. 83-4.

69   Chen Shao-Kwan, *The System of Taxation in China in the Tsing Dynasty, 1644-1911* (New York, 1914), pp. 39-40.

70   Ho, *op. cit.*, pp. 161-3.

71   TAD/FLD 83, f.11/-, Report by Wolfe on Shantung, July 1905, see note 19.

9. THE POLITICAL ECONOMY OF LABOUR MIGRATION TO SETTLER SOCIETIES

1   *Settler Capitalism: the dynamics of dependent development in the Southern hemisphere* (Oxford, 1983).

2   Following the example of many other writers, of whom Paul Baran is one of the most explicit. P. Baran, *The Political Economy of Growth* (New York, 1957), p. 273.

3   S. B. Saul, *Studies in British Overseas Trade 1870-1914* (Liverpool, 1960).

4 P. Winn, 'Uruguay and British Economic Expansion 1880-1914', (unpublished PhD thesis, University of Cambridge, 1971).

5 I.e. The Baring Crisis, when Baring Brothers found themselves in possession of Argentine and Uruguayan securities which could not be sold. The Bank of England and Rothschilds had to intervene to rescue Barings.

6 D. C. M. Platt, *Latin America and British Trade, 1806-1914* (London, 1972).

7 *Ibid.*

8 B. Thomas, 'Migration and International Investment', in A. R. Hall (ed), *The Export of Capital from Britain* (London, 1968).

9 M. F. L. Pritchard, *An Economic History of New Zealand* (Auckland, 1970).

10 E. Olssen, 'Truby King and the Plunket Society', *New Zealand Journal of History*, xv (1981).

11 N. Hicks, *This Sin and Scandal: Australia's population debate, 1891-1911* (Canberra, 1978).

12 P. Corris, ' "White Australia" in action: the repatriation of Pacific Islanders from Queensland', *Historical Studies*, xv (1972). R. Evans, K. Saunders, and K. Cronin, *Exclusion, Exploitation and Extermination: race relations in colonial Queensland* (Sydney, 1975).

13 E. Tornquist and Company, *The Economic Development of the Argentine Republic in the Last Fifty Years* (Buenos Aires, 1919). The census of 1914 enumerated 50,000 'civilised Indians' and some 8,000 'indigenes' (presumably uncivilised?) in a total of some eight million people.

14 C. Taylor, *Rural Life in Argentina* (Baton Rouge, 1948).

15 Tornquist, *op. cit.*

16 Taylor, *op. cit.*

17 Winn, *op. cit.*

18 W. Cantoni, 'Chile: relations between the Mapuche and Chilean national society', in UNESCO, *Race and Class in Post-Colonial Society* (Paris, 1977).

19 A. Angell, *Politics and the Labour Movement in Chile* (London, 1972).

20 C. Solberg, *Immigration and Nationalism in Argentina and Chile* (Austen, 1970).

21 D. H. Houghton and J. Dagut, *Source Material on the South African Economy 1860-1970,* vol. II (Cape Town, 1972).

22 *Investors Review,* quoted by H. D. Hanham, 'New Zealand Promoters and British Investors, 1860-1895' in R. Chapman and K. Sinclair, *Studies of a Small Democracy* (Auckland, 1963).

23 K. Sinclair, *A History of New Zealand* (London, 1959); E. A. Boehm, *Prosperity and Depression in Australia, 1887-1897* (Oxford, 1971).

24 Personal communication from V. Martinez-Alier.

25 Solberg, *op. cit.*

26 Following a line laid down by L. Hartz, *The Founding of New Societies* (New York, 1964).

27 R. Gollan, *Radical and Working Class Politics: a study of eastern Australia 1850-1910* (Melbourne, 1960).

28 B. Godio, *Historia del Movimiento Obrero Argentino* (Buenos Aires, 1973). D. Rock, *Politics in Argentina, 1890-1930* (Cambridge, 1975).

29 Angell, *op. cit.*

30 e.g. J. Fogarty, E. Gallo, and H. Dieguez, *Argentina y Australia* (Buenos Aires, 1979).

31   e.g. G. Rama, 'Desarrollo comparativo de Uruguay y Nueva Zelandia durante el siglo XIX', in Fogarty et al, *op. cit.* See also, J. Kirby, 'On the Viability of Small Countries: Uruguay and New Zealand compared', *Journal of Inter American Studies,* xvii (1975).

32   e.g. D. Skidmore, 'The Chilean Experience of Change: the primacy of politics', in A. Leftwich, *South Africa: economic growth and political change* (London, 1974).

33   J. R. Scobie, *Revolution on the Pampas: a social history of Argentine wheat, 1860-1910* (Austin, 1964).

34   *Ibid.*

35   J. C. Crossley and R. Greenhill, 'The River Plate Beef Trade', in D. C. M. Platt (ed), *Business Imperialism, 1840-1930: an enquiry based on British experience in Latin America* (Oxford, 1977).

36   Tornquist, *op. cit.*

37   E. Gallo, *Farmers in Revolt: the revolution of 1893 in the Province of Santa Fe, Argentina* (London, 1976). Taylor, *op. cit.*

38   Rock, *op. cit.*

39   J. Hirst, 'La sociedad rural y la política en Australia, 1850-1930', in Fogarty et al, *op. cit.*

40   Gollan, *op. cit.*

41   A. Graves and P. Richardson, 'Plantations in the Political Economy of Colonial Sugar Production: Natal and Queensland, 1860-1914', *Journal of Southern African Studies,* vi (1960).

42   J. Katz, 'Commentario', in Fogarty et al, *op. cit.*

43   Taylor, *op. cit.*

44   J. P. Barran and B. Nahum, *La civilización ganadera bajo Batlle (1905-1914)* (Vol. VI of *Historia rural del Uruguay moderno)* (Montevideo, 1977).

45   Rama, *op. cit.*

46   Barran and Nahum, *op. cit.*

47   Kirby, *op. cit.*

48   e.g. J. B. Condliffe, *New Zealand in the Making* (London, 1936).

49   Pritchard, *op. cit.;* Sinclair, *op. cit.*

50   Kirby, *op. cit.*

51   Pritchard, *op. cit.;* Barran and Nahum, *op. cit.*

52   On the 'Red Feds', see Sinclair, *op. cit.*

53   K. Remmer, 'The Timing, Pace and Sequence of Political Change in Chile, 1891-1925', *Hispanic American Historical Review,* lvii (1977), calculates the cost of votes in this era.

54   A. Bauer, *Chilean Rural Society from the Spanish Conquest until 1930* (Cambridge, 1975).

55   Angell, *op. cit.*

56   *Ibid.*

57   H. Blakemore, *British Nitrates and Chilean Politics 1886-1896: Balmaceda and North* (London, 1974).

58   Angell, *op. cit.*

59   Johnstone, *Class, Race and Gold.*

60   N. Mouzelis, 'The Greek Elections', *New Left Review,* 108, (1978). I am indebted to Jean-Jacques van Helten for drawing my attention to this article, and for discussing its implications.

61   This argument is developed at greater length in my 'Capital and Capitalists in the Transvaal in the 1890s and 1900s', *Historical Journal,* xxiii (1980).

62   These technical conditions are reviewed by Johnstone, *op. cit.*

63   The fullest discussion of these considerations is in P. Richardson, 'The Recruiting of Chinese Indentured Labour for the South African Gold Mines, 1903-1908', *Journal of African History,* xviii (1977).

64   *Ibid.*

65   Johnstone, *op. cit.*

66   See, for example, the introduction and the essays by Kimble, Harries, and Shillington in Marks and Rathbone, *Industrialization and Social Change in South Africa,* and the essay by Delius in S. Marks and A. Atmore (eds), *Economy and Society in Preindustrial South Africa* (London, 1980).

10. THE IMPERIAL WORKPLACE

1   Ragnar Nurkse, *Patterns of Trade and Development* (Stockholm, 1959); J. W. McCarty, 'Australia as a Region of Recent Settlement in the Nineteenth Century', *Australian Economic History Review,* xiii (1973), pp. 148-67; D. Denoon, 'Understanding Settler Societies', *Historical Studies,* xviii (1979), pp. 511-27.

2   Nurkse, *op. cit.,* p. 18.

3   The more recent literature is surveyed in Hilda Kuper (ed), *Urbanization and Migration in West Africa* (Los Angeles, 1965); Amin, *Modern Migrations;* J. C. Caldwell, *African Rural-Urban Migration: the movement to Ghana's towns* (Canberra, 1969); H. C. Brookfield and Doreen Hart, *Melanesia: a geographical interpretation of an island world* (London, 1971); R. G. Ward, 'Internal Migration and Urbanization in Papua New Guinea', in M. W. Ward (ed), *Population Growth and Socio-Economic Change,* New Guinea Research Unit Bulletin No 42 (Canberra, 1977), pp. 81-105.

4   See, for example, Oscar Handlin, *The Uprooted: the epic story of the great migrations that made the American people* (New York, 1951), S. N. Eisenstadt, *The Absorption of Migrants* (New York, 1954).

5   F. Alexander, *Moving Frontiers: an American theme and its application to Australian history* (Sydney, 1941); A. L. Mabogunje, 'Migration Policy and Regional Development in Nigeria', *The Nigerian Journal of Social and Economic Studies,* xii (1970), pp. 250-61; T. M. Perry, *Australia's First Frontier: the spread of settlement in New South Wales 1788-1829* (Melbourne, 1963); P. F. Sharp, 'Three Frontiers: some comparative studies of Canadian, American and Australian settlement', *Pacific Historical Review,* xxiv (1955), pp. 369-78; D. V. Glass, 'European Population Movements in the Union of South Africa', *South African Journal of Economics,* vii (1939), pp. 41-65.

6   A. Adepoju, 'Migration and Socio-Economic Links between Migrants and their Home Communities in Nigeria', *Africa,* xliv (1974), pp. 383-96.

7   Brinley Thomas (ed), *Economics of International Migration* (London, 1958); A. K. Cairncross, *Home and Foreign Investment, 1870-1913* (Cambridge, 1953).

8   For recent studies of West African examples see D. N. Souter, 'Colonial Labour Policy and Labour Conditions in Nigeria, 1939-1945', (unpublished DPhil thesis, University of Oxford, 1980); and the special papers by K. C. Zachariah and N. K. Nair, prepared to accompany K. C. Zachariah and Julien Condé, 'Demographic

Aspects of Migration in West Africa' (World Bank Development Economics Department, 1978-79, mimeo).

9   Such nuggets of information are scattered in official reports; see, for example, the analysis of labourers' records in Colonial No 145 (1938), *Report of the Commission Appointed to Enquire into the Financial and Economic Position of Northern Rhodesia*, p. 46; and the life histories of labourers in *BPP*, 1934-35, vii, Cmd 4907, *Report by Mr.A.W. Pim on the Financial and Economic Position of Basutoland*, pp. 38-41; and, for other case histories, Charles van Onselen, *Chibaro* (London, 1976), and Stewart Firth in James Griffin, Hank Nelson, and Stewart Firth, *Papua New Guinea: a political history* (Richmond, 1979), pp. 62-8.

10   C.G.F. Simkin, *The Instability of a dependent Economy* (Oxford, 1951), p. 55. See also W.H. Oliver and B.R. Williams (eds), *The Oxford History of New Zealand* (Oxford, 1981), pp. 70-75, 136.

11   W.D. McIntyre and W.J. Gardner (eds), *Speeches and Documents of New Zealand History* (Oxford, 1971), p. 461.

12   *Appendices to the Journal of the House of Representatives* (AJHR), 1877, D-2, p. 34.

13   *Ibid.*, 1872, D-14, especially deputy-superintendent Napier to minister of public works, 7 February 1972.

14   McIntyre and Gardner, *op. cit.*, p. 461.

15   *AJHR*, 1893, D-7.

16   *Ibid.*, 1876, D-1, especially for detailed returns of requirements.

17   *Ibid.*, 1872, D-4b.

18   *Ibid.*, 1876, D-6.

19   On this period in general, see K. Sinclair, *A History of New Zealand* (London, 1959), p. 135; W.H. Oliver, *The Story of New Zealand* (London, 1963), pp. 116-22. Wage levels in Otago in 1878 covered the following range: married couples (stations) £65-£80, ploughmen £55-£60, farm hands £52-£55, female servants £40-£50, per year, labourers 6s to 8s per day. *AJHR,*1878, D-5.

20   For the social cost of rapid urbanisation and the precarious situation of New Zealand workers in the depression period, see W.B. Sutch, *The Quest for Security in New Zealand, 1840-1966* (Wellington, 1966).

21   The early conditions can be discerned in the prospection reports of the Royal Niger Company, especially volumes 6 and 10, Rhodes House Library, MSS Afr s 85-101; W.H. Laws, 'Nigerian Tin Mining Expedition', 1903, MSS Afr s 888; R.A. Archibold, 'Early Memories of the Nigerian Plateau', MSS Afr s 141; and H.S.W. Edwardes, 'Nigeria Papers, 1906-1924', MSS Afr s 769. See, too, Nigeria, *Annual Reports of the Mines Department* (Lagos, 1921-1950); Provincial Reports in the papers of R.H. Arnett, MSS Afr s 952; the most thorough analysis is by Freund, 'Labour Migration to the Northern Nigerian Tin Mines, 1903-1945'.

22   Royal Niger Company Papers, vol 10, Lugard to Watts, 12 July 1901; for details see Colin Newbury, 'Trade and Technology in West Africa: the case of the Niger company, 1900-1920', *Journal of African History*, xix (1978), pp. 560-1; 'The Economics of Conquest in Nigeria, 1900-1920: amalgamation reconsidered' in E. M'Bokolo and M. Michel (eds), *Mélanges: hommage à Henri Brunschwig* (forthcoming); Freund, *op. cit.*, pp. 76-8; and W.M. Freund, *Capital and Labour in the Nigerian Tin Mines* (London, 1981).

23   Royal Niger Company Papers, vol. 14, Willis 'Report on the New Transport Route', 1 January 1911.

24   Ludwig Schatzl, *The Nigerian Tin Industry*, NISER Monograph Series No 3 (Ibadan, 1971), Table 22; cf Freund, 'Labour Migration . . .', who does not discuss this form of labour contract by 'parasitic intermediaries' (sic), p. 83.

25   Royal Niger Company Papers, vol. 16, Report of the Mining Department, p. 136; Nigeria, *Blue Books* (for wage rates southern and northern provinces); Nigeria, *Annual Reports on the Social and Economic Progress of the People of Nigeria* (Lagos, 1932-1939); Freund 'Labour Migration . . .' pp. 80-1.

26   Nigeria, *Report of the Mines Department* (Lagos, 1931), p. 6.

27   Souter, *op. cit.*, p. 193.

28   *Ibid.*, Chapter 5; Freund, 'Labour Migration . . .' p. 81.

29   Souter, *op. cit.*, p. 200. The average mortality, 1942-1944, among conscripts was 28.5 per thousand annually and as high as 89.4 per thousand for Tiv from Benue Province.

30   Nigeria, Mines Department, *Annual Report* (Lagos, 1951), Appendix L.

31   P.A. Bower in Margery Perham (ed), *Mining, Commerce, and Finance in Nigeria* (London, 1948), pp. 20-21, 23.

32   *Ibid.;* Schatzl, *op. cit.*, pp. 30, 50.

33   *Ibid.*, p. 14.

34   This pattern of migration is discussed in the contributions to Amin, *op. cit.*, and the details are reflected in the 1931 *Census of Nigeria* (Lagos, 1933), p. 31 (Plateau migration) and the tables of occupations under tin mining. Unfortunately, this information was not published in the census of 1952.

35   For the most useful analysis of the Birom, see J.G. Davies, 'The Bi Rom: a study of a Nigerian tribe' (Ms, 1949); and his 'Plateau Province Report of a Farm Survey', Rhodes House Library, MSS Afr s 309; see, too, Daryll Forde in M. Perham (ed), *The Native Economies of Nigeria* (London, 1946); *Geological Survey of Nigeria*, Bulletin no 22: *Land use and Soil Conservation on the Jos Plateau* (Lagos, 1952); and the valuable *Report on the Medical and Health Services for the Year 1934* (Lagos, 1936) for the high incidence of trypanosomiasis among labourers and its gradual reduction.

36   Nigeria, Labour Department, *Annual Report* (Lagos, 1950), p. 38; *Annual Report* (Lagos, 1957), p. 5.

37   For the development of mining, see A.H. Healy, *Bulolo: a history of the development of the Bulolo region, New Guinea,* New Guinea Research Bulletin no 15 (Canberra, 1967); C. Newbury, 'Colour Bar and Labour Conflict on the New Guinea Goldfields, 1935-1941', *Australian Journal of Politics and History*, xxi (1975), pp. 25-38; H. Nelson, *Black, White and Gold: goldmining in Papua New Guinea 1878-1930* (Canberra, 1976). Most of the material for this section is based on the New Guinea series in Australian Archives, Canberra, and has been examined for a study of 'Labour Constraint in German and Australian New Guinea' (forthcoming) with Dr Stewart Firth. See, too, Griffin, Nelson, and Firth, *op. cit.*, especially Chapters 4 and 5.

38   Zachariah and Condé, *op. cit.*, pp. 93-4.

39   F.K. Crowley, 'British Migration to Australia, 1860-1914', (Unpublished DPhil thesis, University of Oxford, 1951).

40   This estimate is arrived at by Souter, *op. cit.*, p. 43 and notes.

41   *New Zealand Year Book* (Wellington, 1970), p. 910.

42   Zachariah and Condé, *op. cit.*, p. 211; and for parallels in New Guinea, R.G. Ward,

'Internal Migration and Urbanization in Papua New Guinea, postscript 1974', in R.J. May (ed) *Change and Movement: readings on internal migration in Papua New Guinea* (Canberra, 1977), pp. 49-51.

43   Amin, *op. cit.,* pp. 65-6.

44   *New Zealand Year Book* (Wellington, 1970), p. 73. By 1945 some 20.6 per cent of the Maori population lived in the cities and boroughs, compared with the general population percentage of 67.6 for urban residents. See, too, Joan Metge, *The Maoris of New Zealand* (London, 1967), p. 50, where a slightly lower figure is cited.

45   Griffin, Nelson, and Firth, *op. cit.,* Chapter 9; Ward, 'Internal Migration', pp. 81-105; Douglas Oliver, *Bougainville: a personal history* (Melbourne, 1973).

46   Souter, *op. cit.,* pp. 38-9; A. Adepoju, *op. cit.*

47   Souter, *op, cit.,* p. 185.

48   This point on the mobility and multiple skills available in a labour force accustomed to mercantile trading is emphasised by Freund, 'Labour Migration . . .', p. 83.

49   The literature on African cases is extensive: see the references in Freund, 'Labour Migration . . .', pp. 73-4 and for an overview of Pacific cases, Newbury, 'The Melanesian Labor Reserve'.

INDEX

270

Index

German indentured and contract labour in America, 38, 40, 51, 54
gift exchange (prestation)
    in Pacific islands, 124-8, 130
gold-mining industry, migrant labour for New Guinea, 224-5
    South Africa: Chinese indentured labour, 167-85, 202-3; migrant labour system, 12, 146-53, 156-8, 160, 201-4
government, **see** state
Guiana (Guyana)
    independence, sugar industry and, 86, 87
    Indian sugar workers: indentured, 78-9, 80, 81-2, 94; isolation, 88; strikes and trade unionism, 83, 84-5, 88-9;
    slavery, 78, 92
Guiana, Dutch **see** Surinam
Guiana Agricultural Workers' Union, 86, 88

Hausa peasants, tin-mining and, 215-16, 217, 218, 219, 220
health
    Pacific islanders, 134
    Surinam indentured sugar workers, 103-6
housing
    black African workers, 154
    sugar workers, 80, 102-3
humanitarian agencies, reforms for indentured labour demanded by, 82
hurricanes, Pacific islands affected by, 134

Illinois, labour bureaus in, 54-5
Illinois Central Railroad, labour for construction of, 45
immigrants, self-financed
    increase in in America, 40
immigration, regulations, 38-9
indentured labour
    conditions experienced by: in N. America, 23-4, 37; similarities with slavery, 76-7, 92, 94-6, 97-8, 104-11 *passim;* on sugar plantations, 79-82, 99, 101-11
    contemporary accounts of, 19, 23-4, 32-3
    contract labour compared with, 41
    contracts for, analysis of, 168-70
    data on: Britain, 22-3, 26-7; China, 169-70, 174-5
    factors contributing to persistence of, 9-10
    Indian, 78-83, 93-111
    legislation affecting: New Guinea, 223, 226, 229; N. America, 38-40; S.

Africa, 141-3, 147, 148, 151, 152, 154, 155, 159, 160-1; on sugar plantations, 82-3, 106-10
New Guinea, 221-6, 228, 229
North America: decline and disappearance, 34, 36-42
recruitment: China, 171, 184; Europe, 36; India, 13, 95-6; New Guinea, 223, 224-5, 229; Pacific islands, 114, 116-18, 121, 128-33, S. Africa, 147, 149, 153
replaced by slavery, 37
resistance and repression, 80-1, 94-5, 106-10
runaways, 40-1
slavery replaced by, 78-9, 90, 93-5, 97
socio-economic background: Britain, 26-7; China, 173-83
South Africa: black Africans, 12, 140-65; Chinese, 167-85
sugar plantations, 11-12, 78-83, 93-111; conditions after abolition of, 82-9
transition from contract labour to, 41-2
wages: absence of, 37; New Guinea, 223, 225; S. Africa, 140-1, 147, 149, 152-3, 156, 157, 159; sugar plantations, 80, 82
white, 19-33
indentures, length of, 41-2, 79-80, 116, 149-50
independence, sugar colonies', 86-7, 89

India
    indentured labour recruitment in, 13, 78-80, 82, 83, 95-6
    sugar workers from, **see** sugar workers
individualistic theories, 5, 113-14
industrial action (**see also** strikes)
    Cornish miners', 68, 69-70
industrial confrontation
    as racial conflict in sugar colonies, 81
industrial reserve army, 143-5
    creation of in S. Africa, 145-8, 150, 152, 153-4, 155-6, 158, 161
information, work opportunities, role of labour agencies in provision of, 52-3
insecurity, contribution of land tenure to North China, 180-1
intelligence offices, 52
internal migration
    Cornish miners, 59
    international migration in relation to, 14; Britain, 24-8, 32
    regional: in fragmented colonial states, 207
International Workers of the World, 71
interpreters, labour bureaus provision of, 53-4

273